Important Instruction

Students, Parents, and Teachers can use the URL or QR code provided below to access two full-length Lumos SBAC practice tests. Please note that these assessments are provided in the Online format only.

URL	QR Code
Visit the URL below and place the book access code **http://www.lumoslearning.com/a/tedbooks** **Access Code: G5ESBAC-36897-P**	

Lumos Learning
Developed by Expert Teachers

SBAC Test Prep: Grade 5 English Language Arts Literacy (ELA) Common Core Practice Book and Full-length Online Assessments: Smarter Balanced Study Guide

Contributing Author   -   Julie Turner
Contributing Author   -   Brenda Green
Contributing Author   -   George Smith
Contributing Author   -   Wendy Bundgaard
Executive Producer   -   Mukunda Krishnaswamy
Designer and Illustrator - Harini N..

ISBN-10: 1940484774

ISBN-13: 978-1-940484-77-8

Printed in the United States of America

For permissions and additional information contact us

Lumos Information Services, LLC
PO Box 1575, Piscataway, NJ 08855-1575
http://www.LumosLearning.com

Email: support@lumoslearning.com
Tel: (732) 384-0146
Fax: (866) 283-6471

Lumos Learning
Developed by Expert Teachers

Table of Contents

Online Program Benefits

Students*

- Two full-length Lumos SBAC practice tests
- Technology-enhanced item types practice
- Additional learning resources such as videos and apps

Parents*

- You can review your student's online work by login to your parent account
- Pinpoint student areas of difficulty
- Develop custom lessons & assignments
- Access to High-Quality Question Bank

Teachers*

- Review the online work of your students
- Get insightful student reports
- Discover standards aligned videos, apps and books through EdSearch
- Easily access standards information along with the Coherence Map
- Create and share information about your classroom or school events

* Terms and Conditions apply

URL	QR Code
Visit the URL below and place the book access code **http://www.lumoslearning.com/a/tedbooks** **Access Code: G5ESBAC-36897-P**	

Start using the online resources included with this book today!

This book is designed to help students get Smarter Balanced Assessment Consortium (SBAC) rehearsal along with standards aligned rigorous skills practice. Unlike a traditional book, this Lumos tedBook offers two full-length practice tests online. Taking these tests will not only help students get a comprehensive review of standards assessed on the SBAC, but also become familiar with the question types.

After students take the test online, educators can use the score report to assign specific lessons provided in this book.

Students will obtain a better understanding of each standard and improve on their weaknesses by practicing the content of this workbook. The lessons contain rigorous questions aligned to the state standards and substandards. Taking the time to work through the activities will afford students the ability to become proficient in each grade level standard.

What is SBAC?

The Smarter Balanced Assessment Consortium (SBAC) is one of the two state consortiums responsible for developing assessments aligned to the rigorous Common Core State Standards.

Thousands of educators, along with test developers, have worked together to create the new computer based English Language Arts and Math Assessments.

SBAC's first round of testing occurred during the 2014 – 2015 school year. The tests are conducted online, requiring students complete tasks to assess a deeper understanding of the CCSS and will involve a variety of new technology-enhanced question.

How Can the Lumos Study Program Prepare Students for SBAC Tests?

At Lumos Learning, we believe that year-long learning and adequate practice before the actual test are the keys to success on these standardized tests. We have designed the Lumos study program to help students get plenty of realistic practice before the test and to promote year-long collaborative learning.

This is a Lumos tedBook™. It connects you to Online SBAC Assessments and additional resources using a number of devices including Android phones, iPhones, tablets and personal computers. The Lumos StepUp Online Assessment is designed to promote year-long learning. It is a simple program students can securely access using a computer or device with internet access. Students will get instant feedback and can review their answers anytime. Each student's answers and progress can be reviewed by parents and educators to reinforce the learning experience.

Discover Engaging and Relevant Learning Resources

Lumos EdSearch is a safe search engine specifically designed for teachers and students. Using EdSearch, you can easily find thousands of standards-aligned learning resources such as questions, videos, lessons, worksheets and apps. Teachers can use EdSearch to create custom resource kits to perfectly match their lesson objective and assign them to one or more students in their classroom.

To access the EdSearch tool, use the search box after you log into Lumos StepUp or use the link provided below.

http://www.lumoslearning.com/a/edsearchb	

The Lumos Standards Coherence map provides information about previous level, next level and related standards. It helps educators and students visually explore learning standards. It's an effective tool to help students progress through the learning objectives. Teachers can use this tool to develop their own pacing charts and lesson plans. Educators can also use the coherence map to get deep insights into why a student is struggling in a specific learning objective.

Teachers can access the Coherence maps after logging into the StepUp Teacher Portal or use the link provided below.

http://www.lumoslearning.com/a/coherence-map	

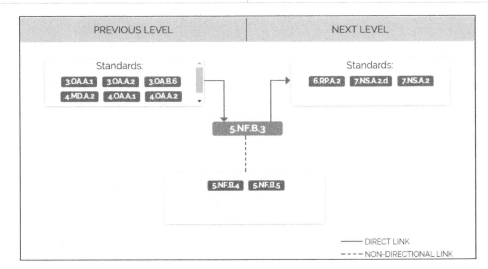

How to use this book effectively

The Lumos Program is a flexible learning tool. It can be adapted to suit a student's skill level and the time available to practice before standardized tests. Here are some tips to help you use this book and the online resources effectively:

Students

- The standards in each book can be practiced in the order designed, or in the order you prefer.
- Complete all the questions each workbook.
- Take the first practice CAT and PT online.
- Download the Lumos StepUp® app using the instructions provided in "How can I Download the App?" to have anywhere access to online resources.
- Have open-ended questions evaluated by a teacher or parent, keeping in mind the scoring rubrics.
- Take the second CAT and PT as you get close to the official test date.
- Complete the test in a quiet place, following the test guidelines. Practice tests provide you an opportunity to improve your test taking skills and to review topics included in the CCSS related standardized test.

Parents

- Help your child use Lumos StepUp® SBAC Online Assessments by following the instructions in "Access Online Program" section.
- You can review your student's online work by login to your parent account.
- You can also conveniently access student progress report on your mobile devices by downloading the Lumos StepUp app. Please follow directions provided in "How can I Download the App?" section in Lumos StepUp® Mobile App FAQ For Parents and Teachers.

Test Taking Tips

1) **The day before the test,** make sure you get a good night's sleep.

2) **On the day of the test,** be sure to eat a good hearty breakfast! Also, be sure to arrive at school on time.

3) **During the test:**

- **Read every question carefully.**

  - Do not spend too much time on any one question. Work steadily through all questions in the section.
  - Attempt all of the questions even if you are not sure of some answers.
  - If you run into a difficult question, eliminate as many choices as you can and then pick the best one from the remaining choices. Intelligent guessing will help you increase your score.
  - Also, mark the question so that if you have extra time, you can return to it after you reach the end of the section.
  - Some questions may refer to a graph, chart, or other kind of picture. Carefully review the graphic before answering the question.
  - Be sure to include explanations for your written responses and show all work.

- **While Answering Multiple-Choice (EBSR) questions.**

  - Select the bubble corresponding to your answer choice.
  - Read **all** of the answer choices, even if think you have found the correct answer.

- **While Answering TECR questions.**

  - Read the directions of each question. Some might ask you to drag something, others to select, and still others to highlight. Follow all instructions of the question (or questions if it is in multiple parts)

Chapter 1 - Reading: Literature

The objective of the Reading Literature standards is to ensure that the student is able to read and comprehend literature (which includes stories, drama and poetry) related to Grade 5.

To help students to master the necessary skills, an example which will help the student understand the concepts related to the standard is given. Along with this, we encourage the student to go through the resources available online on EdSearch to gain an in-depth understanding of these concepts. EdSearch page for each lesson can be accessed with the help of the url or the QR code provided.

A small map is provided after each passage or text in which the student can enter the details as understood from the literary text. Doing this will help the student to refer to key points that help in answering the questions with ease.

Chapter 1

Lesson 1: Supporting Statements

Note: What the text says explicitly is interpreted as identifying the main ideas and then quoting statements that support (explain or provide more detail) about the main ideas.

Let us understand the concept with an example.

Facts about the North American Lobster

The North American lobster (Homarus americanus) is a fascinating marine creature. It can be found in bodies of cold salt water from Labrador to North Carolina. Lobsters are scavengers – they eat other fish and marine animals like clams and mussels – dead or alive. They are also considered a delicacy by many people.

Lobsters go through a life cycle that has several stages, in which they are very vulnerable to predators. Lobsters develop from thousands of eggs in the female. The eggs are pushed out of the female's body into the water where they hatch and are known as larvae. Larvae float or swim at or near the surface of the water; they do not have permanent shelters to live in. Because of this, there needs to be thousands of eggs to hatch thousands of larvae, because the larvae are preyed upon by seabirds and various species of fish and crustaceans. After the larvae stage, lobsters grow to become juvenile lobsters and then adult lobsters. In order for adult lobsters to grow larger, the must shed their shells and grow new, larger ones. This process is called molting.

Juvenile and adult lobsters live on the bottom of salt water bays, rivers and oceans, because there is always water there regardless of the changes in depth from the tide. Lobsters need cold salt water to survive, and salinity is a measure of how much salt is in salt water. Salinity concentrations of at least 20 ppt (parts of salt per thousand units of water) are preferred by lobsters. Adult lobsters prefer water temperatures ranging from 8 to 14 degrees C (46 to 53 degrees F). Water temperature is a major factor influencing lobster activity levels and migrations.

Because juvenile and adult lobsters live at the bottom of the water, they are prey for bottom or reef inhabiting species such as sculpin, cod, sharks, rays, skates, octopus and crabs. Predators also include lobster fishermen. To protect themselves from these predators, lobsters prefer crevices and niches on the bottom made up of small clusters of rocks called cobble (that resemble cobblestones) that frequently sit on sandy or muddy bottoms in areas in rivers, bays and areas of the ocean that are near shore. Areas with substantial underwater plant life are also suitable habitats.

Adult and juvenile lobsters are primarily nocturnal – that is, most active at dusk and during the night until dawn, spending most of their time searching for food. They tend to stay in their shelters during the day, but some studies have shown that lobsters may also be active during daylight hours.

Lobsters are an expensive delicacy today, but they were not always so highly valued or regarded. Hundreds of years ago, lobsters were so plentiful and easy to catch in shallow water near the shoreline that Native Americans used them to fertilize their fields and to bait their hooks for fishing. In colonial times, lobsters were considered "poverty food" and harvested by hand along the shoreline to be served to prisoners and indentured servants, and to widows and children dependent on charitable donations. Today, lobsters are desirable as delicacies, too valuable to be used as fertilizer or fish bait or food for prisoners.

At one time in its history, the North American lobster population shrank to dangerously low levels. Before about 1840, the industry remained local to the places where they were caught, because there was not refrigeration available to prevent lobster meat from spoiling. This situation changed abruptly with the introduction of the canning industry which allowed lobster meat to be shipped to other areas. Canning was so efficient in processing large quantities of lobster meat that eventually only fewer and smaller lobsters were available, a sign that the fishery had been overfished.

What has resulted are measures and techniques to prevent overfishing. First, the introduction of rules that lobster fishermen must follow, such as minimum size limits, requirements to throw back females carrying eggs and periods during the year when lobstering is not allowed. Second is the availability of live lobsters, instead of canned lobster meat, because of the construction of lobster pounds with circulating fresh salt water.

Your assignment: Summarize the main ideas of this article and quote statements that support (provide more detail or examples) the main idea.

This is what you might write.

Note: we have chosen a bullet point format for the summary, in which each bullet point represents a different main idea quoted from the article (shown in bold type and quotation marks) along with statements that support the main idea (shown in plain type).

*   **Life cycle: "Lobsters go through a life cycle that has several stages, in which they are very vulnerable to predators."** Lobsters develop from thousands of eggs in the female. The eggs are pushed out of the female's body into the water where they hatch and are known as larvae. Larvae float or swim at or near the surface of the water; they do not have permanent shelters to live in. Because of this, there needs to be thousands of eggs to hatch thousands of larvae, because the larvae are preyed upon by seabirds and various species of fish and crustaceans.

    After the larvae stage, lobsters grow to become juvenile lobsters and then adult lobsters. "In order for adult lobsters to grow larger, the must shed their shells and grow new, larger ones. This process is called molting."

- **Environment: "Lobsters need cold salt water to survive...."** Salinity concentrations of at least 20 ppt (parts of salt per thousand units of water) are preferred by lobsters..."; "Adult lobsters prefer water temperatures ranging from 8 to 14 degrees C (46 to 53 degrees F)."

- **Geography: "Lobsters can be found in bodies of cold salt water from Labrador to North Carolina."**

- **Habitats: "Because juvenile and adult lobsters live at the bottom of the water, they are prey for bottom or reef inhabiting species such as sculpin, cod, sharks, rays, skates, octopus and crabs. Predators also include lobster fishermen."** To protect themselves from these predators, lobsters prefer crevices and niches on the bottom made up of small clusters of rocks called cobble (that resemble cobblestones) that frequently sit on sandy or muddy bottoms in areas in rivers, bays and areas of the ocean that are near shore. Areas with substantial underwater plant life are also suitable habitats.

- **Value to consumers: "Lobsters are an expensive delicacy today, but they were not always so highly valued or regarded."** Hundreds of years ago, lobsters were so plentiful and easy to catch in shallow water near the shoreline that Native Americans used them to fertilize their fields and to bait their hooks for fishing. In colonial times, lobsters were considered "poverty food" and harvested by hand along the shoreline to be served to prisoners and indentured servants, and to widows and children dependent on charitable donations.

- **Protection of the species: "What has resulted are measures and techniques to prevent overfishing."** What has resulted are measures and techniques to prevent overfishing. First, the introduction of rules that lobster fishermen must follow, such as minimum size limits, requirements to throw back females carrying eggs and periods during the year when lobstering is not allowed. Second is the availability of live lobsters, instead of canned lobster meat, because of the construction of lobster pounds with circulating fresh salt water.

You can scan the QR code given below or use the url to access additional EdSearch resources including videos and mobile apps related to *Supporting Statements.*

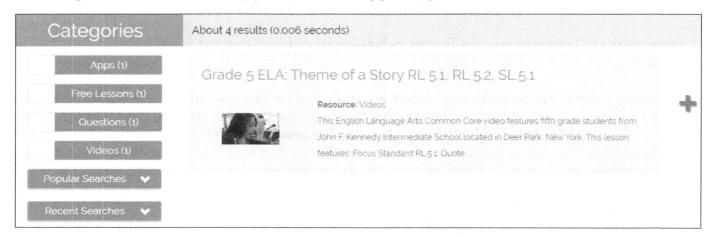

Read the poem below and answer the questions:

What is this life if, full of care,
We have no time to stand and stare?

No time to stand beneath the boughs
And stare as long as sheep or cows.

No time to see, when woods we pass,
Where squirrels hide their nuts in grass

No time to see, in broad daylight,
Streams full of stars, like skies at night.

No time to turn at Beauty's glance,
And watch her feet, how they can dance.

No time to wait till her mouth can
Enrich that smile her eyes began.

A poor life if, full of care,
We have no time to stand and stare.

-- W. H. Davies

1. Where can you find the answer to the question in the first stanza?

Ⓐ In the first stanza
Ⓑ In the fourth stanza
Ⓒ In the last stanza
Ⓓ The poet does not answer the question.

Once there was a severe drought. There was little water in Tony's well, and he didn't know what would happen to the fruit trees in his garden. Just then, he noticed three men looking intently at his house. He was certain that the three strangers were planning to rob his house. He acted quickly. He shouted out to his son, "My son, due to the drought, money has become scarce. There are many thieves. Let us protect our valuables, and put all of our jewels in a box and throw them into the well. They will be safe there." He quickly told his son to put some large stones in a box and throw them into the well. The thieves heard the sound of the box falling into the well and were happy.

That night they came to the well. The box was heavy and had landed deep down in the well. To get it, they would have to take out some of the water. They started drawing water from the well and pouring it onto the ground. Tony had made arrangements to make sure that the water reached his fruit trees. He had channels leading from the well to each of the trees.

By the time thieves found the box, they had drawn out enough water to water the trees. It was almost dawn. Tony sent for the soldiers, and just as the thieves were trying to open the box, they were caught red-handed.

After reading the story, enter the details in the map below. This will help you to answer the questions with ease.

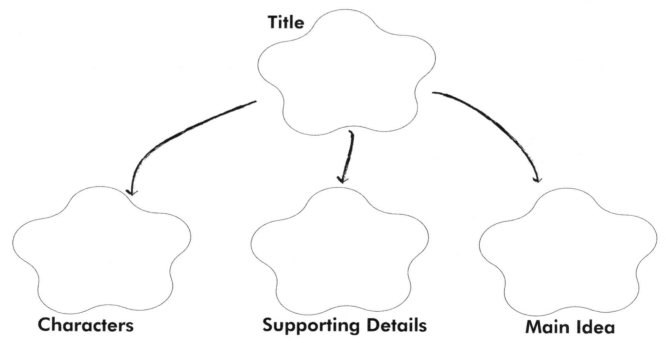

2. What would be an appropriate title for the above story?

Ⓐ "Cunning Tony"
Ⓑ "The Thieves"
Ⓒ "The Well"
Ⓓ "A Clever Idea"

3. What did Tony secretly ask his son to do?

Ⓐ To put the clothes in the box
Ⓑ To put the jewels in the box
Ⓒ To put the papers in the box
Ⓓ To put large stones in the box

4. The fruit trees got enough water because_____.

Ⓐ The thieves drew the water from the well and poured it on the ground.
Ⓑ The thieves did not draw the water from the well.
Ⓒ The thieves watered the garden.
Ⓓ Tony watered the garden.

5. What happened to the thieves as they were trying to open the box?

Ⓐ They found the jewels.
Ⓑ They were caught red-handed.
Ⓒ They did not find the box.
Ⓓ They took the money.

6. Which details in the above story tells us that the country was going through a difficult time?

Ⓐ Once there was a severe drought.
Ⓑ There was little water in Tony's well.
Ⓒ He shouted out to his son, "My son, because of the drought, money has become scarce."
Ⓓ All of the above.

The Glass Cupboard

There was a king who had a cupboard that was made entirely of glass. It was a special cupboard. It looked empty, but you could always take out anything you wanted. There was only one thing that had to be remembered. Whenever something was taken out of it, something else had to be put back in, although nobody knew why.

One day some thieves broke into the palace and stole the cupboard. "Now, we can have anything we want," they said. One of the thieves said, "I want a large bag of gold," and he opened the glass cupboard and got it. The other two did the same and they, too, got exactly what they wanted. The thieves forgot one thing. Not one of them put anything back inside the cupboard.

This went on and on for weeks and months. At last, the leader of the thieves could bear it no longer. He took a hammer and smashed the glass cupboard into a million pieces, and then all three thieves fell down dead.

When the king returned home, he ordered his servants to search for the cupboard. When the servants found it and the dead thieves, they filled sixty great carts with the gold and took it back to the king. He said, "If those thieves had only put something back into the cupboard, they would be alive to this day."

He ordered his servants to collect all of the pieces of glass and melt into a globe of the world with all the countries on it, this was to remind himself and others, to give back something in return when someone shows an act of kindness or gives us something.

After reading the story, enter the details in the map below. This will help you to answer the questions with ease.

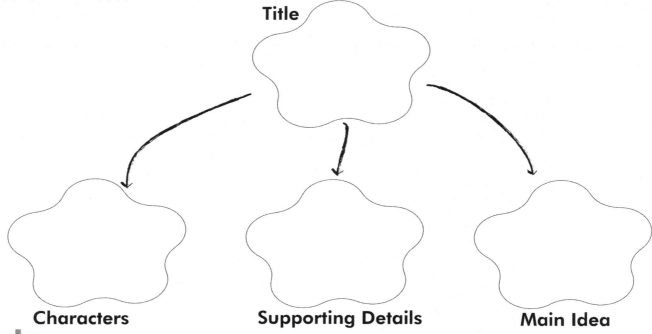

Title

Characters   **Supporting Details**   **Main Idea**

7. What happened when the king was away?

Ⓐ There was a storm, and it smashed the glass cupboard.
Ⓑ The people in the palace accidentally broke the glass cupboard.
Ⓒ Some thieves broke into the palace and stole the glass cupboard.
Ⓓ None of the above

8. What did the thieves take out of the cupboard?

Ⓐ They took out bags of gold.
Ⓑ They took out bags of silver.
Ⓒ They took out bags of diamonds.
Ⓓ They took out bags of stones.

9. What did the thieves forget to do?

Ⓐ They forgot to take out everything that was in the cupboard every time.
Ⓑ They forgot to break the cupboard each time they took something out.
Ⓒ They forgot to take out the jewels.
Ⓓ They forgot to put something back each time they took something out.

The Traveler

A weary traveler stopped at Sam's house and asked him for shelter for the night. Sam was a friendly soul. He not only agreed to let the traveler stay for the night, he decided to treat his guest to some curried chicken. So he bought a couple of chickens from the market and gave them to his wife to cook. Then he went off to buy some fruit.

Now Sam's wife could not resist food. She had a habit of eating as she cooked. So, as she cooked the meat, she smelled the rich steam and could not help tasting a piece. It was tender and delicious, and she decided to have another piece. Soon there was only a tiny bit left. Her little son, Kevin, ran into the kitchen. She gave him that little piece.

Kevin found it so tasty that he begged his mother for more. But there was no more chicken left. The traveler, who had gone to have a wash, returned. The woman heard him coming and had to think of a plan quickly. She began to scold her son loudly. "Your father has taught you a shameful and disgusting habit. Stop it, I tell you!" The traveler was curious. "What habit has his father taught the child?" he asked.

"Oh," said the woman, "Whenever a guest arrives, my husband cuts off their ears and roasts them for my son to eat."

The traveler was shocked. He picked up his shoes and fled.

"Why has our guest left in such a hurry?" asked Sam, when he came back.

"A fine guest indeed!" exclaimed his wife. "He snatched the chickens out of my pot and ran off with them!"

"The chickens!" exclaimed Sam. He ran after his guest, shouting. "Let me have one, at least; you may keep the other!" But his guest only ran faster!

After reading the story, enter the details in the map below. This will help you to answer the question with ease.

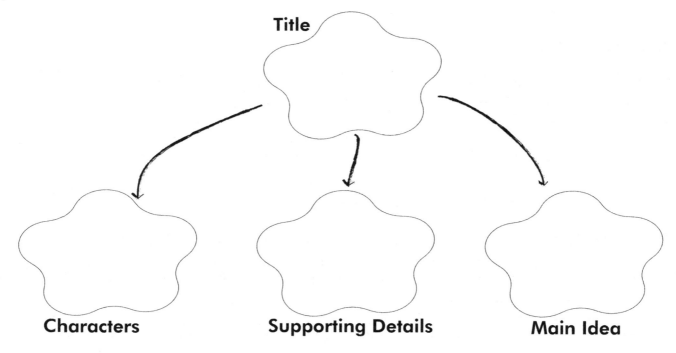

10. Which details in the above paragraph support the fact that the traveler was scared?

Ⓐ The traveler was curious.
Ⓑ The traveler was shocked. He picked up his shoes and fled.
Ⓒ The traveler, who had gone to have a wash, returned.
Ⓓ None of the above.

Chapter 1

Lesson 2: Drawing Inferences

You can scan the QR code given below or use the url to access additional EdSearch resources including videos and mobile apps related to *Drawing Inferences*.

 **Search**

Drawing Inferences

URL	QR Code
http://www.lumoslearning.com/a/rl51	

A Clever Idea

Once there was a severe drought. There was little water in Tony's well, and he didn't know what would happen to the fruit trees in his garden. Just then, he noticed three men looking intently at his house. He was certain that the three strangers were planning to rob his house. He acted quickly. He shouted out to his son, "My son, due to the drought, money has become scarce. There are many thieves. Let us protect our valuables, and put all of our jewels in a box and throw them into the well. They will be safe there." He quickly told his son to put some large stones in a box and throw them into the well. The thieves heard the sound of the box falling into the well and were happy.

That night they came to the well. The box was heavy and had landed deep down in the well. To get it, they would have to take out some of the water. They started drawing water from the well and pouring it onto the ground. Tony had made arrangements to make sure that the water reached his fruit trees. He had channels leading from the well to each of the trees.

By the time thieves found the box, they had drawn out enough water to water the trees. It was almost dawn. Tony sent for the soldiers, and just as the thieves were trying to open the box, they were caught red-handed.

After reading the story, enter the details in the map below. This will help you to answer the questions with ease.

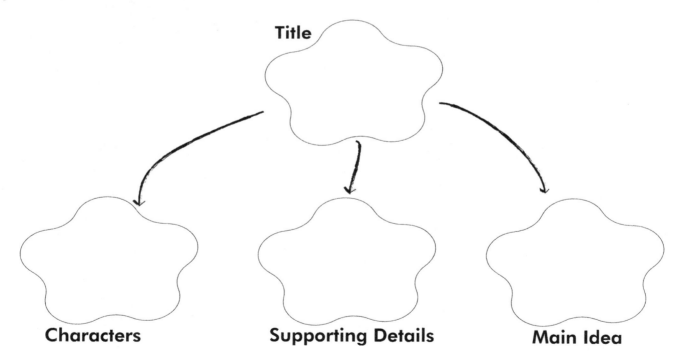

1. The above passage is about _____.

Ⓐ how the thieves watered the field.
Ⓑ how the thieves robbed for money.
Ⓒ how the thieves took the jewels.
Ⓓ how the thieves put the box in the well.

2. Why did Tony throw a box of stones down the well?

Ⓐ The stones were valuable to Tony.
Ⓑ The stones were worth a fortune.
Ⓒ The stones were a diversion.
Ⓓ There was no money at all.

3. Why did Tony send for soldiers?

Ⓐ Tony worked for the Army.
Ⓑ They enforced the laws of the area.
Ⓒ The police were stealing the jewels.
Ⓓ Tony trusted the thieves.

The Traveler

A weary traveler stopped at Sam's house and asked him for shelter for the night. Sam was a friendly soul. He not only agreed to let the traveler stay for the night, and he decided to treat his guest to some curried chicken. So he bought a couple of chickens from the market and gave them to his wife to cook. Then, he went off to buy some fruit.

Now, Sam's wife could not resist food. She had a habit of eating as she cooked. So as she cooked the meat, she smelled the rich steam and could not help tasting a piece. It was tender and delicious, and she decided to have another piece. Soon, there was only a tiny bit left.

Her little son, Kevin, ran into the kitchen. She gave him that little piece. Kevin found it so tasty that he begged his mother for more. But, there was no more chicken left. The traveler, who had gone to have a wash, returned. The woman heard him coming and had to think of a plan quickly. She began to scold her son loudly: "Your father has taught you a shameful and disgusting habit. Stop it, I tell you!"

The traveler was curious. "What habit has his father taught the child?" he asked.

"Oh," said the woman, "Whenever a guest arrives, my husband cuts off their ears and roasts them for my son to eat."

The traveler was shocked. He picked up his shoes and fled. "Why has our guest left in such a hurry?" asked Sam when he came back.

"A fine guest indeed!" exclaimed his wife. "He snatched the chickens out of my pot and ran off with them!"

"The chickens!" exclaimed Sam. He ran after his guest, shouting, "Let me have one, at least; you may keep the other!" But, his guest only ran faster!

After reading the story, enter the details in the map below. This will help you to answer the questions with ease.

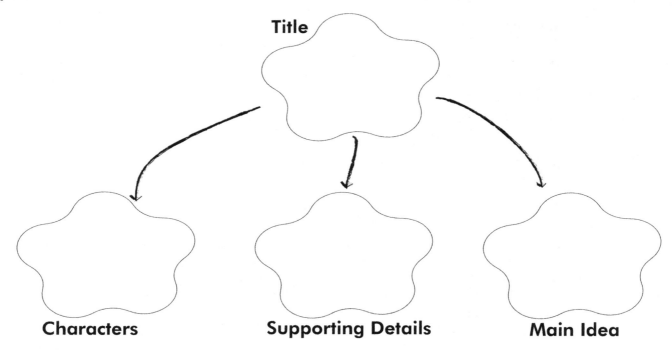

Title

Characters   **Supporting Details**   **Main Idea**

4. According to the above story, what kind of a man was Sam?

Ⓐ He was a friendly and helpful man.
Ⓑ He was a dangerous and cruel man.
Ⓒ He was a miserly and cunning man.
Ⓓ He was a friendly and miserable man.

5. According to the above story, how can you describe the character of Sam's wife?

Ⓐ She liked food a lot.
Ⓑ She was very cunning and clever.
Ⓒ She was a very good cook.
Ⓓ All of the above

Do Your Best

Katie stood before the crowd blushing and wringing her hands. She looked out and saw the room full of faces. Some she knew, and some she did not. But, they were all here to listen to her. Taking a deep breath, she opened her mouth, but no words came out. Tears formed in the corners of her eyes as she closed them.

With her eyes closed, she imagined her mother helping her get dressed and ready for tonight. "Just do your best," is what her mother had told her.

She opened her eyes and found her mother's smiling face in the crowd. Relaxing, she took another deep breath and started singing. She did not stop until she finished, and the crowd was on their feet applauding.

After the show, she found her parents and her friends. They all had wonderful things to say about her song and how proud they were because she kept going even when it seemed like she might give up. She shrugged her shoulders and shared a smile with her mother.

"I just did my best," she answered.

After reading the story, enter the details in the map below. This will help you to answer the questions with ease.

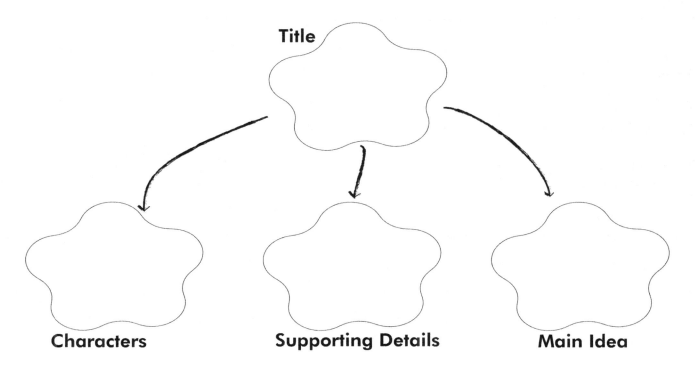

6. The above passage is about _____.

   (A) being determined
   (B) giving up
   (C) listening to friends
   (D) taking a deep breath

7. At the beginning of the story, how was Katie feeling?

   (A) Katie was friendly.
   (B) Katie was excited.
   (C) Katie was depressed.
   (D) Katie was nervous.

What is this life if, full of care,
We have no time to stand and stare?

No time to stand beneath the boughs
And stare as long as sheep or cows.

No time to see, when woods we pass,
Where squirrels hide their nuts in grass

No time to see, in broad daylight,
Streams full of stars, like skies at night.

No time to turn at Beauty's glance,
And watch her feet, how they can dance.

No time to wait till her mouth can
Enrich that smile her eyes began.

A poor life if, full of care,
We have no time to stand and stare.

-- W. H. Davies

8. What do you think is an appropriate title for the above poem?

Ⓐ "Stand and Stare"
Ⓑ "Leisure"
Ⓒ "Hard Work"
Ⓓ "No Time"

Late for School

Marrah heard the brakes on the bus as she shoveled the rest of her breakfast into her mouth. "You just missed the bus!" Marrah's mother yelled. "Why can't you ever be on time?"

"I'm sorry, Mom," Marrah sighed. She ran upstairs to her room so she could get her backpack, knowing she needed to hurry because her mother would have to take her to school.

"Let's go, Marrah!" Her mother called from downstairs. "You don't want to be late for school too!"

Frantic now, Marrah lifted her sheets to look under them before dropping to her knees in front of her bed. She pushed mounds of clothes out of the way as she continued to search for her backpack.

"Marrah!" Her mother called again. She could hear the impatience in her mother's voice downstairs. She ran out of her room and leaned over the rail.

"I can't find my backpack!" She cried out.

"You mean this one?" Her mother pulled the bag from the floor beside her.

"Oh," she replied, her shoulders sagging as she walked down the stairs.

"Let's go to school, Marrah." Her mother said with a small smile on her face as they walked out the door.

After reading the story, enter the details in the map below. This will help you to answer the question with ease.

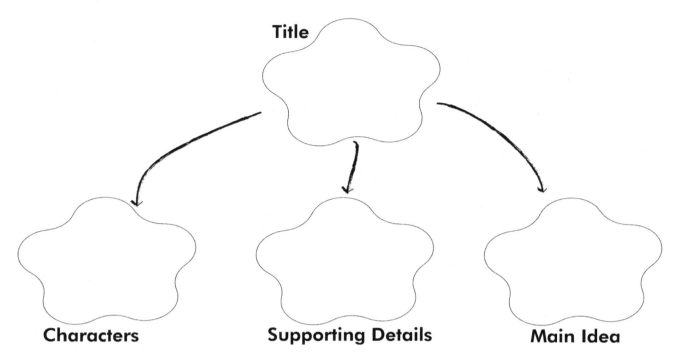

Title

Characters   **Supporting Details**   **Main Idea**

9. Which characteristics below describe Marrah?

Ⓐ Happy, organized, punctual
Ⓑ Sad, depressed, unhappy
Ⓒ Disorganized, frustrated, tardy
Ⓓ Annoyed, confused, pleased

THE LITTLE PINK ROSE

Best Stories to Tell to Children (1912)

By Sara Cone Bryant

Once there was a little pink Rosebud, and she lived down in a little dark house under the ground. One day she was sitting there, all by herself, and it was very still. Suddenly, she heard a little tap, tap, tap, at the door. "Who is that?" she said.

"It's the Rain, and I want to come in," said a soft, sad, little voice.

"No, you can't come in," the little Rosebud said. By and by she heard another little tap, tap, tap, on the window pane. "Who is there?" she said.

The same soft little voice answered, "It's the Rain, and I want to come in!"

"No, you can't come in," said the little Rosebud. Then it was very still for a long time. At last, there came a little rustling, whispering sound, all around the window: rustle, whisper, whisper. "Who is there?" said the little Rosebud.

"It's the Sunshine," said a little, soft, cheery voice, "and I want to come in!"

"N -- no," said the little pink rose, "you can't come in." And she sat still again.

Pretty soon, she heard the sweet little rustling noise at the key-hole. "Who is there?" she said.

"It's the Sunshine," said the cheery little voice, "and I want to come in. I want to come in!"

"No, no," said the little pink rose, "you cannot come in."

By and by, as she sat so still, she heard tap, tap, tap, and rustle, whisper, rustle, all up and down the window pane, and on the door, and at the key-hole. "Who is there?" she said.

"It's the Rain and the Sun, the Rain and the Sun," said two little voices, together, "and we want to come in! We want to come in! We want to come in!"

"Dear, dear," said the little Rosebud, "if there are two of you, I s'pose I shall have to let you in." So she opened the door a little wee crack, and they came in. And one took one of her little hands, and the other took her other little hand, and they ran, ran, ran with her, right up to the top of the ground. Then they said, --

"Poke your head through!"

So she poked her head through, and she was in the midst of a beautiful garden. It was springtime, and all the other flowers had their heads poked through, and she was the prettiest little pink rose in the whole garden!

After reading the story, enter the details in the map below. This will help you to answer the question with ease.

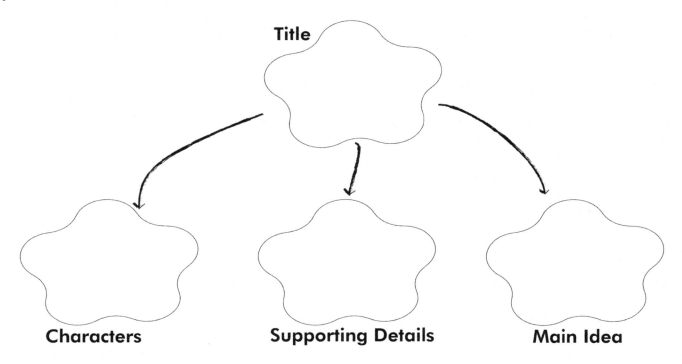

10. What conclusion can you draw from the story?

Ⓐ Flowers make friends.
Ⓑ Flowers need the sun and the rain to grow.
Ⓒ Flowers need other flowers in order to grow.
Ⓓ Flowers need sunshine in their garden.

Chapter 1

Lesson 3: Theme

Let us understand the concept with an example.

What is this life if, full of care,
We have no time to stand and stare?
No time to stand beneath the boughs
And stare as long as sheep or cows.
No time to see, when woods we pass,
Where squirrels hide their nuts in grass.
No time to see, in broad daylight,
Streams full of stars, like skies at night.
No time to turn at Beauty's glance,
And watch her feet, how they can dance.
No time to wait till her mouth can
Enrich that smile her eyes began.
A poor life if, full of care,
We have no time to stand and stare.

W. H. Davies

Theme of poem and summary of the text: The theme is the same as the main idea.

Here is what you might write.

If one's life is so full of care (in which you can assume the poet includes concerns about one's occupation, concerns about one's health or the health of loved ones, or any other concerns that interfere with happiness) that one can't or won't take the time to enjoy nature (standing under a tree and just looking at the scenery or seeing the place where squirrel' hide nuts as you pass by a woods) or take the time with another person (to wait for them to smile about something that his/her eyes are already expressing) or to otherwise have the time to focus on any beauty around you (natural or human), then…no matter how much money or fame you have, you are living a poor life (poor quality of life).

You can scan the QR code given below or use the url to access additional EdSearch resources including videos and mobile apps related to *Theme*.

ed Search   *Theme*

URL	QR Code
http://www.lumoslearning.com/a/rl52	

Katie stood before the crowd blushing and wringing her hands. She looked out and saw the room full of faces. Some she knew, and some she did not. But, they were all here to listen to her. Taking a deep breath, she opened her mouth, but no words came out. Tears formed in the corners of her eyes as she closed them.

With her eyes closed, she imagined her mother helping her get dressed and ready for tonight. "Just do your best," is what her mother had told her. She opened her eyes and found her mother's smiling face in the crowd. Relaxing, she took another deep breath and started singing. She did not stop until she finished, and the crowd was on their feet applauding.

After the show, she found her parents and her friends. They all had wonderful things to say about her song and how proud they were because she kept going even when it seemed like she might give up. She shrugged her shoulders and shared a smile with her mother. "I just did my best," she answered.

After reading the story, enter the details in the map below. This will help you to answer the questions with ease.

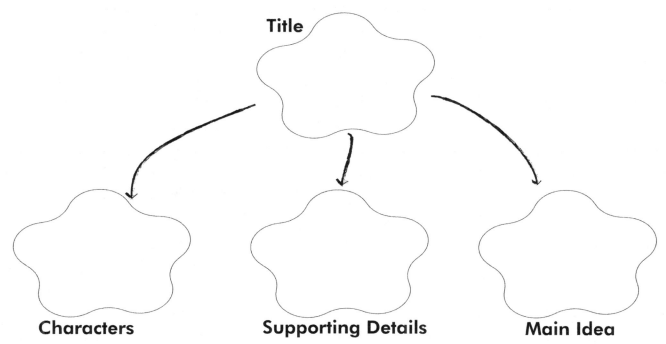

Title

Characters   **Supporting Details**   **Main Idea**

1. Choose a suitable title for this story.

Ⓐ "Trust People"
Ⓑ "Listening to Mom"
Ⓒ "Do Your Best"
Ⓓ "The Show"

2. What is the overall theme of this story?

(A) Give up under pressure.
(B) Always do your best.
(C) Never let your friends get you down.
(D) Close your eyes when you are getting ready to sing.

The Glass Cupboard

There was a king who had a cupboard that was made entirely of glass. It was a special cupboard. It looked empty, but you could always take out anything you wanted. There was only one thing that had to be remembered. Whenever something was taken out of it, something else had to be put back in, although nobody knew why.

One day some thieves broke into the palace and stole the cupboard. "Now, we can have anything we want," they said. One of the thieves said, "I want a large bag of gold," and he opened the glass cupboard and got it. The other two did the same and they, too, got exactly what they wanted. The thieves forgot one thing. Not one of them put anything back inside the cupboard.

This went on and on for weeks and months. At last, the leader of the thieves could bear it no longer. He took a hammer and smashed the glass cupboard into a million pieces, and then all three thieves fell down dead.

When the king returned home, he ordered his servants to search for the cupboard. When the servants found it and the dead thieves, they filled sixty great carts with the gold and took it back to the king. He said, "If those thieves had only put something back into the cupboard, they would be alive to this day."

He ordered his servants to collect all of the pieces of glass and melt into a globe of the world with all the countries on it, this was to remind himself and others, to give back something in return when someone shows an act of kindness or gives us something.

After reading the story, enter the details in the map below. This will help you to answer the question with ease.

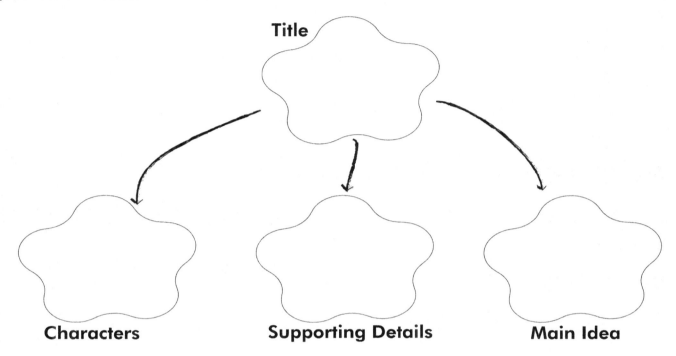

3. What is the purpose of this story?

    (A) This story is about learning how to break a glass cupboard.
    (B) This story is about learning the importance of gold.
    (C) This story is about giving something back in return.
    (D) This story is about a king.

What is this life if, full of care,
We have no time to stand and stare?

No time to stand beneath the boughs
And stare as long as sheep or cows.

No time to see, when woods we pass,
Where squirrels hide their nuts in grass

No time to see, in broad daylight,
Streams full of stars, like skies at night.

No time to turn at Beauty's glance,
And watch her feet, how they can dance.

No time to wait till her mouth can
Enrich that smile her eyes began.

A poor life if, full of care,
We have no time to stand and stare.

- W. H. Davies

4. What is the poet saying in the last stanza of the poem?

Ⓐ This stanza is saying that life is poor even if you have everything, because you have no time to stand and stare.
Ⓑ This stanza is saying that life is not good.
Ⓒ This stanza is saying that there is no time to stand and stare, so life is good.
Ⓓ None of the above

5. Choose a suitable title for this poem.

Ⓐ Life
Ⓑ Stare
Ⓒ Stop and Stare
Ⓓ Life and Stare

My daddy is a tiger,
My mother is a bear

My sister is a pest,
Who messes with my hair

And even though my home,
Is like living in a zoo

I know my family loves me,
And will take care of me too

6. What is this author trying to say in this poem?

   Ⓐ Even though the author's family is crazy, they will still take care of each other.
   Ⓑ The author's family is too crazy to care.
   Ⓒ The author's family is like a bunch of animals.
   Ⓓ The author's family is unpredictable.

In the kitchen,
After the aimless

Chatter of the plates,
The murmur of the stoves,

The chuckles of the water pipes,
And the sharp exchanges

Of the knives, forks, and spoons,
Comes the serious quiet

When the sink slowly clears its throat,
And you can hear the occasional rumble

Of the refrigerator's tummy
As it digests the cold.

7. Choose a suitable title for this poem.

   Ⓐ "The Sink"
   Ⓑ "The Plates"
   Ⓒ "The Kitchen"
   Ⓓ "The Refrigerator"

8. There is a lot of _____ in this kitchen.

   Ⓐ silence and stillness
   Ⓑ sound and activity
   Ⓒ chatter and murmur
   Ⓓ rumble and chill

Yesterday, I decided to make a cake. I mixed the ingredients, poured it into a pan, and placed the pan in the oven. Twenty minutes later, I heard the timer ring and I reached into the oven to pull out the cake. I quickly realized that I had forgotten to put oven mitts on! As a result, I ended up with yummy cake but extremely burned hands.

After reading the paragraph, enter the details in the map below. This will help you to answer the questions with ease.

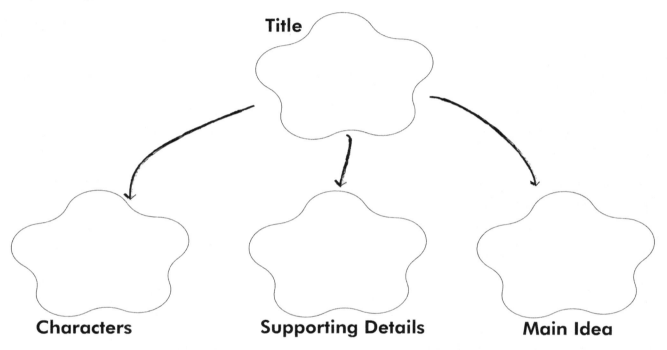

9. What is the theme of the passage?

Ⓐ Enjoy your cake.
Ⓑ Have fun baking.
Ⓒ Be careful when baking.
Ⓓ Never make a cake.

THE LITTLE PINK ROSE

Best Stories to Tell to Children (1912)
By Sara Cone Bryant

Once there was a little pink Rosebud, and she lived down in a little dark house under the ground. One day she was sitting there, all by herself, and it was very still. Suddenly, she heard a little tap, tap, tap, at the door. "Who is that?" she said.

"It's the Rain, and I want to come in," said a soft, sad, little voice.

"No, you can't come in," the little Rosebud said. By and by she heard another little tap, tap, tap, on the window pane. "Who is there?" she said.

The same soft little voice answered, "It's the Rain, and I want to come in!"

"No, you can't come in," said the little Rosebud. Then it was very still for a long time. At last, there came a little rustling, whispering sound, all around the window: rustle, whisper, whisper. "Who is there?" said the little Rosebud.

"It's the Sunshine," said a little, soft, cheery voice, "and I want to come in!"

"N -- no," said the little pink rose, "you can't come in." And she sat still again.

Pretty soon, she heard the sweet little rustling noise at the key-hole. "Who is there?" she said.

"It's the Sunshine," said the cheery little voice, "and I want to come in. I want to come in!"

"No, no," said the little pink rose, "you cannot come in."

By and by, as she sat so still, she heard tap, tap, tap, and rustle, whisper, rustle, all up and down the window pane, and on the door, and at the key-hole. "Who is there?" she said.

"It's the Rain and the Sun, the Rain and the Sun," said two little voices, together, "and we want to come in! We want to come in! We want to come in!"

"Dear, dear," said the little Rosebud, "if there are two of you, I s'pose I shall have to let you in." So she opened the door a little wee crack, and they came in. And one took one of her little hands, and the other took her other little hand, and they ran, ran, ran with her, right up to the top of the ground. Then they said, --

"Poke your head through!"

So she poked her head through, and she was in the midst of a beautiful garden. It was springtime, and all the other flowers had their heads poked through, and she was the prettiest little pink rose in the whole garden!

After reading the story, enter the details in the map below. This will help you to answer the question with ease.

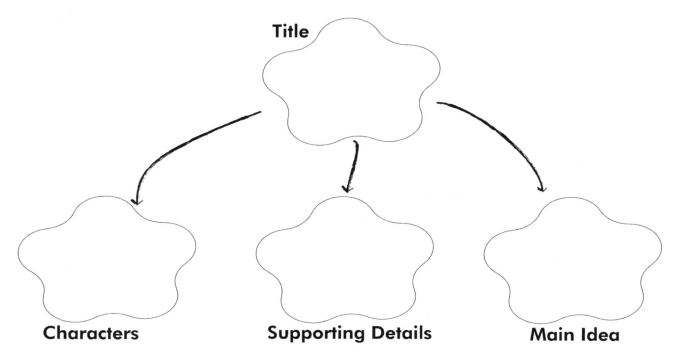

10. What is the theme of the story?

Ⓐ Take a risk and good things may happen.
Ⓑ Do your best.
Ⓒ Do not give up.
Ⓓ Never talk to strangers.

Chapter 1

Lesson 4: Characters

You can scan the QR code given below or use the url to access additional EdSearch resources including videos and mobile apps related to *Characters*.

 **Characters**

URL	QR Code
http://www.lumoslearning.com/a/rl52	

A Clever Idea

Once there was a severe drought. There was little water in Tony's well, and he didn't know what would happen to the fruit trees in his garden. Just then, he noticed three men looking intently at his house. He was certain that the three strangers were planning to rob his house. He acted quickly. He shouted out to his son, "My son, due to the drought, money has become scarce. There are many thieves. Let us protect our valuables, and put all of our jewels in a box and throw them into the well. They will be safe there." He quickly told his son to put some large stones in a box and throw them into the well. The thieves heard the sound of the box falling into the well and were happy.

That night they came to the well. The box was heavy and had landed deep down in the well. To get it, they would have to take out some of the water. They started drawing water from the well and pouring it onto the ground. Tony had made arrangements to make sure that the water reached his fruit trees. He had channels leading from the well to each of the trees.

By the time thieves found the box, they had drawn out enough water to water the trees. It was almost dawn. Tony sent for the soldiers, and just as the thieves were trying to open the box, they were caught red-handed.

After reading the story, enter the details in the map below. This will help you to answer the question with ease.

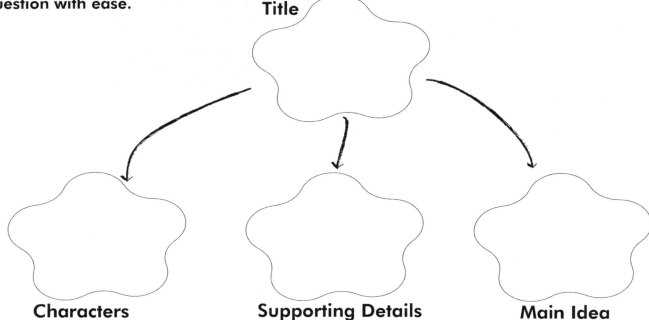

Title

Characters   Supporting Details   Main Idea

1. Which details in the story show that Tony is really clever?

   Ⓐ "Let us protect our valuables, and put all of our jewels in a box and throw them into the well. They will be safe there."

   Ⓑ He quickly told his son to put some large stones in a box and throw them into the well.

   Ⓒ Tony had made arrangements to make sure that the water reached the fruit trees. He had channels leading from the well to each of the trees.

   Ⓓ All of the above

The Glass Cupboard

There was a king who had a cupboard that was made entirely of glass. It was a special cupboard. It looked empty, but you could always take out anything you wanted. There was only one thing that had to be remembered. Whenever something was taken out of it, something else had to be put back in, although nobody knew why.

One day some thieves broke into the palace and stole the cupboard. "Now, we can have anything we want," they said. One of the thieves said, "I want a large bag of gold," and he opened the glass cupboard and got it. The other two did the same and they, too, got exactly what they wanted. The thieves forgot one thing. Not one of them put anything back inside the cupboard.

This went on and on for weeks and months. At last, the leader of the thieves could bear it no longer. He took a hammer and smashed the glass cupboard into a million pieces, and then all three thieves fell down dead.

When the king returned home, he ordered his servants to search for the cupboard. When the servants found it and the dead thieves, they filled sixty great carts with the gold and took it back to the king. He said, "If those thieves had only put something back into the cupboard, they would be alive to this day."

He ordered his servants to collect all of the pieces of glass and melt into a globe of the world with all the countries on it, this was to remind himself and others, to give back something in return when someone shows an act of kindness or gives us something.

After reading the story, enter the details in the map below. This will help you to answer the questions with ease.

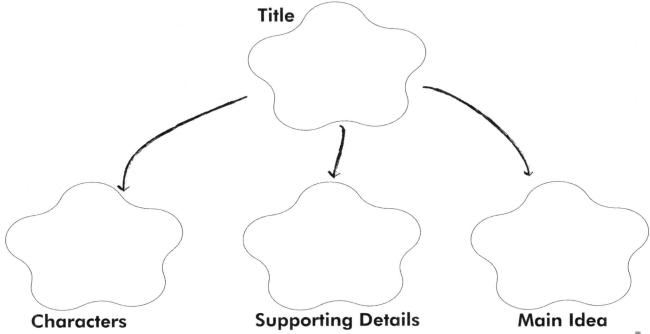

2. Who are the main characters in the above story?

Ⓐ The king and his servants
Ⓑ The king and the thieves
Ⓒ The king's servants
Ⓓ The glass cupboard thieves

3. How can the thieves best be described?

Ⓐ Skillful and careful
Ⓑ Greedy and careful
Ⓒ Greedy and careless
Ⓓ Unskilled and careful

4. The king in this story is _____.

Ⓐ ungrateful and rude
Ⓑ a dominating and greedy person
Ⓒ a mean and selfish person
Ⓓ a just and generous person

Do Your Best

Katie stood before the crowd blushing and wringing her hands. She looked out and saw the room full of faces. Some she knew and some she did not. But, they were all here to listen to her. Taking a deep breath, she opened her mouth but no words came out. Tears formed in the corners of her eyes as she closed them.

With her eyes closed, she imagined her mother helping her get dressed and ready for tonight. "Just do your best," is what her mother had told her. She opened her eyes and found her mother's smiling face in the crowd. Relaxing, she took another deep breath and started singing. She did not stop until she finished and the crowd was on their feet applauding.

After the show, she found her parents and her friends. They all had wonderful things to say about her song and how proud they were because she kept going even when it seemed like she might give up. She shrugged her shoulders and shared a smile with her mother. "I just did my best," she answered.

After reading the story, enter the details in the map below. This will help you to answer the questions with ease.

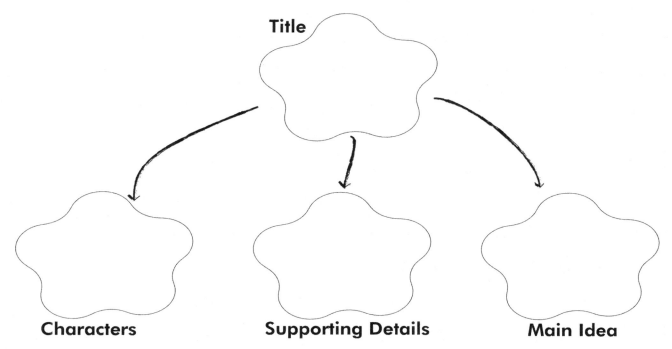

Title

Characters   **Supporting Details**   **Main Idea**

5. Who are the main characters in the above story?

Ⓐ Katie, her mother, and her friends
Ⓑ Katie and her mother
Ⓒ Katie and her parents
Ⓓ Katie and her friends

6. Who are the secondary characters is this story?

Ⓐ Katie and her mother
Ⓑ Katie's father and her mother
Ⓒ Katie's father and her friends
Ⓓ Katie and her friends

7. What does this story say about Katie's mother?

Ⓐ She was very supportive.
Ⓑ She was not supportive.
Ⓒ She did not believe in singing.
Ⓓ She wanted her daughter to make friends.

Late for School

Marrah heard the brakes on the bus as she shoveled the rest of her breakfast into her mouth. "You just missed the bus!" Marrah's mother yelled. "Why can't you ever be on time?"

"I'm sorry, Mom," Marrah sighed. She ran upstairs to her room so she could get her backpack, knowing she needed to hurry because her mother would have to take her to school.

"Let's go, Marrah!" Her mother called from downstairs. "You don't want to be late for school too!"

Frantic now, Marrah lifted her sheets to look under them before dropping to her knees in front of her bed. She pushed mounds of clothes out of the way as she continued to search for her backpack.

"Marrah!" Her mother called again. She could hear the impatience in her mother's voice downstairs. She ran out of her room and leaned over the rail.

"I can't find my backpack!" She cried out.

"You mean this one?" Her mother pulled the bag from the floor beside her.

"Oh," she replied, her shoulders sagging as she walked down the stairs.

"Let's go to school, Marrah." Her mother said with a small smile on her face as they walked out the door.

After reading the story, enter the details in the map below. This will help you to answer the questions with ease.

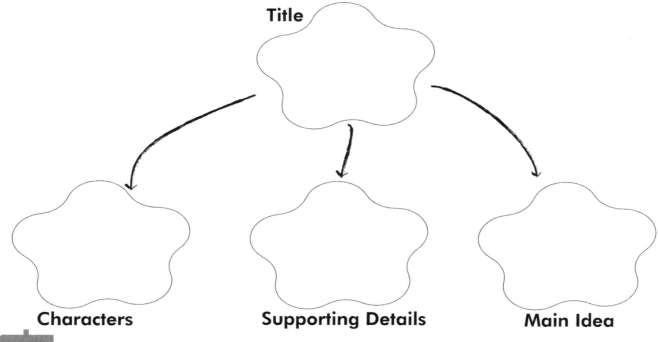

Title

Characters   **Supporting Details**   **Main Idea**

8. In the above story, Marrah appears to be _____ .

Ⓐ a very disorganized girl
Ⓑ a very organized girl
Ⓒ a very punctual girl
Ⓓ a very disciplined girl

9. What detail explains that Marrah's mother is kind even when she was frustrated with her daughter?

Ⓐ Her mother called again and she could hear the impatience in her voice downstairs.
Ⓑ "You just missed the bus!" Marrah's mother yelled. "Why can't you ever be on time?"
Ⓒ "Let's go, Marrah!" Her mother called from downstairs. "You don't want to be late to school too!"
Ⓓ "Let's go to school, Marrah." Her mother said with a small smile on her face as they walked out the door.

THE LITTLE PINK ROSE

Best Stories to Tell to Children (1912)

By Sara Cone Bryant

Once there was a little pink Rosebud, and she lived down in a little dark house under the ground. One day she was sitting there, all by herself, and it was very still. Suddenly, she heard a little tap, tap, tap, at the door. "Who is that?" she said.

"It's the Rain, and I want to come in," said a soft, sad, little voice.

"No, you can't come in," the little Rosebud said. By and by she heard another little tap, tap, tap, on the window pane. "Who is there?" she said.

The same soft little voice answered, "It's the Rain, and I want to come in!"

"No, you can't come in," said the little Rosebud. Then it was very still for a long time. At last, there came a little rustling, whispering sound, all around the window: rustle, whisper, whisper. "Who is there?" said the little Rosebud.

"It's the Sunshine," said a little, soft, cheery voice, "and I want to come in!"

"N -- no," said the little pink rose, "you can't come in." And she sat still again.

Pretty soon, she heard the sweet little rustling noise at the key-hole. "Who is there?" she said.

"It's the Sunshine," said the cheery little voice, "and I want to come in. I want to come in!"

"No, no," said the little pink rose, "you cannot come in."

By and by, as she sat so still, she heard tap, tap, tap, and rustle, whisper, rustle, all up and down the window pane, and on the door, and at the key-hole. "Who is there?" she said.

"It's the Rain and the Sun, the Rain and the Sun," said two little voices, together, "and we want to come in! We want to come in! We want to come in!"

"Dear, dear," said the little Rosebud, "if there are two of you, I s'pose I shall have to let you in." So she opened the door a little wee crack, and they came in. And one took one of her little hands, and the other took her other little hand, and they ran, ran, ran with her, right up to the top of the ground. Then they said, --

"Poke your head through!"

So she poked her head through, and she was in the midst of a beautiful garden. It was springtime, and all the other flowers had their heads poked through, and she was the prettiest little pink rose in the whole garden!

After reading the story, enter the details in the map below. This will help you to answer the question with ease.

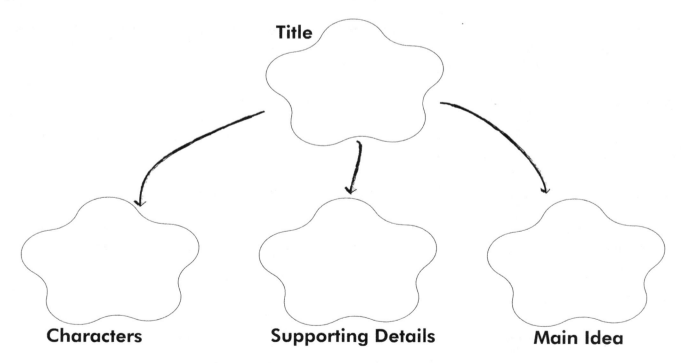

10. How can Rosebud best be described in the story?

Ⓐ She is excited and fearless.
Ⓑ She is happy and friendly.
Ⓒ She is shy and scared.
Ⓓ She is colorful and generous.

Chapter 1

Lesson 5: Summarizing Texts

You can scan the QR code given below or use the url to access additional EdSearch resources including videos and mobile apps related to *Summarizing Texts*.

Summarizing Texts

URL	QR Code
http://www.lumoslearning.com/a/rl52	

Morning Ride

As the sun was gradually rising across the plain, Chloe was preparing to saddle up her favorite horse, Pepper, to go for a morning ride. First she had to be sure the blanket was in place before getting the saddle. Chloe didn't mind the heavy weight of the saddle as she took it down from the rack and quickly threw it over Pepper's back. Sometimes she did wonder why the weight never bothered horses. Tightening the girth under the saddle would be the hardest part of all. If it was not just right, the saddle could slip causing a problem and possible injury to Chloe while riding. Finally, it was snug and secure.

Of course, Chloe took off the halter so that she could put on the bit and bridle along with the reins. Horses will follow people easier to the barn if they have on a halter. Chloe knew that Pepper would be no problem with her as Chloe kept her tack clean. The condition of the tack was so important in horse care.

Chloe's grandfather, Morgan, had always taught her to take pride in her care of horses. He told her many a time that the horse weighed over twelve hundred pounds. She needed to be sure to respect that and keep it in mind, but not to fear the horse.

She had been raised with horses since she was about two years old. She was taught to ride with someone leading her around. Chloe did not ride with saddles when she was little, just bareback. Saddling up came when Chloe was old enough to handle both saddle and tack.

Leading Pepper out of the barn was easy, as Chloe knew she was anxious for a morning run, as well.

One gentle but firm nudge on Pepper's sides and off they went as fast as lightning. The cool breeze blew through Chloe's hair and Pepper's mane. This was the way to start a new day!

After reading the story, enter the details in the map below. This will help you to answer the question with ease.

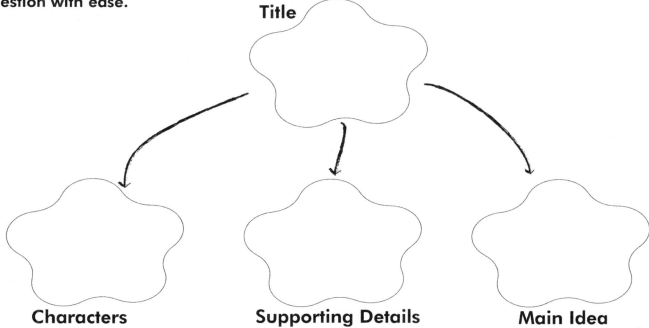

1. What is the passage above about?

Ⓐ It is about taking care of horses.
Ⓑ It is about how to saddle up a horse.
Ⓒ It is about Chloe enjoying riding her horse.
Ⓓ All of the above

Fishing and Chores

Joshua had lived in Mississippi all of his life. He grew up near the coast in a small rural community known as Franklin Creek. If you travel along Highway 10 going toward Alabama, it is the last exit in Mississippi.

Joshua loved to go fishing along the creek that ran behind his grandmother's massive house. He lived there with his grandmother and his parents. When he wanted to go fishing, his parents wanted to be sure that had had done his chores first. Joshua did not like chores at all. Quite often he tried to avoid doing his chores.

This became a real problem for Joshua's mother, as the house was very large, and keeping it clean required help from everyone. She often told Joshua that he would be a hindrance to the family if he did not do his part.

Little reminders did not seem to help. Scolding was of no use either. It seemed he would turn a deaf ear when it came to listening. Joshua's mother was beside herself.

One day his grandmother gave her an idea. Joshua had asked that morning to go fishing. Little did he know that his mother had taken the advice of Grandma and would soon put a stop to his ways of not doing chores. Joshua said, "Mom, chores are done! Can I go now?" His mother replied, "Sure, no problem."

Joshua hurried out to the storage building to gather his fishing gear. The fishing pole was not in its place! The tackle box wasn't there either! His fishing hat was missing, too! He ran back to the house where his mother and grandmother were drinking coffee on the porch.

Joshua asked, "Mom, where is all my fishing stuff?"

"What are you talking about, son?" Replied his mother.

"I can't find anything in the storage building." He said.

She then told him to go look in his room. She said she had put it all in there where he was supposed to have cleaned. When Joshua got to his room, he realized what was going on. In order to find his fishing equipment, he would have to go through the mess in his room. His mother and grandmother were right behind him laughing. He grinned and said, "I get it now, Mom." He cleaned his room and found all the things he needed for fishing, too!

Needless to say, Joshua never had a problem doing chores again!

After reading the story, enter the details in the map below. This will help you to answer the question with ease.

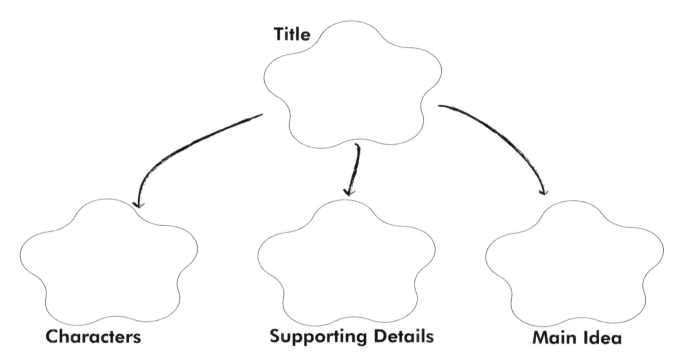

Title

Characters

Supporting Details

Main Idea

2. What is the passage about?

Ⓐ It is about how Joshua did his chores before going fishing.
Ⓑ It is about how Joshua's mother took the advice of his grandmother and taught him a lesson.
Ⓒ It is about how Joshua was scolded for not doing chores.
Ⓓ It is about how Joshua went fishing with his friends.

Birds flutter in the air.
Bees hum around me.
What a sight to see.
Green grass popping everywhere!
Trees and flowers in full bloom.
A look at Nature's happy face.
Then changes happen to the ground.
No more green, only brown.
Birds are gone for now.
Bees hide not to be found.
Leaves are falling all around.
Seasons change.

3. What is this poem about?

Ⓐ The changing of seasons
Ⓑ The changing of weather
Ⓒ The changing of birds
Ⓓ Nothing in particular

What is this life if, full of care,
We have no time to stand and stare?

No time to stand beneath the boughs
And stare as long as sheep or cows.

No time to see, when woods we pass,
Where squirrels hide their nuts in grass

No time to see, in broad daylight,
Streams full of stars, like skies at night.

No time to turn at Beauty's glance,
And watch her feet, how they can dance.

No time to wait till her mouth can
Enrich that smile her eyes began.

A poor life if, full of care,
We have no time to stand and stare.

- W. H. Davies

4. What is the above poem about?

Ⓐ It is about life.
Ⓑ It is about how busy our lives are occasionally.
Ⓒ It is about the importance of taking time to do things that you like.
Ⓓ It is about life not being fair.

Try Again

Surfing is one of Daniel's favorite pastimes! Every weekend when he has the time, he heads toward Port Aransas, Texas with his father. Daniel's family doesn't live far away, so it takes them only about 30 minutes to get there, if there is a short ferry line. They always make sure to get their things ready the night before. Daniel and his dad like to get an early start to their surfing day!

The night before, Daniel makes sure that his dad's truck is clean, especially the bed of the truck where he puts his surfboards. He also takes time to clean his wetsuit that he wears for protection and warmth. His mom usually makes sandwiches, and snacks ahead of time and puts them in the refrigerator to keep them fresh.

Daniel and his dad leave around 5:30 or 6:00 am when the sun is just coming up. Daniel has been surfing with his dad since he was very small. He remembers when his dad would ride with him on the surfboard.

When Daniel was about 9 years old, he fell off of a surfboard and hurt his leg and back. His dad rushed him to a nearby hospital for X-rays and a checkup. Luckily, there were no broken bones. However, the incident claimed Daniel so much that he refused to go surfing for several months. His dad kept encouraging him to give it a try. He told him, "If at once you don't succeed, try, and try again!" Daniel didn't want to try again. He was afraid of getting hurt and falling off of the surfboard.

Finally, Daniel went surfing with his father again. His father went out into the waves, and rode a wave in. Daniel went out on the waves, too. He stayed out for a long time without attempting to ride a wave back to shore. Daniel's dad began to wonder if his son had given up.

Just then a large wave began building up far out in the water. Daniel's dad was astonished! There was Daniel riding the huge wave all the way to shore without a problem. His dad motioned for Daniel to come where he was, but Daniel didn't. Instead he went right back into the water, and began riding wave after wave after wave!

It is amazing that fear can be overcome with one's personal best.

After reading the story, enter the details in the map below. This will help you to answer the questions with ease.

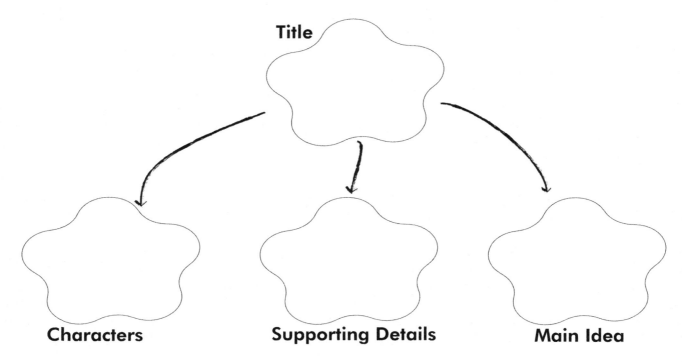

Title

Characters   **Supporting Details**   **Main Idea**

5. What is the story about?

Ⓐ Never give up when you have a surfboard.
Ⓑ Keep trying and you will do your best.
Ⓒ Listen to the waves.
Ⓓ Give up if you don't want to do something.

6. What does the first paragraph tell the reader?

Ⓐ Daniel doesn't like to go surfing with his dad.
Ⓑ Daniel and his dad enjoy going surfing together.
Ⓒ Daniel got hurt one time surfing.
Ⓓ Daniel gives up easily.

7. The second paragraph tells how Daniel _____.

Ⓐ is never ready on time to go surfing.
Ⓑ doesn't like to get his things ready the night before they go surfing
Ⓒ gets his things ready early the night before to go surfing
Ⓓ always forgets something when they go surfing.

8. In the fourth paragraph, Daniel's dad _____.

Ⓐ makes fun of him for not trying to surf again.
Ⓑ encourages him to try again
Ⓒ took him to the hospital when he got hurt
Ⓓ both B and C

How to Design and Make Awesome Snowflakes

With the coming of winter, many people are lucky to see gorgeous snowflakes in the air. Some people do not have snow where they live. All of us can grace our window panes with paper snow flakes. We can decorate our windows and make other crafts with these easy to make snowflakes. You can occupy many hours in a day by cutting out dozens of paper snowflakes.

The following directions will help you make your awesome winter wonderland of snowflakes. First take a square piece of paper and fold it in half diagonally to make a triangle. Then fold it in half again to make the corners meet as shown in figure 2 below.

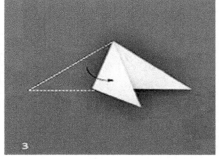

In figure 3, will notice that you will once again fold your triangle to make a smaller triangle. Be sure that you have the corners meeting and even.

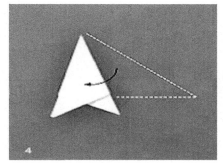

Now fold it over again to make the shape shown in figure 4. Be careful as you might need to adjust these folds to get the sides to match up. Crease the paper after the folds are done just right.

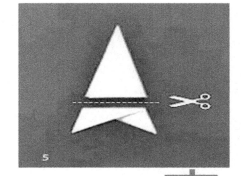

Cut straight across the bottom as shown in figure 5.

You are now ready to cut of various designs and shapes on your folded paper. Be careful not to cut straight across the entire fold.

Carefully unfold to see the awesome snowflake that you have designed and made. You can add color and, glitter. You can even make additional crafts out of multiple snowflakes. Enjoy your winter wonderland of snowflakes.

(Pictures taken from Martha Stewart online.)

9. What is this passage about?

Ⓐ It is about how to make a collage.
Ⓑ It is about how to decorate your house for the holidays.
Ⓒ It is about how to make snowflakes with paper.
Ⓓ It is about playing outside in the snow.

10. What is the last step before opening up the snowflake?

Ⓐ Folding a piece of paper in half diagonally.
Ⓑ Cutting off the bottom of the folded triangles.
Ⓒ Opening up the snowflake.
Ⓓ Cutting the folded triangles in designs and shapes.

Chapter 1

Lesson 6: Events

Compare means to find the similarities in two texts while Contrast means to find the differences in two texts.

Let us understand the concept with an example.

It was the bottom of the 7th inning of the baseball game, the last inning for the kids in this age group. The Pirates were trailing 4-3 with one out and a base runner at 2nd base.

Tommy was due to bat. In a league of older kids, the coach would have substituted a kid from the bench with the highest batting average, but in this league, a coach had to play each kid for at least 3 innings, and Tommy had only played 2 innings so far. The coach tried a pep talk with a "you can do it, we are depending on you" theme. But that did not motivate Tommy; it just made him feel more uncomfortable. And so, with that attitude, it was no surprise that Tommy struck out.

Next up was Zach. Zach had the highest batting average on the team, and was a nonstop dispenser of encouragement and optimism. The coach knew that Zach did not need any words of encouragement. The pitch, a fastball, was too fast for Zach; strike 1. Zach swung at the second pitch, and grounded it foul. His team watched from the dugout, convinced that maybe this pitcher was too skillful, even for Zach. But Zach stepped out of the batter's box, looked over at his teammates, smiled and gave them the high sign. His unspoken message was: relax, have confidence, I won't let you down.

Before he threw the next pitch, the pitcher sized up the situation and figured that Zach was primed to swing, so he pitched a low ball that initially appeared to be a strike but dropped down too low as it crossed home plate. Zach as not fooled; he held back; ball 1. Then the pitcher threw a higher pitch, figuring to catch Zach off guard, and he did, causing Zach to swing but only get a piece of it, and it went foul. Still strike 2, ball 1. The next pitch was also too low; ball 2. The opposing crowd sensed the end of the game was coming , that Zach would make an out, so they were yelling encouragement to the pitcher, urging him on; they were the visitors but so many showed up they were louder than the home team crowd. Next pitch, a fastball, but this time Zach was ready; he swung hard and with a loud crack, the ball sailed toward right center field and a right fielder racing toward the outfield wall. The crowd was momentarily silent, watching to see where the ball would end up, and then the home team roared its approval as the ball cleared the right center field wall. A 2 run homer! And the Pirates began to celebrate. Zach was in his glory, surrounded by cheering teammates. Tommy was standing in the corner of the dugout, looking sad and being ignored.

Compare and contrast the two main characters and key events.

Zach was the model of a confident, optimistic person. He did not get discouraged by the 1-2 count nor by the yelling of the opposing team's fans. He continued to believe he would come through. Tommy, on the other hand, was not a starting player, and was put into the game for the last 3 innings because the coach had to allow him to play. He let his negative attitude distract him from the task at hand, which was to get a hit and move the base runner at least one base ahead, and not make an out. And as is human nature, the player who came through got the praise and attention; the one who did not got nothing. The most important events were the performances of the two batters.

You can scan the QR code given below or use the url to access additional EdSearch resources including videos and mobile apps related to *Events*.

ed)Search	**Events**
URL	**QR Code**
http://www.lumoslearning.com/a/rl53	

Salmon

A fish that is a great favorite with people is salmon. It begins its life in a small pool up a river. Far from the sea, the fish lays its eggs in a pool in the river. When the baby fish are a few inches long, they begin to swim down the river. As they grow bigger, they make their way towards the sea.

They jump over rocks, often with their tails first. Suddenly, they find themselves in the sea. The fish live in the sea for three years. They swim far away from land. How do they find their way back? These fish have a wonderful sense of smell. They remember the scent of their journey easily, because the river flowed to the sea and carried them there. After three years, most salmon swim toward the pools.

As soon as they reach a pool, the females lay their eggs. They lay their eggs near the edge of the water and cover them with sand. Soon the eggs hatch and the pool is full of small fish, getting ready for the long journey out to the sea.

After reading the story, enter the details in the map below. This will help you to answer the question with ease.

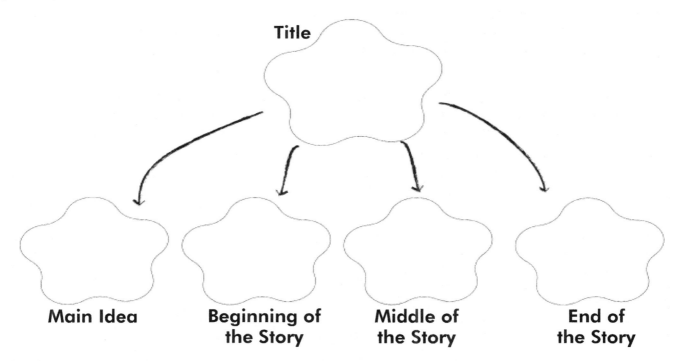

1. What is the first important event that happens in this story?

Ⓐ Salmon are a favorite of many people.
Ⓑ The fish lay their eggs in the river.
Ⓒ The fish live in the ocean for three years.
Ⓓ The fish swim to the ocean.

Fishing and Chores

Joshua had lived in Mississippi all of his life. He grew up near the coast in a small rural community known as Franklin Creek. If you travel along Highway 10 going toward Alabama, it is the last exit in Mississippi.

Joshua loved to go fishing along the creek that ran behind his grandmother's massive house. He lived there with his grandmother and his parents. When he wanted to go fishing, his parents wanted to be sure that had had done his chores first. Joshua did not like chores at all. Quite often he tried to avoid doing his chores.

This became a real problem for Joshua's mother, as the house was very large, and keeping it clean required help from everyone. She often told Joshua that he would be a hindrance to the family if he did not do his part.

Little reminders did not seem to help. Scolding was of no use either. It seemed he would turn a deaf ear when it came to listening. Joshua's mother was beside herself.

One day his grandmother gave her an idea. Joshua had asked that morning to go fishing. Little did he know that his mother had taken the advice of Grandma and would soon put a stop to his ways of not doing chores. Joshua said, "Mom, chores are done! Can I go now?" His mother replied, "Sure, no problem."

Joshua hurried out to the storage building to gather his fishing gear. The fishing pole was not in its place! The tackle box wasn't there either! His fishing hat was missing, too! He ran back to the house where his mother and grandmother were drinking coffee on the porch.

Joshua asked, "Mom, where is all my fishing stuff?"

"What are you talking about, son?" Replied his mother.

"I can't find anything in the storage building." He said.

She then told him to go look in his room. She said she had put it all in there where he was supposed to have cleaned. When Joshua got to his room, he realized what was going on. In order to find his fishing equipment, he would have to go through the mess in his room. His mother and grandmother were right behind him laughing. He grinned and said, "I get it now, Mom." He cleaned his room and found all the things he needed for fishing, too!

Needless to say, Joshua never had a problem doing chores again!

After reading the story, enter the details in the map below. This will help you to answer the questions with ease.

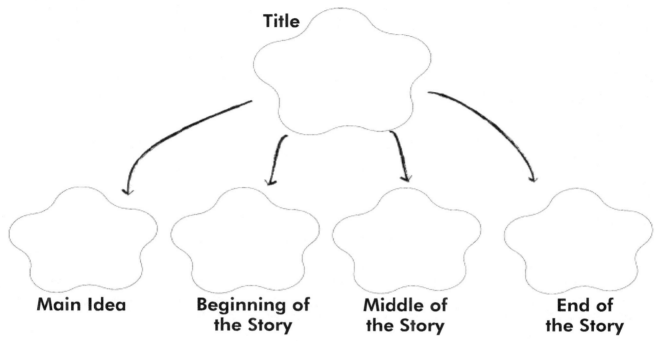

Title

Main Idea   **Beginning of the Story**   **Middle of the Story**   **End of the Story**

2. Which answer shows the correct timeline of events?

Ⓐ   Joshua did not like to do chores. He wanted to go fishing. His mother took Grandma's advice and tricked Joshua. Joshua cleaned is room and learned his lesson.

Ⓑ   Joshua wanted to go fishing with his friends. Grandma and his mother tricked him. He found his fishing gear. He went fishing with his friends.

Ⓒ   Joshua loved to do chores. He did then without being told to do so. He and his grand mother went fishing every day.

Ⓓ   Joshua did not like doing chores. He did them that morning so he could go fishing. He had trouble finding his fishing gear, but finally found it.

3. What happened at the end of the story?

Ⓐ   Joshua kept on not doing or avoiding chores.

Ⓑ   Joshua learned from what happened and didn't continue to avoid his chores.

Ⓒ   Joshua called his dad to come take him fishing.

Ⓓ   Joshua cried about not being able to find his fishing equipment.

Morning Ride

As the sun was gradually rising across the plain, Chloe was preparing to saddle up her favorite horse, Pepper, to go for a morning ride. First she had to be sure the blanket was in place before getting the saddle. Chloe didn't mind the heavy weight of the saddle as she took it down from the rack and quickly threw it over Pepper's back. Sometimes she did wonder why the weight never bothered horses. Tightening the girth under the saddle would be the hardest part of all. If it was not just right, the saddle could slip causing a problem and possible injury to Chloe while riding. Finally, it was snug and secure.

Of course, Chloe took off the halter so that she could put on the bit and bridle along with the reins. Horses will follow people easier to the barn if they have on a halter. Chloe knew that Pepper would be no problem with her as Chloe kept her tack clean. The condition of the tack was so important in horse care.

Chloe's grandfather, Morgan, had always taught her to take pride in her care of horses. He told her many a time that the horse weighed over twelve hundred pounds. She needed to be sure to respect that and keep it in mind, but not to fear the horse.

She had been raised with horses since she was about two years old. She was taught to ride with someone leading her around. Chloe did not ride with saddles when she was little, just bareback. Saddling up came when Chloe was old enough to handle both saddle and tack.

Leading Pepper out of the barn was easy, as Chloe knew she was anxious for a morning run, as well.

One gentle but firm nudge on Pepper's sides and off they went as fast as lightning. The cool breeze blew through Chloe's hair and Pepper's mane. This was the way to start a new day!

After reading the story, enter the details in the map below. This will help you to answer the questions with ease.

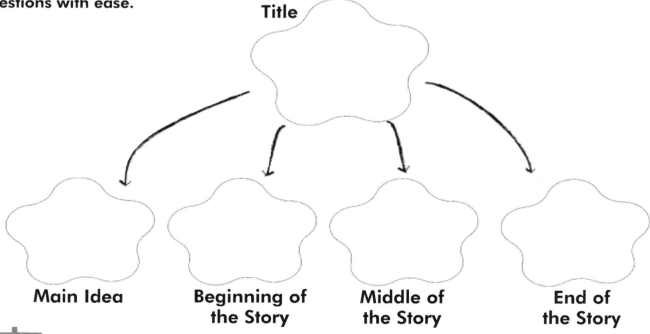

Title

Main Idea   **Beginning of the Story**   **Middle of the Story**   **End of the Story**

4. What is the first thing that Chloe does when getting ready to ride Pepper?

Ⓐ Chloe puts the saddle on.
Ⓑ Chloe tightens the girth underneath the horse.
Ⓒ Chloe puts the saddle blanket on.
Ⓓ The sun is shining brightly.

5. Which is the correct order of events?

Ⓐ Chloe puts the saddle blanket on. She then tightens the girth. She carefully places the saddle on Pepper. She takes off the halter and puts on the bit and bridle.
Ⓑ Chloe takes the saddle down and throws it over Pepper. She puts the blanket on Pep per. She tightens the girth. She gallops away.
Ⓒ Chloe takes the saddle down and throws it across Pepper's backside. She tightens the girth. She puts the blanket on Pepper. She rides away.
Ⓓ Chloe puts the saddle blanket on Pepper. Then she takes down the saddle and quickly throws it on Pepper's back. She tightens the girth securely. She puts on the bit and bridle after taking off the halter.

6. Using the letter at the beginning of each sentence, put the sentences into the correct order to make a paragraph.

A. Emily asks her mother to put the pan in the oven.
B. Emily loves to cook.
C. Emily loves brownies.
D. Emily asks her mother if she can make a snack.
E. She mixes the brownie mix, eggs, and oil together and pours them in a pan.

Ⓐ B, C, D, E, A
Ⓑ B, D, C, E, A
Ⓒ A, B, D, E, C
Ⓓ E, C, A, D, B

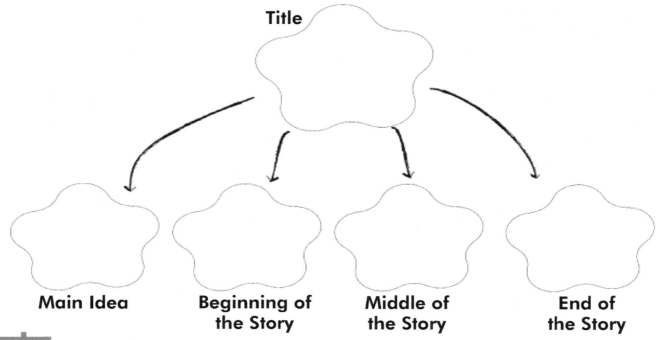
Late for School

Marrah heard the brakes on the bus as she shoveled the rest of her breakfast into her mouth. "You just missed the bus!" Marrah's mother yelled. "Why can't you ever be on time?"

"I'm sorry, Mom," Marrah sighed. She ran upstairs to her room so she could get her backpack, knowing she needed to hurry because her mother would have to take her to school.

"Let's go, Marrah!" Her mother called from downstairs. "You don't want to be late for school too!"

Frantic now, Marrah lifted her sheets to look under them before dropping to her knees in front of her bed. She pushed mounds of clothes out of the way as she continued to search for her backpack.

"Marrah!" Her mother called again. She could hear the impatience in her mother's voice downstairs. She ran out of her room and leaned over the rail.

"I can't find my backpack!" She cried out.

"You mean this one?" Her mother pulled the bag from the floor beside her.

"Oh," she replied, her shoulders sagging as she walked down the stairs.

"Let's go to school, Marrah." Her mother said with a small smile on her face as they walked out the door.

After reading the story, enter the details in the map below. This will help you to answer the questions with ease.

Title

Main Idea   **Beginning of the Story**   **Middle of the Story**   **End of the Story**

7. Which major event occurred first in the story?

Ⓐ The school bus arrived.
Ⓑ Marrah finished her breakfast.
Ⓒ Marrah searched for her bag.
Ⓓ Marrah ran down the stairs.

8. Which major event occurred at the end of the story?

Ⓐ Her mother took Marrah to school because she missed her school bus.
Ⓑ Marrah was still searching for her backpack.
Ⓒ Marrah took a day off from school.
Ⓓ Marrah's school bus waited for her to take her to school.

9. Using the letter at the beginning of each sentence, put the sentences above into the correct order to make a paragraph.

A. Janie plays with her puppy.
B. Janie realizes her puppy is covered with mud.
C. Janie grabs the shampoo and water hose.
D. She changes into play clothes.
E. Janie washes and dries her puppy.

Ⓐ E, C, D, B, A
Ⓑ B, D, C, E, A
Ⓒ C, B, A, D, E
Ⓓ A, C, E, D, B

10. All the above events took place because _____.

A. Emily asks her mother to put the pan in the oven.
B. Emily loves to cook.
C. Emily loves her brownies.
D. Emily asks her mother if she can make a snack.
E. She mixes the brownie mix, eggs, and oil together and pours them in a pan.

Ⓐ Emily loves her brownies.
Ⓑ Emily loves to cook.
Ⓒ Emily's mother puts the pan in the oven.
Ⓓ Emily wanted a snack.

Chapter 1

Lesson 7: Setting

You can scan the QR code given below or use the url to access additional EdSearch resources including videos and mobile apps related to *Setting*.

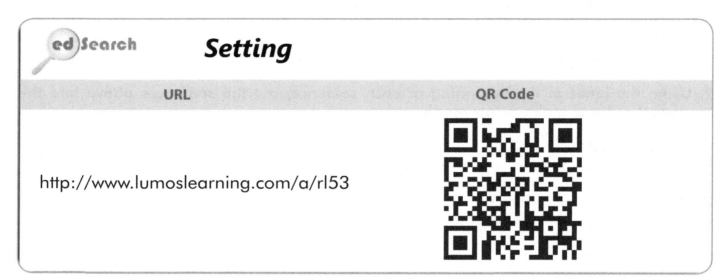

ed Search   *Setting*

URL	QR Code
http://www.lumoslearning.com/a/rl53	

Fishing and Chores

Joshua had lived in Mississippi all of his life. He grew up near the coast in a small rural community known as Franklin Creek. If you travel along Highway 10 going toward Alabama, it is the last exit in Mississippi.

Joshua loved to go fishing along the creek that ran behind his grandmother's massive house. He lived there with his grandmother and his parents. When he wanted to go fishing, his parents wanted to be sure that had had done his chores first. Joshua did not like chores at all. Quite often he tried to avoid doing his chores.

This became a real problem for Joshua's mother, as the house was very large, and keeping it clean required help from everyone. She often told Joshua that he would be a hindrance to the family if he did not do his part.

Little reminders did not seem to help. Scolding was of no use either. It seemed he would turn a deaf ear when it came to listening. Joshua's mother was beside herself.

One day his grandmother gave her an idea. Joshua had asked that morning to go fishing. Little did he know that his mother had taken the advice of Grandma and would soon put a stop to his ways of not doing chores. Joshua said, "Mom, chores are done! Can I go now?" His mother replied, "Sure, no problem."

Joshua hurried out to the storage building to gather his fishing gear. The fishing pole was not in its place! The tackle box wasn't there either! His fishing hat was missing, too! He ran back to the house where his mother and grandmother were drinking coffee on the porch.

Joshua asked, "Mom, where is all my fishing stuff?"

"What are you talking about, son?" Replied his mother.

"I can't find anything in the storage building." He said.

She then told him to go look in his room. She said she had put it all in there where he was supposed to have cleaned. When Joshua got to his room, he realized what was going on. In order to find his fishing equipment, he would have to go through the mess in his room. His mother and grandmother were right behind him laughing. He grinned and said, "I get it now, Mom." He cleaned his room and found all the things he needed for fishing, too!

Needless to say, Joshua never had a problem doing chores again!

After reading the story, enter the details in the map below. This will help you to answer the questions with ease.

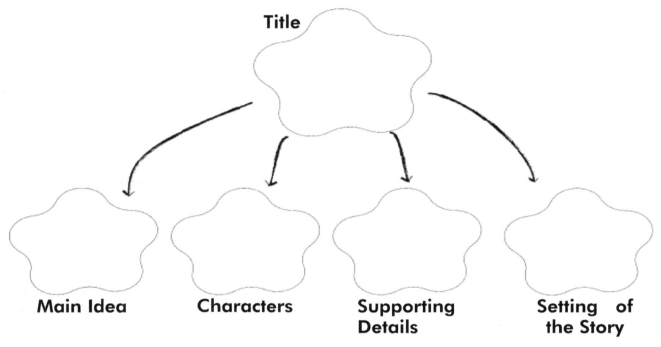

Title

Main Idea   **Characters**   **Supporting Details**   **Setting of the Story**

1. What is the setting of the above story?

    Ⓐ Franklin Creek, Mississippi
    Ⓑ A rural community in Alabama
    Ⓒ A cabin in the woods
    Ⓓ Highway 10 going to Alabama

2. Which detail in the story supports the possibility that this story could have taken place in the past?

    Ⓐ Little reminders did not seem to help.
    Ⓑ Joshua had lived in Mississippi all his life.
    Ⓒ "Mom, where is all of my stuff?"
    Ⓓ None of the above

Try Again

Surfing is one of Daniel's favorite pastimes! Every weekend when he has the time, he heads toward Port Aransas, Texas with his father. Daniel's family doesn't live far away, so it takes them only about 30 minutes to get there, if there is a short ferry line. They always make sure to get their things ready the night before. Daniel and his dad like to get an early start to their surfing day!

The night before, Daniel makes sure that his dad's truck is clean, especially the bed of the truck where he puts his surfboards. He also takes time to clean his wetsuit that he wears for protection and warmth. His mom usually makes sandwiches, and snacks ahead of time and puts them in the refrigerator to keep them fresh.

Daniel and his dad leave around 5:30 or 6:00 am when the sun is just coming up. Daniel has been surfing with his dad since he was very small. He remembers when his dad would ride with him on the surfboard.

When Daniel was about 9 years old, he fell off of a surfboard and hurt his leg and back. His dad rushed him to a nearby hospital for X-rays and a checkup. Luckily, there were no broken bones. However, the incident claimed Daniel so much that he refused to go surfing for several months. His dad kept encouraging him to give it a try. He told him, "If at once you don't succeed, try, and try again!" Daniel didn't want to try again. He was afraid of getting hurt and falling off of the surfboard.

Finally, Daniel went surfing with his father again. His father went out into the waves, and rode a wave in. Daniel went out on the waves, too. He stayed out for a long time without attempting to ride a wave back to shore. Daniel's dad began to wonder if his son had given up.

Just then a large wave began building up far out in the water. Daniel's dad was astonished! There was Daniel riding the huge wave all the way to shore without a problem. His dad motioned for Daniel to come where he was, but Daniel didn't. Instead he went right back into the water, and began riding wave after wave after wave!

It is amazing that fear can be overcome with one's personal best.

After reading the story, enter the details in the map below. This will help you to answer the question with ease.

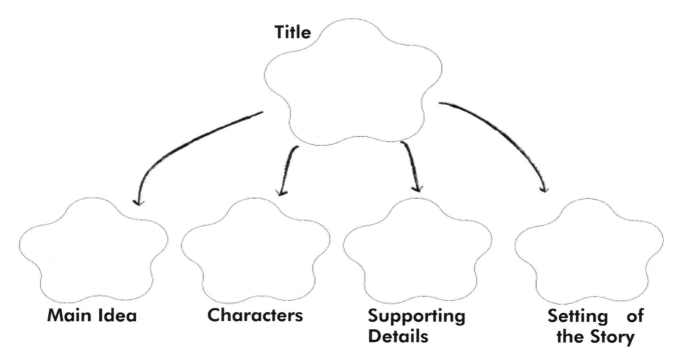

3. Where does this story take place?

Ⓐ   On an unknown beach somewhere.
Ⓑ   On an island in the Pacific Ocean.
Ⓒ   On a beach in Port Aransas, Texas.
Ⓓ   None of the above

Late for School

Marrah heard the brakes on the bus as she shoveled the rest of her breakfast into her mouth. "You just missed the bus!" Marrah's mother yelled. "Why can't you ever be on time?"

"I'm sorry, Mom," Marrah sighed. She ran upstairs to her room so she could get her backpack, knowing she needed to hurry because her mother would have to take her to school.

"Let's go, Marrah!" Her mother called from downstairs. "You don't want to be late for school too!"

Frantic now, Marrah lifted her sheets to look under them before dropping to her knees in front of her bed. She pushed mounds of clothes out of the way as she continued to search for her backpack.

"Marrah!" Her mother called again. She could hear the impatience in her mother's voice downstairs. She ran out of her room and leaned over the rail.

"I can't find my backpack!" She cried out.

"You mean this one?" Her mother pulled the bag from the floor beside her.

"Oh," she replied, her shoulders sagging as she walked down the stairs.

"Let's go to school, Marrah." Her mother said with a small smile on her face as they walked out the door.

After reading the story, enter the details in the map below. This will help you to answer the question with ease.

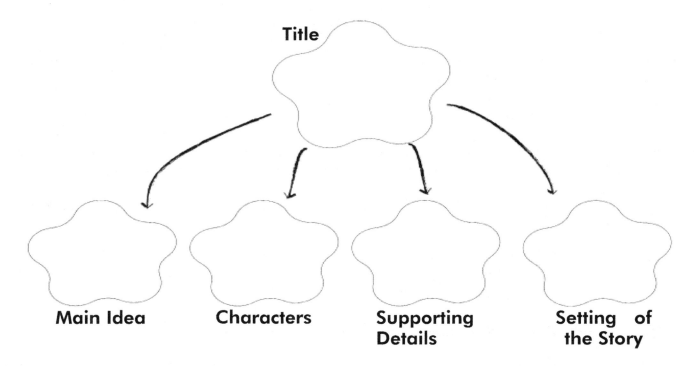

Title

Main Idea   Characters   Supporting
Details   Setting of
the Story

4. What is the setting of this story?

    Ⓐ It takes place at Marrah's house.
    Ⓑ It takes place at Marrah's school.
    Ⓒ It takes place on Marrah's bus.
    Ⓓ It takes place in Marrah's backyard.

Once there was a severe drought. There was little water in Tony's well, and he didn't know what would happen to the fruit trees in his garden. Just then, he noticed three men looking intently at his house.

He was certain that the three strangers were planning to rob his house. He acted quickly. He shouted out to his son, "My son, due to the drought, money has become scarce. There are many thieves.

Let us protect our valuables, and put all of our jewels in a box and throw them into the well. They will be safe there." He quickly told his son to put some large stones in a box and throw them into the well.

After reading the story, enter the details in the map below. This will help you to answer the question with ease.

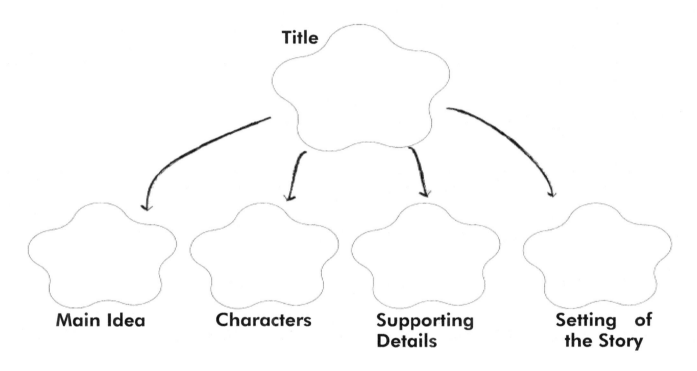

5. **The author uses the phrase "a severe drought" to show that this story is set in a time when _____.**

Ⓐ there is too much rain.
Ⓑ there is too much light.
Ⓒ there is not enough light.
Ⓓ there is not enough rain.

In the kitchen,
After the aimless
Chatter of the plates,
The murmur of the stoves,
The chuckles of the water pipes,
And the sharp exchanges
Of the knives, forks and spoons,
Comes the serious quiet
When the sink slowly clears its throat,
And you can hear the occasional rumble
Of the refrigerator's tummy
As it digests the cold.

6. What is the setting of this poem?

Ⓐ It is set in a house.
Ⓑ It is set in the stove.
Ⓒ It is set in a restaurant.
Ⓓ It is set in a kitchen.

Sally is reading a story about two wounded soldiers, their capture, and their escape from the enemy's camp.

7. What is likely the setting for the story she is reading?

Ⓐ a cinema theatre
Ⓑ a school auditorium
Ⓒ a battlefield
Ⓓ a circus

Mike is reading a story about spaceships, satellites, space stations, and invading aliens. There were wars in the sky, and astronauts were trying to save their spaceship. The astronauts won the war against some aliens who wanted to rule earth.

8. The setting of this story is _____.

Ⓐ on earth
Ⓑ in outer space
Ⓒ in the ocean
Ⓓ none of the above

9. Select the phrase that best completes the sentence below.

Setting is important, because it tells the audience _____.

  Ⓐ where and what the story is about
  Ⓑ where and how the story is told
  Ⓒ where and when the story takes place
  Ⓓ who tells the story

Chapter 1

Lesson 8: Figurative Language

Let us understand the concept with an example.

Figurative language and figures of speech: Words or phrase that have a meaning other than the literal meaning.

Examples:

Simile: A simile is a comparison between unlike things that are different from each other physically but are similar in some other characteristic. A simile uses the words "like" or "as" in the comparison.

Examples:

1. The famous heavyweight boxing champion Muhammed Ali once described his style of fighting as "Float like a butterfly, sting like a bee." He was able to move very gracefully in the ring, seeming to float on air like a butterfly in flight. Yet his powerful punches could hurt an opponent, much like a bee sting hurts.

2. The water in the lake was as smooth as glass. This means the water was so calm, without a ripple, that it resembled a flat piece of glass, such as found in a tabletop or window pane.

Metaphor: Like a simile, a metaphor is a comparison between unlike things that are different from each other physically but are similar in some characteristic, but unlike a simile, the comparison does not use the words "like" or "as."

Examples:

1. The seagulls flew in patterns resembling the dancing of ballerinas.

2. He was a tiger in the ring; a pussycat at home.

Idiom: An idiom is a statement that is not meant to be taken seriously (literally).

Examples:

1. The ball is in your court. It means it is up to you to make the next decision or step.

2. You are barking up the wrong tree. It means looking in the wrong place. Accusing the wrong person.

Proverb: A short popular saying, usually of unknown and ancient origin, that expresses effectively some commonplace truth or useful thought.

Examples:

1. A leopard cannot change its spots. This usually refers negatively to a person's personality, implying that this person is not capable of changing the impression you have of him or her.

2. You can't judge a book by its cover. This also usually applies when talking about a person, not a book, and means that you can't just rely on a person's outward appearance to really know them – you have to "look inside" (not literally, unless you're a surgeon, but mentally).

You can scan the QR code given below or use the url to access additional EdSearch resources including videos and mobile apps related to *Figurative Language*.

ed Search	**Figurative Language**
URL	**QR Code**
http://www.lumoslearning.com/a/rl54	

1. Select the phrase that best completes the sentence.

A simile is _____.

Ⓐ a phrase that compares two things.
Ⓑ a phrase that compares two things using the words 'like' or 'as.'
Ⓒ a word that compares two things.
Ⓓ a phrase that gives an object human characteristics.

Under the snow-white coverlet, upon a snow-white pillow, lay the most beautiful girl that Tom had ever seen. Her cheeks were very white, and her hair was like threads of gold spread all over her pillow.

2. Select the phrase that best completes the sentence.

The second sentence is an example of _____.

Ⓐ a metaphor
Ⓑ personification
Ⓒ a detailed sentence
Ⓓ a simile

My daddy is a tiger
My mother is a bear
My sister is a pest
Who messes with my hair
And even though my home
Is like living in a zoo
I know my family loves me
And will take care of me too

3. How many similes are in the poem above?

Ⓐ One
Ⓑ Two
Ⓒ Three
Ⓓ Four

4. How many metaphors are in the poem above?

Ⓐ One
Ⓑ Two
Ⓒ Three
Ⓓ Four

5. An example of a simile in this poem would be _____.

  Ⓐ my mother is a bear
  Ⓑ my father is a tiger
  Ⓒ my sister is a pest
  Ⓓ my home is like living in a zoo

6. This simile compares what two objects?

A cloud floats like a feather in the sky.

  Ⓐ It compares a cloud and the sky.
  Ⓑ It compares a cloud and a feather.
  Ⓒ It compares a feather and the sky.
  Ⓓ It compares the sky with nothing.

7. Which of the following is another appropriate simile?

  Ⓐ A cloud floats like a rock in the water.
  Ⓑ A cloud floats like a bird in the sky.
  Ⓒ A cloud floats like a leaf in the wind.
  Ⓓ A cloud floats like a cotton ball in a jar.

My daddy is a tiger
My mother is a bear
My sister is a pest
Who messes with my hair

8. What would be another similar metaphor for the author's sister?

  Ⓐ My sister is a bug.
  Ⓑ My sister is like a pest.
  Ⓒ My sister is annoying.
  Ⓓ My sister is like a bug.

The trapeze artist in the circus was amazing. He leapt effortlessly through the air and landed on his feet so smoothly. All I can say is that he is a cat!

9. The expression, 'he is a cat' is _____.

Ⓐ a metaphor
Ⓑ a simile
Ⓒ an idiom
Ⓓ a proverb

My mother is very particular about giving me healthy food. I only eat French fries once in a blue moon.

10. The expression, once in a blue moon, is an example of _____.

Ⓐ an idiom
Ⓑ a simile
Ⓒ a metaphor
Ⓓ none of the above

Chapter 1

Lesson 9: Structure of Text

Publisher's note: Theatrical plays, dance compositions, books and musical compositions use scenes, chapters and stanzas respectively to deliver their themes or stories. Scenes, chapters and stanzas divide the stories and performances into separate parts in which characters, settings, events, melodies and choruses are introduced and re-introduced. Dividing these performances into separate parts holds the audiences' attention, creating variety and interest. While each part is unique, it still relates and complements the overall production; each part makes up the structure of the overall production. The play Les Misérables is an example of how individual parts (scenes) fit together to form the entire play.

Let us understand the concept with an example.

Les Misérables

The story begins as the peasant Jean Valjean, just released from 19 years' imprisonment, is turned away by innkeepers because his yellow passport marks him as a former convict. He sleeps on the street, angry and bitter.

A benevolent local priest gives him shelter. At night, Valjean runs off with the priest's silverware, but when the police capture Valjean, the priest lies to protect him and tells him that his life has been spared for God, and that he should use money from the silverware to make an honest man of himself. But although Valjean broods over the priest's advice, he steals a coin from a 12-year-old boy. His theft is reported to the authorities and Valjean hides as they search for him, because if apprehended he will be returned to jail for life as a repeat offender.

Six years pass and Valjean, using an alias, has become a wealthy factory owner and mayor of the town. Walking down the street, he sees a man pinned under the wheels of a cart. When no one volunteers to help, he decides to rescue the man himself by crawling underneath the cart and lifting it to free him. The town's police inspector, Inspector Javert, who was a guard at the prison during Valjean's incarceration, becomes suspicious of the mayor after witnessing this remarkable feat of strength. He has known only one other man, a convict named Jean Valjean, who could accomplish it. Note: This past relationship has now been rekindled.

Years earlier in Paris, a woman named Fantine was very much in love with a man, with whom she had a child, but the man left her to fend for herself and her daughter Cosette. She arrives in the town in which Valjean is the mayor. In order to work, Fantine leaves Cosette in the care of the Thénardiers, a corrupt innkeeper and his selfish, cruel wife. Fantine ends up working at Valjean's factory. She is later fired from her job at Valjean's factory, because of the discovery of her daughter, who was born out of wedlock. Fantine is attacked in the street and arrested by Javert who sentences her to prison but

Valjean intervenes and takes the ill woman to the hospital and promises Fantine that he will bring Cosette to her. But Fantine dies before this happens. Note: And thus another connection among characters is created: Valjean, Fantine, Cosette, Javert and the Thénardiers. Javert is now an enemy of Valjean and tries to arrange his capture, but Valjean escapes and searches for Cosette who he promised Fantine he would take care of.

Valjean returns to his home city and finds Cosette alone and walks with her to the inn. He orders a meal and observes how the Thénardiers abuse her, while pampering their own daughters Éponine and Azelma. The next morning, Valjean informs the Thénardiers that he wants to take Cosette with him. Madame Thénardier immediately accepts, while Thénardier pretends to love Cosette and be concerned for her welfare, reluctant to give her up. Valjean pays off the Thénardiers, and he and Cosette leave the inn. Note: Thus a new relationship occurs: Valjean and the Thenardiers.

Valjean and Cosette flee to Paris, where he and Cosette live happily. However, Javert discovers Valjean's lodgings there a few months later. Valjean takes Cosette and they try to escape from Javert. They soon find shelter in a convent with the help of the man whom Valjean once rescued from being crushed under a cart and who has become the convent's gardener. Note: the past relationship between the man Valjean rescued and Valjean is rekindled. Valjean also becomes a gardener and Cosette becomes a student at the convent school.

Publisher's Note: The story continues, with new relationships, such as those between a young man named Marius and Cosette, in spite of the extreme jealousy of Éponine, Thenardier's daughter. Yes, the Thenardiers enter into Valjean's life again, as does Javert, and the French Revolution draws in Marius and Valjean and Cosette. But we're going to end the story here because our intent was not to give a synopsis of the entire play but to demonstrate how a series of individual scenes fit together to provide the overall structure of the play (and in a similar manner, a book or a dance performance or a musical performance), as required by the standard above.

You can scan the QR code given below or use the url to access additional EdSearch resources including videos and mobile apps related to *Structure of Text*.

ed Search	*Structure of Text*
URL	**QR Code**
http://www.lumoslearning.com/a/rl55	

The Orange

Even though no one knows exactly where oranges come from, Southeast Asia is believed to be their first home. They are grown today in most of the warmer parts of the world. The ancient Greeks and Romans knew about oranges. It is possible that oranges were carried from India to Western Asia, and then to Europe.

The Spaniards took the sour oranges to the West Indies and from there to Florida, in America. Today, oranges are the most important fresh fruit in international trade. There are three different kinds of oranges: the sweet or common orange, the mandarin orange, and the sour or bitter orange.

One type of sweet orange is called the blood orange. It has a pulp with a deep red color. This type of orange is grown mostly in the Mediterranean region. Mandarin oranges are mainly found in Florida. Sour oranges are grown almost everywhere with Spain having the greatest number used for trade. These sour oranges are generally used to make marmalade.

However, they can be put to many other interesting uses, from making medicine to creating perfumes. Oranges have many medicinal values. Oranges are the fruit with the greatest concentration of vitamin C. The skin of the orange helps to keep the fruit inside from becoming damaged and to remain clean. The thick, oily, and bitter skin does not allow any insects to get into an orange. Many kinds of useful oils can be extracted from the thick skin. Oranges are healthy and delicious.

After reading the story, enter the details in the map below. This will help you to answer the question with ease.

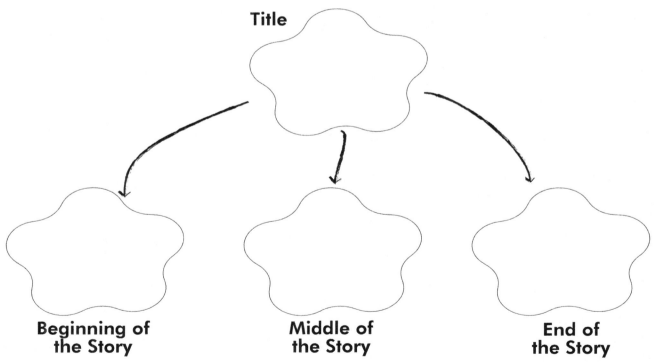

Title

Beginning of the Story

Middle of the Story

End of the Story

1. Where can you find the conclusion of this passage?

Ⓐ At the beginning of the passage.
Ⓑ In the middle of the passage.
Ⓒ At the end of the passage.
Ⓓ A passage never has an ending.

What is this life if, full of care,
We have no time to stand and stare?

No time to stand beneath the boughs
And stare as long as sheep or cows.

No time to see, when woods we pass,
Where squirrels hide their nuts in grass

No time to see, in broad daylight,
Streams full of stars, like skies at night.

No time to turn at Beauty's glance,
And watch her feet, how they can dance.

No time to wait till her mouth can
Enrich that smile her eyes began.'

A poor life if, full of care,
We have no time to stand and stare

-- W. H. Davies

2. What is the first stanza of the poem doing?

Ⓐ Asking a question.
Ⓑ Answering a question.
Ⓒ Introducing life.
Ⓓ Introducing the poet.

3. Who wrote this poem?

Ⓐ An unknown poet
Ⓑ W. H. Davies
Ⓒ Life
Ⓓ No one

4. When you read a humorous piece of writing, you usually _____.

- (A) cry
- (B) become serious
- (C) write down information
- (D) laugh

5. A passage that is an example of descriptive writing _____.

- (A) is a letter written to a person
- (B) creates a clear and vivid picture of a person, place, or thing
- (C) describes an experience in a personal voice
- (D) is a dialogue between two people

6. In a poem, we often find _____.

- (A) rhyming words
- (B) rhythmic writing
- (C) dialogues
- (D) 'a' and 'b'

7. Which of the following is not a genre of fiction?

- (A) poetry
- (B) mystery
- (C) fairy tale
- (D) informational

8. Which of the following is not a genre of nonfiction?

- (A) newspaper article
- (B) mystery
- (C) biography
- (D) informational

In the kitchen,
After the aimless

Chatter of the plates,
The murmur of the stoves,

The chuckles of the water pipes,
And the sharp exchanges

Of the knives, forks, and spoons,
Comes the serious quiet

When the sink slowly clears its throat,
And you can hear the occasional rumble

Of the refrigerator's tummy
As it digests the cold.

9. The above lines are a _____.

   Ⓐ story
   Ⓑ poem
   Ⓒ passage
   Ⓓ song

A Clever Idea

Once there was a severe drought. There was little water in Tony's well, and he didn't know what would happen to the fruit trees in his garden. Just then, he noticed three men looking intently at his house. He was certain that the three strangers were planning to rob his house. He acted quickly. He shouted out to his son, "My son, due to the drought, money has become scarce. There are many thieves. Let us protect our valuables, and put all of our jewels in a box and throw them into the well. They will be safe there." He quickly told his son to put some large stones in a box and throw them into the well. The thieves heard the sound of the box falling into the well and were happy.

That night they came to the well. The box was heavy and had landed deep down in the well. To get it, they would have to take out some of the water. They started drawing water from the well and pouring it onto the ground. Tony had made arrangements to make sure that the water reached his fruit trees. He had channels leading from the well to each of the trees.

By the time thieves found the box, they had drawn out enough water to water the trees. It was almost dawn. Tony sent for the soldiers, and just as the thieves were trying to open the box, they were caught red-handed.

After reading the story, enter the details in the map below. This will help you to answer the question with ease.

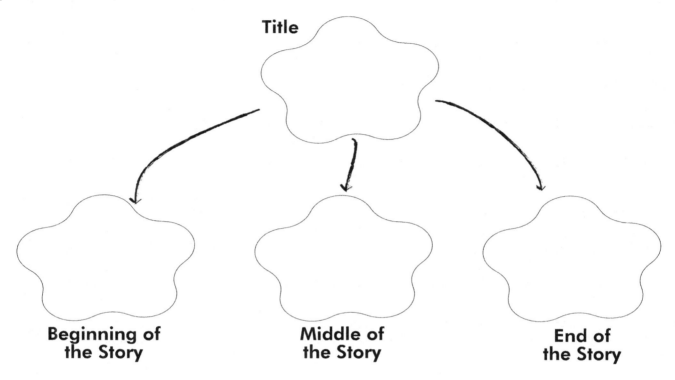

Title

Beginning of the Story

Middle of the Story

End of the Story

10. What is one of the main things that the above story is missing?

Ⓐ It is missing the introduction to the story.
Ⓑ It is missing the conclusion to the story.
Ⓒ It is missing the title of the story.
Ⓓ It is missing the description of the characters.

Chapter 1

Lesson 10: Styles of Narration

Let us understand the concept with an example.

The Candidate's Point of View: I am Brian Jones, a candidate running for mayor of the small city where I live. I am unpopular and considered a threat by the current mayor and his administration because I have been criticizing them for excessive spending and a lack of cost controls. This administration has been in office for many years and is well connected in this city.

I scheduled a town hall meeting in the city and publicized it with posters; the local paper would not publicize it. The meeting was well attended and went according to plan until the question and answer period. During this period, several of the mayor's friends asked loaded questions designed to make me look bad; some of the questions implied actions or views on my part that were false. When I tried to counteract them, or when others tried to defend me, they were shouted down by the mayor's friends. Emotions on both sides flared to the point that several fights started and the police were called, disbursed everyone, and arrested a couple of my friends for disturbing the peace, even though it was the mayor's friends who provoked them and started the fights. I was appalled by the biased reporting from the reporter who covered this meeting for the local newspaper.

The Newspaper Reporter's Point of View: Here is the article published in the paper.

Headline: Riot erupts at Jones's town hall meeting

Mayoral candidate Brian Jones held a town hall meeting last night that ended when police were called to quell a riot. After Jones made a speech about his political platform, a question and answer period followed. Jones either refused to answer some questions or provided answers that antagonized members of the audience, especially answers which criticized the mayor and his administration. Rather than try to maintain calm, Jones continued on with inflammatory comments that caused heated arguments between his supporters and detractors which led to several fist fights and the arrival of police. This is in contrast to a town hall held by the mayor two weeks ago that was conducted in a professional manner.

Publisher's Note: This example shows how different two points of view about the same event can be, depending on the outlook/biases/intents of the people telling or writing about the event. The newspaper reporter and the newspaper itself had a strong negative bias toward this candidate and a strong positive bias toward the mayor. The candidate had a positive bias toward his political platform and a negative bias toward the newspaper, the mayor and the mayor's friends who attended the meeting.

You can scan the QR code given below or use the url to access additional EdSearch resources including videos and mobile apps related to *Styles of Narration*.

Styles of Narration

URL	QR Code
http://www.lumoslearning.com/a/rl56	

Late for School

Marrah heard the brakes on the bus as she shoveled the rest of her breakfast into her mouth. "You just missed the bus!" Marrah's mother yelled. "Why can't you ever be on time?"

"I'm sorry, Mom," Marrah sighed. She ran upstairs to her room so she could get her backpack, knowing she needed to hurry because her mother would have to take her to school.

"Let's go, Marrah!" Her mother called from downstairs. "You don't want to be late for school too!"

Frantic now, Marrah lifted her sheets to look under them before dropping to her knees in front of her bed. She pushed mounds of clothes out of the way as she continued to search for her backpack.

"Marrah!" Her mother called again. She could hear the impatience in her mother's voice downstairs. She ran out of her room and leaned over the rail.

"I can't find my backpack!" She cried out.

"You mean this one?" Her mother pulled the bag from the floor beside her.

"Oh," she replied, her shoulders sagging as she walked down the stairs.

"Let's go to school, Marrah." Her mother said with a small smile on her face as they walked out the door.

After reading the story, enter the details in the map below. This will help you to answer the question with ease.

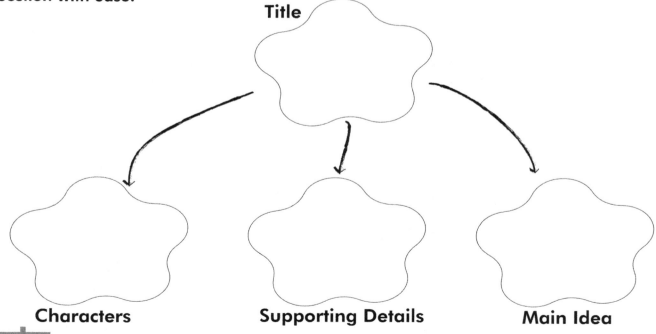

1. **How might this story be different if the author told it from the point of view of Marrah's mother?**

    Ⓐ The story would have described Marrah's frustration.
    Ⓑ The story would not change.
    Ⓒ The story would describe her mother's frustration.
    Ⓓ The story would focus on the bus driver's experience.

The first person point of view _____.

2. **Select the phrase that best completes the above sentence.**

    Ⓐ has the character tell the story in his own words and uses the word "I".
    Ⓑ has the character tell the story in his own words and uses pronouns like "he" and "she."
    Ⓒ has the ability to show what is happening in many places but does not reveal the thoughts of the characters.
    Ⓓ has the narrator tell the story to another character using the pronoun "you."

The second person point of view _____.

3. **Select the phrase that best completes the above sentence.**

    Ⓐ has the character tell the story in his own words and uses the pronoun "I."
    Ⓑ has the character tell the story in his own words and uses pronouns like "he" and "she."
    Ⓒ has the ability to show what is happening in many places but cannot see the thoughts of the characters.
    Ⓓ has the narrator tell the story to the reader using the pronoun "you."

4. **Which sentence is written in first person point of view?**

    Ⓐ Kelsey walked to school today.
    Ⓑ She walked to school today.
    Ⓒ I walked to school today.
    Ⓓ The neighbor walks to school every day.

5. **Which sentence is written in third person point of view?**

    Ⓐ I just won the race!
    Ⓑ Did you think the race was really long?
    Ⓒ She won the race.
    Ⓓ none of the above

6. Why is it important for the author to keep the same point of view throughout the whole text?

   Ⓐ It makes writing the story easy.
   Ⓑ It makes the characters fun.
   Ⓒ It makes the reader think about the message of the story.
   Ⓓ It keeps the story clear and easier to understand.

7. Select the phrase that best completes the sentence below.

Narrative writing is the style of writing which_____.

   Ⓐ describes an experience in a personal voice
   Ⓑ is written in verse and is rhythmic
   Ⓒ is a fairy tale
   Ⓓ none of the above

8. Which point of view is typically found in a diary or journal?

   Ⓐ omniscient
   Ⓑ first
   Ⓒ second
   Ⓓ third

9. If a piece of writing deals with the solution of a crime or the unraveling of secrets, it is called a _____.

   Ⓐ an autobiography
   Ⓑ a biography
   Ⓒ mystery
   Ⓓ a fairy tale

10. What point of view is the below sentence?

Kelsey was extremely upset. While she and Danny were together, he got lost.

   Ⓐ omniscient
   Ⓑ first
   Ⓒ second
   Ⓓ third

Chapter 1

Lesson 11: Visual Elements

Let's understand how visual and multimedia elements contribute to the meaning and tone of a text.

The Comeback

It was magnificent! They had not seen a performance like that by a basketball player since the days of Michael Jordan with the Chicago Bulls. Down 9 points in the fourth quarter, with only a few minutes remaining and the college championship on the line, the Invaders faced what looked like an impossible task to win this game. But that was not the way forward Jerry Smilek saw it. He saw the need to focus, to tell his teammates to get the ball to him and he would do the rest. What the crowd saw next was an almost inhuman dynamo dashing down the court, weaving, faking, moving, jumping and dunking four times to tie the game. Then, after being fouled, sinking two free throws with no time remaining to win the game and the MVP trophy as well.

Analysis: The photo shows clearly and efficiently Jerry's powerful and athletic technique for executing dunks. Without the photo, it would have taken many words to describe his technique, and the words would probably not inspire the awe that the photo does. The seriousness and concentration shown in the photo complements the inspiring tone of the text. "The Comeback" link adds to the text by allowing readers who want to see more photos to quickly access them, without adding more length to the text.

How Can An Aircraft Fly?

You must likely have heard the term "gravity" and probably know that gravity is a force that pulls downward toward the center of the earth and acts on objects that are on the ground, in the water or in the air. It is gravity that makes you come back down to earth when you jump up in the air.

If gravity has this effect on your body, you can imagine the effect it has on a jet airplane, which weighs much more than you do. You may have wondered how something as heavy as a jet airplane can rise in the air against the force of gravity pulling it down. You probably think the answer is because of its powerful engines.

But then, how do you explain why gliders without engines can still fly? Or how would you explain the fact that if someone designed an airplane whose top and bottom wing surfaces were both flat, it would have a very difficult time gaining altitude, even with a powerful engine (you'll have to take my word on this that this would be true)?

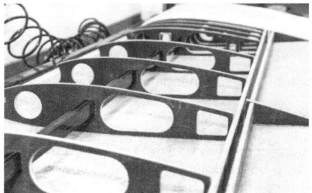

The logical explanation that answers these questions is the shape of the aircraft's wing surfaces. The front of the top surface of the wing is thicker than the rear of the top surface, meaning that the top wing surface is curved. The bottom surface of the wing is the same thickness – it is flat. You can see this in the shape of the wing ribs that determine the shape of the wing (see Figure 1).

Figure 1. Wing Structure Showing Wing Ribs

So how does the design of the wings allow the aircraft to gain altitude and fly? Here's how: As the aircraft picks up speed on takeoff, the air rushing over the top wing surface is slowed down by the thick front edge of the wing. The air rushing over the bottom surface is not slowed down because that surface is flat. Because the air under the wind is moving faster than the air over the wing, the air pressure across the bottom surface of the wing is greater than the air pressure across the top surface of the wing, and that air pressure pushes upward on the wing and the body of the aircraft, so the airplane rises. Yes, engines provide the speed for takeoff (gliders must be towed by a powered airplane), but it is the shape of the wing that provides the upward lift.

Analysis: The explanation of the shape of an aircraft's wing seems easy to understand, but including the illustration makes it so clear that any reader can understand the concept of shaping an aircraft wing.

You can scan the QR code given below or use the url to access additional EdSearch resources including videos and mobile apps related to *Visual Elements*.

ed)Search

Visual Elements

URL	QR Code
http://www.lumoslearning.com/a/rl57	

Eliza stood beside the winding train. It seemed to go on for miles and miles! The noise was unbearable at times and she was constantly dirty. Ma and Pa told her that this would not be a fun way to travel but she was so excited to go that she said she did not care. Now, all that Eliza can think of is a clean bed and a quiet rest.

1. Select the phrase that best completes the below sentence.

Without the added image, the reader might _____.

- Ⓐ think Eliza is describing a car ride.
- Ⓑ think Eliza is describing an actual train ride.
- Ⓒ believe the author is confused.
- Ⓓ think the author needs more details.

2. What is media in relation to text?

- Ⓐ Media uses sounds, images, and language.
- Ⓑ Media uses sounds, movies, and language.
- Ⓒ Media uses sounds, verbs, and metaphors.
- Ⓓ Media uses sounds, similes, and alliteration.

3. Select the phrase that best completes the below sentence.

Charts, graphs, pictures, and maps are examples of _____.

- Ⓐ images of text
- Ⓑ visual elements of text
- Ⓒ needless attachments to text
- Ⓓ none of the above

4. How does a timeline enhance text as a visual element?

Ⓐ It provides factual information.

Ⓑ It provides the key events mentioned in the text in the order that they occurred.

Ⓒ It provides illustrations.

Ⓓ It provides location information of places mentioned in the text.

5. Please select the phrase that best completes the below sentence.

The above illustration is titled "The Nutcracker".

Without looking at the image in detail, the reader might assume from only reading the title, that the image is about _____.

Ⓐ the song "The Nutcracker"

Ⓑ the commercial "The Nutcracker"

Ⓒ the ballet "The Nutcracker"

Ⓓ the star "The Nutcracker"

6. How does a map enhance text as a visual element?

Ⓐ It provides factual information.

Ⓑ It provides the key events mentioned in the text in the order that they occurred.

Ⓒ It provides key information as illustrations.

Ⓓ It provides the location information of places mentioned in the text.

7. Some examples of facts that are presented in visual form are _____.

Ⓐ graphs
Ⓑ charts
Ⓒ essays
Ⓓ both 'a' and 'b'

8. Select the phrase that best completes the sentence.

Some common types of graphs that present data are _____ .

Ⓐ bar graphs
Ⓑ line graphs
Ⓒ pie graphs
Ⓓ all of the above

9. Select the phrase that best completes the sentence.

A graph is a _____ that shows the relationship between changing things.

Ⓐ movie
Ⓑ circular
Ⓒ chart or drawing
Ⓓ all the above

10. Which visual aid works best in fictional text?

Ⓐ an internet link
Ⓑ illustration
Ⓒ text only
Ⓓ bar graph

Chapter 1

Lesson 12: Compare and Contrast

Publisher's Note: The genres chosen as an example for this standard are fiction and drama, and the stories chosen for comparison are The Hunger Games (Book 1) and Catching Fire (Book 2).

There are several major themes in each story. Several will be identified.

Theme: How an authoritarian government (the Capitol region) tries to exercise complete control over the lives of citizens in the surrounding districts.

The Hunger Games (Book 1): The Capitol region soundly defeats a rebellion by one of the districts and sends a message to the other 12 districts as a warning against rebelling and as a reminder they are in complete control: each district must select one boy and one girl between the ages of 12 and 18 to participate in an annual televised event known as the Hunger Games, in which they are forced to fight to the death, leaving only one survivor to claim victory. The contest gives the participants two incentives to win: avoiding death and earning certain benefits for their district, such as extra food and luxuries. But it also forces unpleasant decisions on the participants: they must kill another person to survive, and it is even more painful if any participants are friends.

The theme of unselfish sacrifice was played out when Katniss, the lead character, substituted for her sister when the sister was selected for the Hunger Games.

The Hunger Games are an example of using contests with high stakes: winning will make you famous; losing means certain death, to motivate and control participants and their sponsors (each district). Catching Fire (Book 2): The location of the story, the existence of the Capital Region and the 12 districts and many of the characters remain the same in Book 2. Also, the authoritarian practices by the Capitol government to control the districts continue.

What has changed is that by winning the first Hunger Games as the lone survivor, lead character Katniss has motivated others in her district to plan to rebel against the Capitol. To counter those plans, the President of the Capitol region pays a personal visit to Katniss to force an unpleasant choice on her: either stop this rebellion or they will kill her loved ones. She opts to try and pacify the Capitol by leading a noncontroversial life, including participating in the Victory Tour held for the Hunger Games winner, but the threat of rebellion by her district continues to grow. The Capitol adds a frightening change in rules for the next Hunger Games: the only participants will be previous winners of the Games. They add further danger by creating hazards in the Games arena that will kill or weaken the participants.

The theme of unselfish sacrifice also plays out in Book 2 when participants in the second Hunger Games contest rescue Katniss from the Games and carry her to safety, as a reward for her being the symbol of rebellion among the districts.

You can scan the QR code given below or use the url to access additional EdSearch resources including videos and mobile apps related to *Compare and Contrast*.

Compare and Contrast

URL	QR Code
http://www.lumoslearning.com/a/rl59	

Late for School

Marrah heard the brakes on the bus as she shoveled the rest of her breakfast into her mouth. "You just missed the bus!" Marrah's mother yelled. "Why can't you ever be on time?"

"I'm sorry, Mom," Marrah sighed. She ran upstairs to her room so she could get her backpack, knowing she needed to hurry because her mother would have to take her to school.

"Let's go, Marrah!" Her mother called from downstairs. "You don't want to be late for school too!"

Frantic now, Marrah lifted her sheets to look under them before dropping to her knees in front of her bed. She pushed mounds of clothes out of the way as she continued to search for her backpack.

"Marrah!" Her mother called again. She could hear the impatience in her mother's voice downstairs. She ran out of her room and leaned over the rail.

"I can't find my backpack!" She cried out.

"You mean this one?" Her mother pulled the bag from the floor beside her.

"Oh," she replied, her shoulders sagging as she walked down the stairs.

"Let's go to school, Marrah." Her mother said with a small smile on her face as they walked out the door.

Do Your Best

Katie stood before the crowd blushing and wringing her hands. She looked out and saw the room full of faces. Some she knew and some she did not. But, they were all here to listen to her. Taking a deep breath, she opened her mouth but no words came out. Tears formed in the corners of her eyes as she closed them.

With her eyes closed, she imagined her mother helping her get dressed and ready for tonight. "Just do your best," is what her mother had told her. She opened her eyes and found her mother's smiling face in the crowd. Relaxing, she took another deep breath and started singing. She did not stop until she finished and the crowd was on their feet applauding.

After the show, she found her parents and her friends. They all had wonderful things to say about her song and how proud they were because she kept going even when it seemed like she might give up. She shrugged her shoulders and shared a smile with her mother. "I just did my best," she answered.

1. How are Katie and Marrah similar?

Ⓐ Both girls have dark hair.
Ⓑ Both girls are the same age.
Ⓒ Both girls rely on their mothers.
Ⓓ Both girls have many friends.

What is this life if, full of care,
We have no time to stand and stare?

No time to stand beneath the boughs
And stare as long as sheep or cows.

No time to see, when woods we pass,
Where squirrels hide their nuts in grass

No time to see, in broad daylight,
Streams full of stars, like skies at night.

No time to turn at Beauty's glance,
And watch her feet, how they can dance.

No time to wait till her mouth can
Enrich that smile her eyes began.

A poor life if, full of care,
We have no time to stand and stare.
-- W. H. Davies

In the kitchen,
After the aimless
Chatter of the plates,
The murmur of the stoves,
The chuckles of the water pipes,
And the sharp exchanges
Of the knives, forks, and spoons,
Comes the serious quiet
When the sink slowly clears its throat,
And you can hear the occasional rumble
Of the refrigerator's tummy
As it digests the cold.

2. How are these two poems similar?

    Ⓐ Both poems use similes.
    Ⓑ Both poems use personification.
    Ⓒ Both poems use colorful descriptions.
    Ⓓ Both poems use metaphors.

3. **What things might you look for when comparing two pieces of text?**

   Ⓐ type of text
   Ⓑ purpose of text
   Ⓒ style of text
   Ⓓ all of the above

4. **When using a Venn diagram to compare and contrast two characters, what does the overlapping section of the circles show?**

   Ⓐ It describes the traits the characters have in common.
   Ⓑ It describes the traits the characters do not have in common.
   Ⓒ It describes all the characteristics of both characters.
   Ⓓ It does not do any of the above.

5. **When using a Venn diagram to compare and contrast two characters, what do the outside non-overlapping parts of the circles represent?**

   Ⓐ They describe the traits the characters have in common.
   Ⓑ They describe the traits the characters do not have in common.
   Ⓒ Be all the characteristics of both characters.
   Ⓓ They do not do any of the above.

Number of library books borrowed in 2016	
Month	Number of books borrowed
September	660
October	670
November	570
December	475

6. **From the above table, which two months had the largest number of library books borrowed?**

   Ⓐ September and December
   Ⓑ September and October
   Ⓒ October and November
   Ⓓ October and December

7. Refer to the chart above to complete the sentence below.

Students borrowed the least number of books in _____ 2016.

Ⓐ November
Ⓑ October
Ⓒ September
Ⓓ December

8. Pick the sentence that compares the above sets of words correctly.

a. Math, Science, Social Studies, History
b. Basketball, Soccer, Baseball, Tennis

Ⓐ 'a' contains subjects related to cognitive activity whereas 'b' contains games that are related to physical activity
Ⓑ 'a' contains subjects that we study whereas 'b' contains the games that we play
Ⓒ 'a' contains subjects that are easy whereas 'b' contains games that are difficult to play
Ⓓ both 'a' and 'b' are correct

9. Which sentence would lead you to compare two items?

Ⓐ Presidents Lincoln and Kennedy had several similarities during their terms in office.
Ⓑ The American Revolution and the Civil War had many differences.
Ⓒ The two pets could not be more diverse from each other.
Ⓓ How are tornados different from hurricanes?

10. Which sentence would lead you to contrast two items?

Ⓐ My brother is exactly like my father.
Ⓑ How are tornados similar to hurricanes?
Ⓒ How is my mother's cake unlike my grandmother's?
Ⓓ How are tornados similar from hurricanes?

End of Reading: Literature

Answer Key and
Detailed Explanations

Chapter 1: Reading: Literature

Lesson 1: Supporting Statements

Question No.	Answer	Detailed Explanations
1	C	In the first stanza, the poet asks a question as shown with the question mark at the end. Beginning in each of the other stanzas the poet begins each one with the phrase "No time." He is telling all of the things that one may not have time to do. However, in the final stanza, the poet answers the question using a statement that begins with "A poor life."
2	D	The word "cunning" means one full who is of tricks. In the beginning of the passage, Tony would be best described as "cautious", because he was trying to prevent the thieves from robbing him. The "well" is just an element in the story which creates the problem. The "thieves" are the villains in the story. At the end, Tony does become clever and outwits the thieves. However, the best title for this story is "The Clever Idea," because it sums up what was done to catch "the thieves" and solve the problem.
3	D	The passage shows that Tony asks his son "to put all of the valuables in the box." The passage does not mention clothes. However, when Tony refers to their valuables, he calls them jewels. Tony also ordered his son to load another box with stones and to throw it into the well. This is the box that the thieves would get while the family's valuables protected.
4	A	The passage supports the correct answer to how Tony's fruit trees got water, because "the thieves" drew water from the well and poured it on the ground. The thieves nor Tony directly watered the fruit trees. The word "not" in the answer choice "the thieves did not draw water from the well" makes that choice incorrect.
5	B	The correct answer is that "the thieves were caught red-handed," and the passage supports the answer. However, the passage states that the jewels were protected in another box. The passage mentions that money was scarce, and there wasn't any in the box that the thieves pulled from the well. The answer choice "the thieves did not find the box" is incorrect, because they actually drew the box up from the bottom of the well, but did not open it.
6	D	The correct answer is all of the above, because one may conclude from each of the detailed choices in the passage that there was a severe drought, little water in the well, and money was scarce. This is evidence that the country was going through a difficult time.

Question No.	Answer	Detailed Explanations
7	C	There isn't any evidence in the passage that indicates that there was a storm that crashed the cupboard when the king was gone. The statement that people in the passage accidentally broke the glass cupboard is not accurate. However, it does say that the thieves broke into the palace and stole the glass cupboard. "None of the above" does not apply.
8	A	There is evidence in the passage that correctly supports the answer that the thieves took gold out of the cupboard. However, there isn't evidence that there was silver, diamonds, or stones taken from the cupboard, so these answer choices are incorrect.
9	D	There isn't evidence in the passage to support that the thieves were told to take everything out of the cupboard, to break the cupboard, or to take gold out of the cupboard. However, there is evidence to support that the thieves should have remembered to put something back into the cupboard each time that they took something out.
10	B	The passage indicates that the traveler picked up his shoes and ran out of the house because he was scared. However, when the traveler went to wash up, the wife was supposed to have chicken cooked and ready for the traveler to eat. The passage indicates that the traveler was weary or tired, but there isn't evidence to support that the traveler was curious. He was frightened into running off. None of the above is incorrect, because there is an answer from the given choices.

Lesson 2: Drawing Inferences

Question No.	Answer	Detailed Explanations
1	A	Choice A is correct. There isn't any evidence in the passage to support that the thieves successfully robbed for money, so this answer is incorrect. Also, according to the passage, the thieves did not take the jewels, because they were put in another box for protection. The thieves did not put the box in the well, but they drew the box out of the well. There is evidence to support the correct answer of how the thieves watered the garden which was by taking water out of the well as they were trying to get to the box.
2	C	Choice C is correct. The stones were used as a means to divert the robbers to try to remove the box from the well and in that process water the garden. There isn't evidence to support that the stones were valuable to Tony or that it was worth a fortune. In fact there is no money is true but that is not the reason why the box contained stones. The last option is also incorrect.
3	B	Choice B is correct. Based on the passage above, Tony sent for the soldiers because they enforced the laws. However, there is no direct evidence that Tony trusted the thieves. Also, there isn't any evidence in the passage to indicate that Tony was a member of the Army. The passage does not provide evidence to support the statement that the police were stealing the jewels, because there weren't any police officers present. The soldiers were the "police."
4	A	Choice A is correct. According to the first paragraph of the passage, it states directly that Sam was friendly. So, one can infer that he was helpful because he wanted to feed the weary traveler. However, there isn't any evidence from the passage to support that Sam was dangerous and cruel, or miserly and cunning. The last answer is partially correct, because Sam was friendly, but he was not miserable. Remember that if one part of the answer is wrong, then the whole answer is wrong.
5	D	Choice D is correct. In the passage, the reader can infer that Sam's wife likes food a lot, because can't resist it and loves to eat while cooking. One can also infer that the wife is cunning and clever, because she figures out a way to avoid telling the truth which is that she and her son ate the chicken.

Question No.	Answer	Detailed Explanations
6	A	The evidence shows that this passage is about being determined. The narrator did not give up. She listens to friends and takes a deep breath, but these are the details in the story, not the main idea. Remember that the sum of the details is the main idea which is what the story is mostly about.
7	D	Choice D is correct. The evidence in this story that supports that Katie was nervous at the beginning is her blushing and wringing her hands. There is not enough information in the story to support that Katie was depressed. Do not confuse the crowd's excitement to mean that Katie felt the same way. While at the beginning she was nervous, she seems relieved at the end or glad that it was over. Because Katie had so many people happy for her, one might assume that she was friendly, but there isn't any evidence to support that in the story.
8	D	Choice D is correct. The best title for this poem is "No Time," because the author speaks about how being busy can make a person miss out on the simple things in life, like enjoying leisure time and standing and staring. There isn't any evidence to indicate "hard work." Although "stand and stare" is mentioned, it is always referenced to no time.
9	C	Choice C is correct. The title of this passage gives the reader an idea about some of Marrah's characteristics. There isn't any evidence to support that all three words in group A. Remember that if one part of the answer is wrong, then the entire answer is wrong. There is evidence that Marrah is annoyed, but not confused and pleased. There isn't evidence to support that Marrah is sad, depressed, and unhappy. There isn't evidence to support Marrah is happy, organized, and punctual. Many choices will include the antonym or the opposite, so try to be aware of those types of answer choices.
10	B	Choice B is correct. According to the passage above, there is not enough evidence to support that flowers make friends or that they need other flowers in order to grow. However, there is evidence to conclude that sun and rain made the little pink flower grow up to be the prettiest little pink rose in the garden.

Lesson 3: Theme

Question No.	Answer	Detailed Explanations
1	C	The evidence in this passage best supports the choice "Do Your Best," because in the end, it was Katie doing her best that allowed her to complete her performance. The rest of the phrases are details of the story, but they are not the main idea, nor do they suggest the most appropriate title. Always remember to choose the best answer. Sometimes, the title will summarize the main idea of the story.
2	B	The overall message of this story is to "Always Do Your Best." The last sentence, "I just did my best," echoes this message. There isn't any evidence to support "closing your eyes...," "giving up under pressure," or "never letting your friends down"as correct answer choices. These are the details that help move the plot of the story along.
3	C	The evidence clearly suggests that the purpose of this story is to show how giving back something in return for something else pays off. There isn't any evidence that shows the reader how to break the glass cupboard, or that this story was about the king. Although the king was mentioned in the story, he is not the main part of the story. Also, it can't be about the importance of gold, because there aren't any details to support its significance.
4	A	The last stanza of this poem states that one who has everything, but doesn't have time to stop and stare (look longingly at something), has a poor life. Another way of looking at this is to ask what good is it to have everything if you can't enjoy it? There isn't any evidence to support that life is good, so the other two statements are incorrect. Remember that if a statement is supported by a comma, both parts of the statement must be correct. If one part is false, the entire statement is false.
5	C	From the given choices, the best title for this poem is "Stop and Stare," because it supports the overall meaning of the story which tells the reader that a full life includes having time to stop and stare or just to rest and look at something for a while. "Life" is too general because the focus is not on life, but taking time to enjoy something in life. "Stare" and "Life and Stare" do not have supporting evidence in the story. The title can give the reader a clue to the message or theme of a piece, and "Stop and Stare" provides that information.

Question No.	Answer	Detailed Explanations
6	A	There is no evidence in this poem to support a message that the family unpredictable. The last line clearly shows that the author believes that his family will take care of him, so that makes the choice "they are too crazy to care" incorrect. Even though the author describes each family member like different animals, the author is not trying to say that they are animals. Refer to the last line, where the evidence points out that their differences do not keep them from caring for each other.
7	C	This poem uses personification (non-human objects are given human qualities) to describe the various noises in the kitchen. "The Kitchen" is the most appropriate title because it is the setting, which is very important to this passage. Since the poem only briefly mentions, "The Sink," "The Plate," and "The Refrigerator," they are mere details and are not the focus of the poem.
8	B	From the first to the last line of this poem, there is a lot of sound and activity in this kitchen. The author's use of onomatopoeia (sound words) and personification (non-human objects are given "human qualities") creates the different sounds and activity. However, the rumble and chill, chatter and murmur, and silence and stillness are just details in the poem that add up to sound and activity.
9	C	The lesson from this story is to be careful when baking. The fact that the narrator tries to take the cake out of the oven without a mitt and burns her hands supports this lesson. There is not enough evidence to support that the lesson of this story is mainly focused on enjoying the cake and having fun, because it was fun and enjoyable until she burned her hands. There is no evidence to support not making the cake.
10	A	There is evidence in this story to support the theme "to take a risk and good things will happen." The risk was that the little pink rose let the rain and sun in and discovered that she was the prettiest pink flower in the beautiful garden. There is no evidence that there were lessons to be learned in "not talking to strangers," "do you best," and "don't give up."

Lesson 4: Characters

Question No.	Answer	Detailed Explanations
1	D	Each of the details in the answer choices directly supports how clever Tony is. He is able to trick the thieves and arrange his plan so that his trees received the much needed water, the thieves did not get the jewels or treasure, and the thieves were caught red-handed.
2	B	The main characters in the story, the king and the thieves, moved the plot along. The servants were minor characters. Without the main characters, there is no plot, and therefore, no story.
3	C	The thieves' actions in this story are evidence of their greed and carelessness. They wanted more and more, and could have gotten more if they had only remembered to put something back when they received something. There isn't any evidence in this story to indicate that the thieves were skilled, unskilled, or careful. Remember that a character's actions -- what they say, what they do, how they feel, what others say about them, etc. -- help to describe who they are.
4	D	The king in this story is just and generous as evidenced by his making it possible for others to give something back each time one receives something. Once the thieves broke the glass cupboard and did not follow the king's instructions to put something back when they took something, their fate was decided. It was just, or right, that the thieves lost everything that they had received and died. There is no evidence in this story to show that the king was ungrateful, rude, mean, or selfish. In fact, he was the opposite of each of these traits.
5	B	In the first two paragraphs, the evidence clearly supports Katie and her mother as the main characters. They are key to the plot of the story. The story is mainly about Katie getting ready to perform and her mother's assistance. Katie's parents and friends are minor characters and were present to watch her perform, but they were not the focus of the story.
6	C	Katie's father and her friends, who were in the audience watching Katie's performance, are the secondary or minor characters in this story. The plot is not created around these secondary characters because they do not move the plot along.

Question No.	Answer	Detailed Explanations
7	A	The evidence in this story shows that Katie's mother is very supportive, because she had helped her to get ready the night before her singing performance. There is no evidence to show that Katie's mother was not supportive or that she didn't like Katie's singing. In the story, there is no evidence that Katie's mother wanted her to make friends, even though some of Katie's friends were in the audience. We cannot assume anything unless there is supporting evidence in the story.
8	A	Evidence in this story clearly supports that Marrah is very disorganized. Being organized is the opposite, so it isn't correct. There is no evidence to directly support it Marrah is disciplined. However, one can conclude that if she is not able to remain organized, then she is not disciplined enough to do what it takes to keep up with her backpack. Being disorganized causes Marrah to be tardy, whereas, if she were organized, she would be punctual.
9	D	After Marrah got her backpack, her mother smiled and said, "Let's go to school, Marrah." Marrah's mother called upstairs to her to come down, and reminded her that she always missed the bus are evidence of her mother's frustration, and she didn't remain in this mood. She smiled and took her to school. Be sure that you read the question carefully and examine each answer choice closely to ensure that it addresses the question. The answer choices that are incorrect are so because they don't address the question asked. However, they may be true for another question if it were asked. But, be very careful not to create your own questions to fit an incorrect answer choice because you may unintentionally select the wrong answer.
10	C	Rosebud is shy and scared, even though she overcomes these traits at the end of the story. There is no evidence in the story to support that Rosebud is colorful, generous, and fearless. In fact, she was very cautious. Because Rosebud lives in the dark underground, there isn't evidence that she expects company, so she is not seen as excited, happy, or friendly right away. In the end, after she had let in Sun and Rain and saw the beautiful garden, she realized that she was the most beautiful flower, which probably made her happy and excited. But, there is no evidence given in the story to support this.

Lesson 5: Summarizing Texts

Question No.	Answer	Detailed Explanations
1	D	All of the answers give information found in the passage. Therefore, D is the best answer.
2	B	Only answer B can be validated by reading the text. Answers A and D are not found in the passage. Answer C is not a summary of the text.
3	A	Answer A is the only accurate answer to choose after reading the poem.
4	C	This poem is about the importance of taking time to do things that you like. Even though the author does not directly state this, there is evidence to support this, such as no time to stop and stare. The author continues to list different things that the readers may have time to do if their life is too busy. The other answer choices are not as precise as the correct one. Remember to choose the best answer or the one that is the most accurate and complete.
5	B	Daniel was encouraged by his dad to try again. He finally tried and succeeded. The answers A, C, D are not found in the story. Answer B is correct.
6	B	It states that Daniel goes surfing with his dad. By reading the paragraph, one notes that they are enjoying getting ready and going. Only answer B is correct.
7	C	The second paragraph shows all of the things Daniel does to get ready early. Answer C is correct.
8	D	Answer D shows that both B,C happened. Therefore, it is the best answer. Answer A did not happen.
9	C	The passage shows the reader how to make a snowflake with paper. Answer C is correct.
10	D	The last step before opening the snowflake is cutting the folded triangles into designs and shapes. This is also shown in the diagram. The answer is D.

Lesson 6: Events

Question No.	Answer	Detailed Explanations
1	B	Although salmon is a favorite of many people, it is not the first event of this story. This first sentence is an introductory statement. So, the first important event is that the fish lay their eggs in the river. However, after the eggs are laid, and the fish hatch, they swim to the ocean and live there for three years.
2	A	The events are listed correctly in chronological order in Answer A. The events happen and flow from one to another as shown by reading the story.
3	B	The story states that Joshua learned his lesson at the end of the story. Thus , the only correct answer would be B.
4	C	The saddle blanket is put on first, as noted in the passage. Answer C states that.
5	D	Each answer has details, but the correct order is D. This answer shows exactly how to saddle up a horse-blanket, saddle, tighten girth, bit and bridle after removing halter. The other details will not work with a blank after saddle, or tightening the girth before placing it on the horse.
6	B	Answer choice B has the correct order of sentences. Which demonstrates the order that Emily prepared, cooked, and ate her brownies? Answer choices A, C, D are incorrect.
7	A	Answer Choice A is correct because the bus arrived first. Even though Marrah was trying to finish eating her breakfast, she wasn't ready to ride the bus, so as the text states, Marrah had to search for her backpack upstairs and then run downstairs to get a ride to school with her mother.
8	A	Answer choice A correctly states an important event that happened at the end of the story, which was Marrah's mother having to take her to school because Marrah missed the bus. Choice B: Marrah was not still searching for her backpack at the end because she had already found it. Choice C: There is no evidence to support that Marrah missed the day of school. She missed the bus, but her mother took her to school. Choice D: Marrah's school bus did not wait for her so Marrah's mother took her to school.
9	B	Answer Choice B lists the correct order of the sentences in the paragraph. Choices A, C, D, and E are incorrect, because they are out of order and in some cases, do not even make sense, because the events couldn't have logically happened in that order.

Question No.	Answer	Detailed Explanations
10	D	According to the passage, all of the above events happened because Emily wanted a snack (Answer Choice D). Choices A, B, and C were details in the passage.

Lesson 7: Setting

Question No.	Answer	Detailed Explanations
1	A	The story specifically states the location Franklin Creek, MS. The other answers show incorrect or misleading information.
2	B	The passage is written mostly in past tense, giving the impression that this has already occurred and is not occurring now. Answer B is correct. Answer A, C do not show time frame. Since Answer B is in past tense, one can gather this possibly happened in the past.
3	C	The author directly states that the beach that they surf at is in Port Aransas, TX. Answer C is correct.
4	A	The setting of this story is in Marrah's house. Evidence of this is that she runs upstairs and downstairs, looks through mounds of clothes in her bedroom, and misses the bus, so her Mom has to take her to school. She missed the bus, and there was no mention of the back-yard. Marrah's mother dropped her off at school, but there is no evidence of any action that takes place at school..
5	D	A severe drought means there is a lack of rain. Evidence in the story to support this is that the fruit trees in the garden needed water, and it just so happened that the trick that Tony played on the thieves provided some much needed water from the well that was able to water the fruit trees. The definition of a drought contrasts with the concept of too much rain. Also, there is no mention of there being too much or too little light.
6	D	The setting of this poem is in the kitchen because there is evidence of noise from kitchen utensils and appliances. The house is too broad and general, whereas the kitchen is more specific. There is no mention of a restaurant. The stove is in the kitchen and is does murmur but it is not the setting.
7	C	The evidence that supports a battlefield setting is the wounded sol-diers, an escape, and the enemy's camp. There is no evidence that supports a circus, an auditorium, or a theatre. One doesn't have to read too much into this statement, so don't. Identify the key words to help to determine the appropriate setting.

Question No.	Answer	Detailed Explanations
8	B	The mention of spaceships, satellites, space stations and aliens is evidence of the setting being "in outer space." Also, astronauts travel to space. Earth and ocean are incorrect because there is no evidence of earth life or ocean life. Space is the focus. Yes, earth is a planet and is part of the solar system, but the details in the story are more supportive of outer space.
9	C	Setting is important, because it tells the reader where (and when) the story takes place. The who is the narrator/author. The other answers are incorrect because what the story is about reveals the plot, and how the story is told is the point of view.

Lesson 8: Figurative Language

Question No.	Answer	Detailed Explanations
1	B	The definition of a simile is a phrase that compares two different things using the words "like" or "as". The other choices are incorrect because a simile is not just a word or phrase that compares two things. It's the way the two things are compared that creates a simile. In choice D, an object with human characteristics is personification.
2	D	The second sentence is a simile because it compares two unlike things using the word "like," It compares hair to threads of gold It has details in the sentence, but it's not just details. It is not a metaphor because it doesn't call her hair threads of gold -- Her hair WAS threads of gold would make this sentence a metaphor, but hair WAS LIKE threads of gold makes it a simile. There is no personification or human characteristics given to the hair. Example: Her hair whispered in the wind -- is personification.
3	A	Since the definition of a simile is a comparison between two unlike things that uses the words like or as, the phrase that reads: "And even though my home is like living in a zoo" is a simile. However, each of the first three lines of the poem are metaphors. So, there are three metaphors. The answer choices two and four are incorrect and do not apply to the question.
4	C	Choice C is correct because using the definition of a metaphor, which is comparing two unlike things without using the words like, as, or than, is applied three times in the first three lines of the poem. The first thing is compared to the second thing using the word "is"-- My daddy IS a tiger, continuing with lines 2 and 3.
5	D	My home is like a living in a zoo uses a simile to compare a home to a zoo. However, choices A, B, and C are metaphors, which are more intense comparisons than a simile. A metaphor actually calls one thing another, even if it's not very nice. The word "is" equates the first thing to the second or makes them equal.
6	B	This simile compares a cloud to a feather using the word "like." The feather is located "in the sky." Choice A and D are incorrect because they do not apply to the definition of a simile.

Question No.	Answer	Detailed Explanations
7	C	Choice C is the best choice because it correctly uses the word "like" in the comparison of two unlike things, a cloud and a leaf. Just like a cloud floats across the sky, so does a leaf when the wind blows. In choice A, comparing a cloud to a "rock in the water" is incorrect, because a rock doesn't float like a cloud. It sinks in the water. In choice B, a comparison of a cloud to a bird is incorrect, because a bird doesn't float in the sky, it flies or glides. Choice D is incorrect because a cotton ball doesn't float. Be very careful that the first and second things have something in common.
8	A	My sister is a bug is a similar metaphor to my sister is a pest, because both comparisons indicate that the sister is annoying. A bug is a type of pest. Choices B, and D, are similes. In choice C, there isn't comparison being made. It is just a descriptive sentence.
9	A	The sentence, "He is a cat" is a metaphor that is saying that he is the same or equal to a cat in comparison. Using the comparison word "like," would make it a simile, "He is like a cat." An idiom and a proverb do not apply to this sentence in any way, although there are idioms and proverbs about cats. An example of a "cat" idiom is "Has the cat got your tongue?" This may be said when someone is shy or afraid to talk. Idioms are expressions that are not meant to be taken literally or seriously. An example of an English proverb is: "A cat has nine lives: For three it plays, for three it strays, and for three it stays."
10	A	The expression, "Once in a blue moon" is an idiom, but it is not to be taken literally. It's just a way of expressing something that doesn't happen very often. There is no comparison being made between two unlike things, so choices B and C are incorrect.

Lesson 9: Structures of Text

Question No.	Answer	Detailed Explanations
1	C	A conclusion to a passage is usually found at the end. Choices A and B are not logical. A passage does not have a conclusion in the beginning or in the middle. Putting the end in the beginning or middle changes the flow and may confuse the reader. However, every passage usually has an ending, so choice D does not make sense.
2	A	The first stanza of the poem is asking a question, while the last stanza answers the question. However, none of the stanzas introduce life or the author. The stanzas are describing things that an individual with a busy life may not have time to do.
3	B	W. H. Davies wrote this poem, and his name is printed at the bottom of the poem. Since there is an author, the other choices are incorrect.
4	D	When you read a humorous piece of writing, you laugh. You would not generally cry (unless you were just laughing so hard that tears welled up in your eyes), or take things seriously, because the laughter may be because of a joke. You would not write down notes during laughter unless of course you are writing down something that was so funny that it made a large audience laugh, and you just wanted to remember what it was.
5	B	Descriptive passages are created to present clear, vivid pictures of a person, place, or thing. Descriptive writing may not be the intent of one writing a letter, an experience in personal voice, or a dialogue between two people.
6	D	Choice D is correct. In a poem we often find rhyming words and rhythmic writing.
7	D	Informational text is not considered a fictional genre. However, poetry, mystery, and fairytales are appropriate fictional genres which might easily adapt to informational text.
8	B	A mystery is a genre of fiction. A newspaper article, a biography, and informational text are all examples of nonfiction genres.

Question No.	Answer	Detailed Explanations
9	B	The above lines are a poem. The text has the form of a poem. However, the lines are not a story because a story has a setting, characters, a problem, and solution, as well as a beginning, middle, and end. A passage is a very small story that may have been condensed from a larger story. Song lyrics are usually written in stanzas, but may also have a chorus and a refrain. Song lyrics, being lyrical, express or tell a story, depending on the genre of music. Also, song lyrics sound like a melody when read or even like a poem that could be put to music.
10	C	The above story is missing a title. The story has an introduction, when we meet the characters, and a conclusion which shows how the problem was solved when the story ended.

Lesson 10: Styles of Narration

Question No.	Answer	Detailed Explanations
1	C	If this story were told from Marrah's mother's point of view, it would clearly show more of her mother's frustration with Marrah being late and not being able to find things, whereas the point of view that it's written from depicts Marrah's frustration over misplacing her backpack, missing the bus, and being late for school. Since Marrah is telling the story, the reader likely connects better with her. If her mother were telling the story, the reader might make a connection with the mother.
2	A	The points of view are first, second, third, limited omniscient, and omniscient. However, the first person point of view is powerful and engaging because the author is telling the story in his or her own words. The words describe the action. It also uses the first person pronouns: I, me, and my. He and she are used with the third person point of view, while you is used in second person point of view. In omniscient, the narrator knows the thoughts and feelings of all of the characters and is outside of the action, while limited omniscient is when the narrator knows the thoughts and feelings of some of the characters.
3	D	The second person point of view has the narrator tell the story to the reader using the pronoun "you." This point of view generally should not be used in telling stories because it makes the reader feel that they are responsible for the thoughts, feelings, and actions of the characters.
4	C	The use of "I" in the sentence shows first person, where the narrator is speaking about themselves. The use of Kelsey, she, and the neighbor show the third person point of view.
5	C	The use of she in the sentence is third person point of view. Choice A is first person. Choice B is second person.
6	D	Maintaining the same point of view throughout a story helps to keep the story clear and is easier for the reader to follow and to understand. The theme helps the reader to think about the message of the story. Descriptive words, well-developed character, and a great plot help make the characters fun.
7	A	Narrative writing tells an experience in a personal voice. Poems are recognized because their form consists of stanzas, verses, and rhythm.

Question No.	Answer	Detailed Explanations
8	B	First person point of view is usually found in personal diaries or journals because they are an individual's private thoughts. Journals are personal recounts of things that happen.
9	C	Mysteries are stories that have an unsolved crime. Clues lead the reader to the solution of the crime. An autobiography, which is written in first person, is a story written by a person about his or her own life. However, a biography, which is written in third person, is a story written by another person about someone else's life.
10	D	The sentence, which uses the name Kelsey, Danny, and the pronouns she and he, is written from the third person point of view.

Lesson 11: Visual Elements

Question No.	Answer	Detailed Explanations
1	B	Without the illustration, the reader might assume that Eliza is describing her experience of an actual train ride. So without this, the reader may be confused, but the author doesn't appear to be confused. Since the first sentence opens with a "winding train," this does not support the choice of a car. There isn't evidence of roads, highways, or other cars.
2	A	Media uses sounds, images, and language to convey a message, while text relies on the use of words to get a message across. Movies are considered a form of media. Verbs help to describe the action. Similes, metaphors, and alliteration are figures of speech that are used in both media and text.
3	B	Charts, maps, graphs, and maps are visual elements of text that help to illustrate or to explain a part of the text. An image of a text is just a picture of the text itself.
4	B	When a timeline is inserted in the text, it shows the key events in chronological order as they occurred. A timeline should contain factual information. Also, a timeline is a type of illustration or visual element that may enhance text. A map, which is another type of illustration or visual element, is used to show the location of places.
5	C	After reading the title and without looking at the image in detail, a reader might assume, from prior knowledge, that the image is about the famous, classic ballet, "The Nutcracker." The presence of lyrics would suggest a song. A commercial may be an advertisement to sell or promote something. "The Nutcracker," as a star would likely be the focal point of the image.
6	D	As a visual element of text, a map provides location information of places mentioned in the text. A map may be considered a type of illustration that shows the factual information of things from the text, but option D is a more relevant answer because other illustrations can show factual information but only a map shows location.
7	D	Charts and graphs are visual elements of factual data and information. An essay has an introduction, body, and conclusion.

Question No.	Answer	Detailed Explanations
8	D	Bar, line, and pie graphs are different types of graphs that show a form of data. For example, line graphs are used to show information that happens over time. A bar graph may be used to compare things, and a pie graph may be used to show the parts of a whole.
9	C	A chart or drawing may be used to show the relationship between changing things. A chart could be used to show the number of people who go to see movies on the big screen or theatre and the number of people who watch movies in the privacy of their homes. If something is circular, it moves in the same direction as a shape of a circle.
10	B	Choice B is correct. In fictional text, an illustration works best as a visual aid. An internet link may be inserted as a reference to something in non-fiction text. A bar graph is also used in non-fiction text to show how data compare. Text only excludes the use of any visual aids.

Lesson 12: Compare and Contrast

Question No.	Answer	Detailed Explanations
1	C	There is evidence that both girls rely on their mothers, because Katie's mother has to help her to get ready for her performance, and Marrah's mother has to take her to school when she misses the bus. There is no evidence that both girls have the same hair color, are the same age, or have many friends.
2	B	Personification is giving human characteristics to non-human things. In the first poem, Beauty is personified and in the second poem the appliances and utensils in the kitchen are personified.
3	D	When comparing two texts to determine if they are like or different, one should look at the type, style, and purpose of the text. These are the various aspects of text that create the content.
4	A	When using a Venn Diagram, a graphic representation of the comparison of two things, the overlapping section shows what the two things being compared have in common, while the outer circles show the characteristics of each thing. The outer circles also show how the two things contrast.
5	B	In a Venn Diagram, the outside non-overlapping circles describe what the two characters do not have in common They show each one's unique characteristics, which is also the same as showing how the characters contrast.
6	B	According to the chart, the two months with the highest book check outs are September and October. The evidence in the chart shows that these two months are above 600 while the months of November and December are below 600.
7	D	According to the chart, students borrowed a total of 475 books during the month of December, which was the lowest number.
8	D	While sentence A describes subjects that require a mental activity, sentence B represents games that are played physically.
9	A	The use of the word similarities in the sentence leads you to compare or tell how President Lincoln and President Kennedy were alike. Option B provides contrasting information.
10	C	Choice C is correct. The use of the word unlike in the sentence leads you to contrast or tell how different mother's cake is from grandmother's.

Chapter 2 - Reading Informational Text

The objective of the Reading Informational Text standards is to ensure that each student is able to read and comprehend informational text (history/social studies, science, and technical texts) related to Grade 5.

This section is to support students to master the necessary skills, an example which will help the student understand the concepts related to the standard is given. Along with this, we encourage the student to go through the resources available online on EdSearch to gain an in-depth understanding of these concepts. EdSearch page for each lesson can be accessed with the help of the url or the QR code provided.

A small map is provided after each passage or text in which the student can enter the details as understood from the literary text. Doing this will help the student to refer to key points that help in answering the questions with ease.

Chapter 2

Lesson 1: Inferences and Conclusions

Inferences from a text: After reading a text, an inference is an idea or conclusion that the reader has made or reached <u>that was not</u> in the text but is based on information <u>that was</u> in the text.

Let us understand the concept with an example.

Facts about the North American Lobster

The lobster is a fascinating marine creature. It can be found in bodies of salt water from Labrador to North Carolina. Lobsters are scavengers – they eat other fish and marine animals like clams and mussels – dead or alive. They are also considered a delicacy by many people.

The female lobster produces a sweet smelling liquid (think of it as perfume in human terms) to attract the attention of the male lobster. The male lobster is needed in order for the female to produce eggs. Once eggs are developed inside the female, the eggs are pushed out of the female's body into the water where they hatch and are known as larvae. Larvae float or swim at or near the surface of the water; they do not have permanent shelters to live in. Because of this, they are preyed on by seabirds and various species of fish and crustaceans.

After the larvae stage, lobsters grow to become juvenile lobsters and then adult lobsters. Juvenile and adult lobsters live at the bottom of the water where they are prey for bottom or reef inhabiting species such as sculpin, cod, sharks, rays, skates, octopus and crabs. Predators also include lobster fishermen. To protect lobster populations to decrease severely from overfishing, there are rules that lobster fishermen must follow, such as minimum size limits and periods during the year when lobstering is not allowed. Human-caused pollution is a threat to the health of lobsters.

Juvenile and adult lobsters live on the bottom of salt water bays, rivers and oceans, because there is always water there regardless of the changes in depth from the tide. Lobsters need salt water to survive, and salinity is a measure of how much salt is in salt water. Salinity concentrations of at least 20 ppt (parts of salt per thousand units of water) are preferred by lobsters. Adult lobsters prefer water temperatures ranging from 8 to 14 degrees C (46 to 53 degrees F). Water temperature is a major factor influencing lobster activity levels and migrations.

Lobsters prefer crevices and niches on the bottom made up of small clusters of rocks called cobble (that resemble cobblestones) that frequently sit on sandy or muddy bottoms in areas in rivers, bays and areas of the ocean that are near shore. Areas with substantial underwater plant life are also suitable habitats.

Adult and juvenile lobsters are primarily nocturnal – that is, most active at dusk and during the night until dawn, spending most of their time searching for food. They tend to stay in their shelters during the day, but some studies have shown that lobsters may also be active during daylight hours. In order for adult lobsters to grow larger, the must shed their shells and grow new, larger ones. This process is called molting.

Lobsters migrate nearer to the coast when the water warms up as summer approaches. This migration is especially important for egg-bearing female lobsters, because eggs mature faster and hatch sooner in warmer water. Warmer water is also beneficial for the hatching of eggs, molting and mating, which is why these events occur primarily in the springtime and early summer in shallow coastal waters.

Lobsters are an expensive delicacy today, but they were not always so highly valued or regarded. Hundreds of years ago, lobsters were so plentiful and easy to catch in shallow water near the shoreline that Native Americans used them to fertilize their fields and to bait their hooks for fishing. In colonial times, lobsters were considered "poverty food" and harvested by hand along the shoreline to be served to prisoners and indentured servants, and to widows and children dependent on charitable donations.

Until about 1840, the lobster industry was fairly localized to the areas where the lobsters were caught, because lobster meat would spoil easily if not refrigerated, and there were no refrigerated trucks or air freight capabilities or dry ice sufficient to protect them in shipment. But then a new food manufacturing process changed all that.

What manufacturing process are we referring to? It is believed that the single most important factor which resulted in the exploitation of the lobster resource was the sudden success of the canning industry. The spreading fame of Maine lobsters and the lack of adequate facilities for distribution of fresh product were the factors that stimulated the beginning of the canning industry in 1840. The number of canneries grew, and the canneries were very efficient at processing.

Why, then, did the lobster meat canning industry collapse 40 years later? Because they were so efficient and canned so many pounds of the larger lobsters, there reached a time when the only lobsters being caught were smaller lobsters. Only twenty years later, the canneries were stuffing meat from half-pound lobsters into the tins for processing, a sign that the fishery had been overfished by then. The success of the canning industry made obvious the need for preservation and law enforcement if the fishery was to survive. Following the collapse of the canning industry, the fresh lobster industry took over the commercialization of the fishery. This meant the building of lobster pounds. Using the circulating salt water facilities at the pounds for storing lobsters live, dealers could wait for the price of lobster to increase or allow a newly-molted lobster time to harden its shell. These live-storage facilities became the backbone of the modern lobster industry.

Your assignment: Explain any inferences and conclusions you reach after reading the text. Use quotes from the text as support for your inferences and conclusions.

This is what you might write.

Note that we have chosen a numbered format to use to present inferences and conclusions. Inferences and conclusions are displayed in bold type.

1. "The lobster is a fascinating marine creature."

- The female produces a sweet smelling liquid (think of it as perfume in human terms) to attract the attention of the male lobster.
- Lobsters are scavengers – they eat other fish and marine animals like clams and mussels – dead or alive."
- Even though they are scavengers willing to eat dead creatures, lobsters are now considered a delicacy by many people. What is surprising is that hundreds of years ago, lobsters were so plentiful and easy to catch in shallow water near the shoreline that Native Americans used them to fertilize their fields and to bait their hooks for fishing. In colonial times, lobsters were considered "poverty food" and harvested by hand along the shoreline to be served to prisoners and indentured servants, and to widows and children dependent on charitable donations.
- Nature has provided the female lobster with the ability to produce thousands of eggs, from which hatch thousands of lobster larvae. Thousands are needed because the larvae are defenseless and many are eaten by seabirds and various species of fish and crustaceans.
- In order for adult lobsters to grow larger, the must shed their shells and grow new, larger ones. This process is called molting.

2. The lobster is in danger of being caught and eaten by predators.

- Larvae float or swim at or near the surface of the water and are preyed on by seabirds and various species of fish and crustaceans.
- After the larvae stage, juvenile and adult lobsters live at the bottom of the water where they are prey for bottom or reef inhabiting species such as sculpin, cod, sharks, rays, skates, octopus and crabs. Predators also include lobster fishermen.
- At one time in the 1800's, lobsters were in danger of becoming extinct because of overfishing and efficient processing by the canning industry.
- To protect themselves, lobsters prefer to live in crevices and niches made up of small clusters of rocks that frequently sit on sandy or muddy bottoms in areas in rivers, bays and areas of the ocean that are near shore.

3. The North American lobster is now protected from becoming an endangered species

- While canned lobster meat is still available, live lobsters have become the favored choice of consumers, now that lobster pounds with fresh circulating salt water are available.
- To protect lobster populations from severely decreasing because of overfishing, there are rules that lobster fishermen must follow, such as minimum size limits, throwing back females bearing eggs and periods during the year when lobstering is not allowed. With these legal protections in place, we can infer that lobsters will be available for years to come.

You can scan the QR code given below or use the url to access additional EdSearch resources including videos and mobile apps related to *Inferences and Conclusions*.

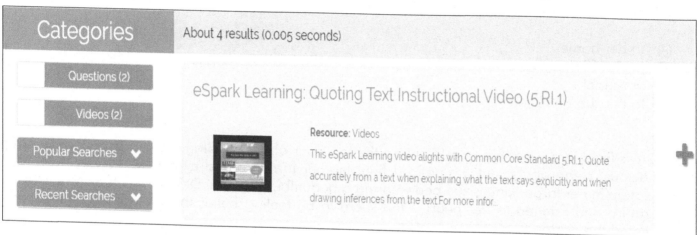

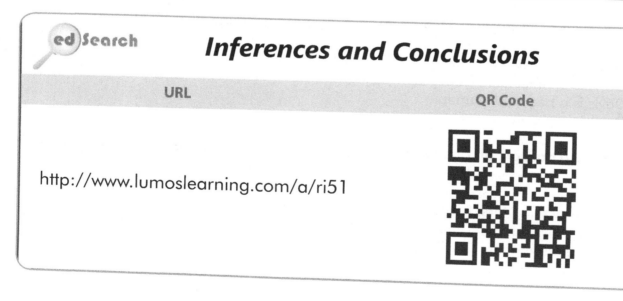

Inferences and Conclusions

URL	QR Code
http://www.lumoslearning.com/a/ri51	

It was a cool, crisp morning. Lucy threw her backpack over her shoulders, jumped on her bicycle, and pedaled down Pine Street. Her tires made soft crunching noises as she drove through piles of brown, yellow, and orange leaves.

1. In the paragraph above, what time of year do you think it was?

- Ⓐ fall
- Ⓑ spring
- Ⓒ summer
- Ⓓ winter

2. Where do you think Lucy is going?

- Ⓐ to her home
- Ⓑ to visit friends
- Ⓒ to school
- Ⓓ to the supermarket

Mrs. Davis lived in a great big apartment on the top floor of her building. As the doctor walked into her spacious, clean apartment, he noticed fine, leather furniture and expensive works of art. Mrs. Davis sat up in her large, king-sized bed wearing a beautiful, silk robe. Dr. Thomas took Mrs. Davis's temperature and listened to her heart. "You seem to be feeling better this afternoon, Mrs. Davis," commented the doctor.

What can you infer about Mrs. Davis after reading the passage above?

Mrs. Davis is a wealthy woman.
Mrs. Davis is an intelligent woman.
Mrs. Davis is a beautiful woman.
Mrs. Davis is a young woman.

...ding the paragraph above, what can you infer about the reason for Dr. Thomas's

...as is visiting Mrs. Davis, because she was sick.
...s is visiting Mrs. Davis, because he is her new neighbor.
...is visiting Mrs. Davis, because he needs a favor.
...'s visiting Mrs. Davis, because it is her birthday.

5. Based on the sentence below, draw a conclusion about the way that Jan feels about the creature.

Jan took one look at the hideous creature and ran away as fast as she could.

- Ⓐ She thinks the creature is cute.
- Ⓑ She thinks the creature is scary.
- Ⓒ She feels sorry for the creature.
- Ⓓ None of the above

6. Select the phrase that best completes the sentence.

Kara's mother wakes up at 5:30 A.M. every morning so she'll have time to study for her college classes. This is the only time she has to study before she has to go to work. She takes college classes two nights a week. Every weekend, she volunteers at the local homeless shelter. She has been helping out there for the past three years.

From the information in the paragraph above, one can infer that Kara's mother is probably _____.

- Ⓐ married to a college professor
- Ⓑ a very hard-working woman
- Ⓒ tired of going to college
- Ⓓ None of the above

7. Select the phrase that best complete the sentence.

Victor took off his reading glasses and rubbed his eyes. He picked up his walking cane. Then he slowly used the cane to help himself up from the bench. Every day, it takes him a little bit longer to stand up. Every day, it becomes more difficult for him to walk.

From the information in the paragraph above, you can infer that Victor is _____.

- Ⓐ a young man
- Ⓑ happy
- Ⓒ an old man
- Ⓓ in good health

8. Select the phrase that best completes the sentence.

You can infer from the paragraph that _____.

    Ⓐ Victor was reading before he decided to stand up
    Ⓑ It is difficult for Victor to get up from the bench
    Ⓒ Victor doesn't walk very well
    Ⓓ All of the above

9. What conclusion can you draw about Corky from the sentences below?

Corky waddled toward the lake. When he reached the water, he flapped his wings, quacked, and jumped in.

    Ⓐ Corky is a dog.
    Ⓑ Corky is a duck.
    Ⓒ Corky is a fish.
    Ⓓ Corky is a horse.

10. What do you think "read between the lines" means?

Authors help readers make inferences by giving certain details. However, authors expect readers to "read between the lines."

    Ⓐ Figure out what text means.
    Ⓑ Look for evidence in text to make inferences.
    Ⓒ Come up with ideas or opinions of your own based on what you read.
    Ⓓ All of the above

Chapter 2

Lesson 2: Main Idea and Supporting Details

Publisher's Note: to identify the main idea(s) or theme of written text, you have to figure out what the author considers the most important purpose or message or lesson that he/she wants you to recognize. It could be a lesson in morals, or a call for you to take some action, or just to entertain you. Key details are used to further explain things about the main idea(s). Summarizing the text means writing only the main ideas.

Let us understand the concept with an example.

You have been assigned to read the following article, and write text that meets what the standard requires.

Scientists tell us that changes in our climate are happening. Average temperatures around the world are getting higher. The planet's average surface temperature has risen about 2.0 degrees Fahrenheit since the late 19th century. The warmest year on record was 2016; eight months were the warmest on record. The number of warm days in a year has increased while the number of cold days has decreased. This is called global warming.

Because of the rise in temperature, the ice caps in Greenland and Antarctica are melting and are have caused sea levels to rise 8" in the last 100 years; glaciers are shrinking; ocean water temperatures are rising. Carbon dioxide levels in the air have risen from an average of 300 ppm (parts per million) to 400 ppm, the highest levels ever. Carbon dioxide forms a blanket above the earth that traps heat, an additional contributor to global warming.

Studies by scientists point out that global warming is having bad effects on humans, animals and plants. Carbon dioxide reduces air quality which is not healthy for humans and animals to breathe. Water is essential for living creatures; without enough water they die. Global warming decreases the amount of water on the planet. Some creatures cannot adapt quickly to changes in climates and will die, and those that migrate can be forced to change their migration patterns.

Why is this happening? Ninety seven percent of global scientists think this is happening because of things we humans are doing. Our use of fuels from fossils, such as oil and coal, are major causes, and our manufacturing activities are another cause. We need your help to convince our government and companies that use chemicals to manufacture their products to agree to rules that minimize the release of harmful chemicals into the air. Please sign up to help us at: (assume that the author provides a link to a signup form).

Your assignment: To identify the main idea(s) and explain how the author uses key details (reasons and evidence) to support his/her main idea(s) in the article, and then to summarize the article.

The following is an example of what you might write.

The author claims that global warming is happening; this is one main idea in the article. The second main idea is to convince you to sign up with an organization that tries to convince government and certain companies to minimize the release of chemicals into the air.

To support the claim that global warming is happening, the author presents data proving that global temperatures have been rising, major ice caps are melting and carbon dioxide levels in the atmosphere have increased, all as a result of global warming.

The author states that science studies show that global warming is having bad effects on humans, animals and plants. The author gives several key details to support this statement, such as a reduction (decrease) in air quality, reduction in fresh water supplies, inability (not able to do something) of some creatures to adapt to changes in climate and disruption (change) of migration patterns.

You might summarize the article this way: Global warming is happening. Scientists have conducted studies that prove this using actual data, and the article gives examples. Global warming has harmful effects on human, animal and plant life on Earth. The article gives examples.

You can scan the QR code given below or use the url to access additional EdSearch resources including videos and mobile apps related to *Main Idea and Supporting Details*.

ed Search	**Main Idea and Supporting Details**
URL	**QR Code**
http://www.lumoslearning.com/a/ri52	

Read the passage below and answer the questions

The Orange

Even though no one knows exactly where oranges come from, Southeast Asia is believed to be their first home. They are grown today in most of the warmer parts of the world. The ancient Greeks and Romans knew about oranges. It is possible that oranges were carried from India to Western Asia, and then to Europe.

The Spaniards took the sour oranges to the West Indies and from there to Florida, in America. Today, oranges are the most important fresh fruit in international trade. There are three different kinds of oranges: the sweet or common orange, the mandarin orange, and the sour or bitter orange.

One type of sweet orange is called the blood orange. It has a pulp with a deep red color. This type of orange is grown mostly in the Mediterranean region. Mandarin oranges are mainly found in Florida. Sour oranges are grown almost everywhere with Spain having the greatest number used for trade. These sour oranges are generally used to make marmalade.

However, they can be put to many other interesting uses, from making medicine to creating perfumes. Oranges have many medicinal values. Oranges are the fruit with the greatest concentration of vitamin C. The skin of the orange helps to keep the fruit inside from becoming damaged and to remain clean. The thick, oily, and bitter skin does not allow any insects to get into an orange. Many kinds of useful oils can be extracted from the thick skin. Oranges are healthy and delicious.

After reading the story, enter the details in the map below. This will help you to answer the questions with ease.

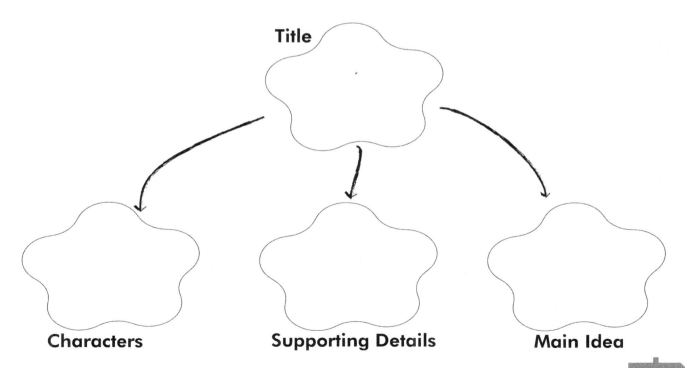

1. **What is the author saying about oranges in the first paragraph?**

   Ⓐ The author is explaining how oranges have been dispersed around the world.
   Ⓑ The author is explaining how the ancient Romans and Greeks knew about oranges.
   Ⓒ The author is explaining how oranges are traded around the world.
   Ⓓ None of the above

2. **From your understanding of the above passage, oranges are grown in ___.**

   Ⓐ Spain
   Ⓑ the West Indies
   Ⓒ most of the colder parts of the word.
   Ⓓ most of the warmer parts of the world.

3. **Where in the passage can you find out about who grows the sour oranges and where they are grown?**

   Ⓐ The second paragraph
   Ⓑ The third paragraph
   Ⓒ Both A and B.
   Ⓓ In the last paragraph

4. **Which detail in the above passage supports the fact that the orange is a clean fruit?**

   Ⓐ Anyone touching it only touches the outer covering, which is easily taken off.
   Ⓑ The thick, oily, and bitter skin does not allow insects to get into the orange.
   Ⓒ Both A and B
   Ⓓ None, because the orange is a very messy fruit.

5. **The second paragraph tells us _____.**

   Ⓐ about the types of oranges
   Ⓑ about where the oranges are grown
   Ⓒ about the usefulness of oranges
   Ⓓ All of the above

Salmon

A fish that is a great favorite with people is salmon. It begins its life in a small pool up a river. Far from the sea, the fish lays its eggs in a pool in the river. When the baby fish are a few inches long, they begin to swim down the river. As they grow bigger, they make their way towards the sea.

They jump over rocks, often with their tails first. Suddenly, they find themselves in the sea. The fish live in the sea for three years. They swim far away from land. How do they find their way back? These fish have a wonderful sense of smell. They remember the scent of their journey easily, because the river flowed to the sea and carried them there. After three years, most salmon swim toward the pools.

As soon as they reach a pool, the females lay their eggs. They lay their eggs near the edge of the water and cover them with sand. Soon the eggs hatch and the pool is full of small fish, getting ready for the long journey out to the sea.

After reading the story, enter the details in the map below. This will help you to answer the questions with ease.

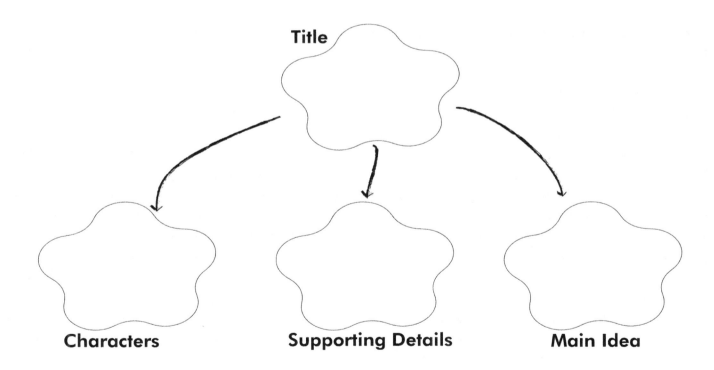

Title

Characters   **Supporting Details**   **Main Idea**

6. Which detail in the paragraph tells us that salmon jump backward over the rocks?

Ⓐ "When the baby fish are a few inches long, they begin to swim down the river."
Ⓑ "Suddenly, they find themselves in the sea."
Ⓒ "They swim far away from land."
Ⓓ "As they grow bigger, they make their way towards the sea. They jump over rocks, often with their tails first."

7. According to the passage, how long do salmon live in the sea?

Ⓐ six years
Ⓑ three years
Ⓒ one year
Ⓓ five years

Fruits begin to appear on the orange trees when they are three years old. Flowers and fruits may appear throughout the year. A very tasty and healthy kind of honey can be made from the orange flowers.

8. According to the text above, what is made out of orange flowers?

Ⓐ A tasty but unhealthy kind of honey
Ⓑ A tasty and healthy kind of honey
Ⓒ A bad tasting, but healthy kind of honey
Ⓓ Nothing is made out of the orange flowers.

For a full, healthy, and useful life, sports are as important and necessary as work. They help us mentally, physically, and emotionally, and help us develop a healthy outlook towards life. Sports are very useful as a diversion of the mind. Most sports require skill and good judgment. Players not only develop their bodies but also their minds. Players must acquire the art of playing a game.

9. According to the passage, why are sports important?

Ⓐ Sports help people mentally, physically, and emotionally.
Ⓑ Sports do not require any special skills.
Ⓒ Sports require players to develop their bodies only, not their minds.
Ⓓ Sports are not useful.

Sports can develop character. The players must abide by the rules of the game. Any departure from following these rules means foul play. Every foul stroke in a game involves a penalty. Therefore, players play a fair game. Fair play is a noble and moral quality. Players become honest and punctual.

10. What is the main idea of the above passage?

 Ⓐ Sports players are honest and punctual.
 Ⓑ Sports players must play a fair game.
 Ⓒ Sports players must abide by the rules.
 Ⓓ Sports can develop a strong character in players.

Chapter 2

Lesson 3: Text Relationships

The following essay is an example of interactions between two groups on the science issue of global warming.

Global Warming

For many years, scientists have been studying the effects of temperature on living organisms on planet Earth. In the last few years, there has been increase in the earth's atmospheric and oceanic temperatures, which has been called global warming. Global warming has been recognized as a very important environmental phenomenon that can have dramatic and devastating effects on the environment of planet Earth.

Group A believes the theory that global warming is caused by the increase of certain gases (such as carbon dioxide) in the atmosphere that occurs when warmth from the sun is trapped in the Earth's atmosphere by a layer of gases (such as carbon dioxide) and water vapor. They refer to this as the "greenhouse effect." This group believes that human activities, such as manufacturing, deforestation and pollution are the primary contributors to the greenhouse effect.

Group A provides the following key details to support their theory:

An IPCC (United Nations' Intergovernmental Panel on Climate Change) report, based on the work of some 2,500 scientists in more than 130 countries, concluded that humans have caused all or most of the current planetary warming. Human-caused global warming is often called anthropogenic climate change. Industrialization, deforestation, and pollution have greatly increased atmospheric concentrations of water vapor, carbon dioxide, methane, and nitrous oxide, all greenhouse gases that help trap heat near Earth's surface. Humans are pouring carbon dioxide into the atmosphere much faster than plants and oceans can absorb it.

Also, that 97% of the climate scientists surveyed believe "global average temperatures have increased" during the past century; and 97% think human activity is a significant contributing factor in changing mean global temperatures.

Group B believes the theory that global warming is not just a recent phenomenon, but is a natural phenomenon that has been occurring for thousands of years as part of a cycle of warming and cooling of the earth's atmosphere, and that human activity is only a minor contributor.

Group B provides the following key details to support their theory:

31,000 scientists reject global warming and say "no convincing evidence" that humans can or will cause global warming. This claim originates from an organization which published an online petition that they claim 31,000 scientists have signed.

Also, they mention that some experts point out that natural cycles in the Earth's orbit can alter the planet's exposure to sunlight, which may explain the current trend. Earth has indeed experienced warming and cooling cycles roughly every hundred thousand years due to these orbital shifts, but such changes have occurred over the span of several centuries.

Lastly, they claim that in 2009, hackers unearthed hundreds of e-mails stored at a university that exposed private conversations among some top-level climate scientists discussing whether certain data that did not support Group A's theory should be released to the public. The e-mail exchanges also refer to statistical tricks used to illustrate climate change trends, according to a report in one major newspaper. Climate change skeptics have heralded the e-mails as an attempt to fool the public into accepting Group A's theory.

Your assignment: Explain the relationship between Group A and Group B based on the Global Warming article.

This is what you might write.

The relationship between Group A and Group B is confrontational. Each group has a theory about the causes of global warming, and the theories are opposing views. Each group believes their theory is correct and the other group's theory is not correct.

Specifically, Group A's theory states that "global warming is caused by the increase of certain gases (such as carbon dioxide) in the atmosphere that occurs when warmth from the sun is trapped in the Earth's atmosphere by a layer of gases (such as carbon dioxide) and water vapor." They believe "that human activities, such as manufacturing, deforestation and pollution are the primary contributors to the greenhouse effect."

Group B's theory states that "global warming is not just a recent phenomenon, but is a natural phenomenon that has been occurring for thousands of years as part of a cycle of warming and cooling of the earth's atmosphere, and that human activity is only a minor contributor."

You can scan the QR code given below or use the url to access additional EdSearch resources including videos and mobile apps related to *Text Relationships.*

 **Search**

Text Relationships

URL	QR Code
http://www.lumoslearning.com/a/ri53	

Fishing and Chores

Joshua had lived in Mississippi all of his life. He grew up near the coast in a small rural community known as Franklin Creek. If you travel along Highway 10 going toward Alabama, it is the last exit in Mississippi.

Joshua loved to go fishing along the creek that ran behind his grandmother's massive house. He lived there with his grandmother and his parents. When he wanted to go fishing, his parents wanted to be sure that had had done his chores first. Joshua did not like chores at all. Quite often he tried to avoid doing his chores.

This became a real problem for Joshua's mother, as the house was very large, and keeping it clean required help from everyone. She often told Joshua that he would be a hindrance to the family if he did not do his part.

Little reminders did not seem to help. Scolding was of no use either. It seemed he would turn a deaf ear when it came to listening. Joshua's mother was beside herself.

One day his grandmother gave her an idea. Joshua had asked that morning to go fishing. Little did he know that his mother had taken the advice of Grandma and would soon put a stop to his ways of not doing chores. Joshua said, "Mom, chores are done! Can I go now?" His mother replied, "Sure, no problem."

Joshua hurried out to the storage building to gather his fishing gear. The fishing pole was not in its place! The tackle box wasn't there either! His fishing hat was missing, too! He ran back to the house where his mother and grandmother were drinking coffee on the porch.

Joshua asked, "Mom, where is all my fishing stuff?"

"What are you talking about, son?" Replied his mother.

"I can't find anything in the storage building." He said.

She then told him to go look in his room. She said she had put it all in there where he was supposed to have cleaned. When Joshua got to his room, he realized what was going on. In order to find his fishing equipment, he would have to go through the mess in his room. His mother and grandmother were right behind him laughing. He grinned and said, "I get it now, Mom." He cleaned his room and found all the things he needed for fishing, too!

Needless to say, Joshua never had a problem doing chores again!

1. What happens when Joshua looks for his fishing gear?

Ⓐ He quickly finds it in the storage shed.
Ⓑ His mother tells him that she has hidden it.
Ⓒ His grandmother has taken it fishing.
Ⓓ He cannot find his fishing gear and asks his mother about it.

2. Why did Joshua's mother hide his fishing gear?

Ⓐ She had cleaned the storage shed and rearranged everything.
Ⓑ He was neglecting his chores and she wanted to teach him a lesson.
Ⓒ Joshua didn't do chores, so the storage shed was a mess and he couldn't locate his things.
Ⓓ None of the above.

Try Again

Surfing is one of Daniel's favorite pastimes! Every weekend when he has the time, he heads toward Port Aransas, Texas with his father. Daniel's family doesn't live far away, so it takes them only about 30 minutes to get there, if there is a short ferry line. They always make sure to get their things ready the night before. Daniel and his dad like to get an early start to their surfing day!

The night before, Daniel makes sure that his dad's truck is clean, especially the bed of the truck where he puts his surfboards. He also takes time to clean his wetsuit that he wears for protection and warmth. His mom usually makes sandwiches, and snacks ahead of time and puts them in the refrigerator to keep them fresh.

Daniel and his dad leave around 5:30 or 6:00 am when the sun is just coming up. Daniel has been surfing with his dad since he was very small. He remembers when his dad would ride with him on the surfboard.

When Daniel was about 9 years old, he fell off of a surfboard and hurt his leg and back. His dad rushed him to a nearby hospital for X-rays and a checkup. Luckily, there were no broken bones. However, the incident claimed Daniel so much that he refused to go surfing for several months. His dad kept encouraging him to give it a try. He told him, "If at once you don't succeed, try, and try again!" Daniel didn't want to try again. He was afraid of getting hurt and falling off of the surfboard.

Finally, Daniel went surfing with his father again. His father went out into the waves, and rode a wave in. Daniel went out on the waves, too. He stayed out for a long time without attempting to ride a wave back to shore. Daniel's dad began to wonder if his son had given up.

Just then a large wave began building up far out in the water. Daniel's dad was astonished! There was Daniel riding the huge wave all the way to shore without a problem. His dad motioned for Daniel to come where he was, but Daniel didn't. Instead he went right back into the water, and began riding wave after wave after wave!

It is amazing that fear can be overcome with one's personal best.

3. What happened to Daniel to make him not want to surf?

Ⓐ His dad bought him a motorcycle.
Ⓑ He was hurt in a car accident while going to the beach with his dad.
Ⓒ Daniel was hurt while surfing and became afraid of trying again.
Ⓓ None of the above

4. The reason that Daniel tried to surf again was because_____.

Ⓐ His dad made him do it again.
Ⓑ His dad encouraged him without belittling him.
Ⓒ He was bullied into trying again.
Ⓓ The weather changed so he could surf again.

The Traveler

A weary traveler stopped at Sam's house and asked him for shelter for the night. Sam was a friendly soul. He not only agreed to let the traveler stay for the night, he decided to treat his guest to some curried chicken. So he bought a couple of chickens from the market and gave them to his wife to cook. Then he went off to buy some fruit.

Now Sam's wife could not resist food. She had a habit of eating as she cooked. So, as she cooked the meat, she smelled the rich steam and could not help tasting a piece. It was tender and delicious, and she decided to have another piece. Soon there was only a tiny bit left. Her little son, Kevin, ran into the kitchen. She gave him that little piece.

Kevin found it so tasty that he begged his mother for more. But there was no more chicken left. The traveler, who had gone to have a wash, returned. The woman heard him coming and had to think of a plan quickly. She began to scold her son loudly: "Your father has taught you a shameful and disgusting habit. Stop it, I tell you!" The traveler was curious. "What habit has his father taught the child?" he asked. "Oh," said the woman, "Whenever a guest arrives, my husband cuts off their ears and roasts them for my son to eat."

The traveler was shocked. He picked up his shoes and fled.

"Why has our guest left in such a hurry?" asked Sam, when he came back.

"A fine guest indeed!" exclaimed his wife. "He snatched the chickens out of my pot and ran off with them!"

"The chickens!" exclaimed Sam. He ran after his guest, shouting. "Let me have one, at least; you may keep the other!" But his guest only ran faster!

5. Why did the traveler pick up his shoes and flee?

Ⓐ He disliked Sam's wife very much.
Ⓑ He thought Sam would be angry with him when he returned.
Ⓒ Sam's wife tricked him into thinking her husband would cut off his ears.
Ⓓ There were no chickens left to eat.

6. What happened as a result of Sam's wife's habit of eating as she cooked?

Ⓐ Travelers stopped by for dinner often.
Ⓑ Guests did not visit Sam and his wife's home.
Ⓒ Sam's wife became very fat.
Ⓓ There were no curried chickens left to eat.

Morning Ride

As the sun was gradually rising across the plain, Chloe was preparing to saddle up her favorite horse, Pepper, to go for a morning ride. First she had to be sure the blanket was in place before getting the saddle. Chloe didn't mind the heavy weight of the saddle as she took it down from the rack and quickly threw it over Pepper's back. Sometimes she did wonder why the weight never bothered horses. Tightening the girth under the saddle would be the hardest part of all. If it was not just right, the saddle could slip causing a problem and possible injury to Chloe while riding. Finally, it was snug and secure.

Of course, Chloe took off the halter so that she could put on the bit and bridle along with the reins. Horses will follow people easier to the barn if they have on a halter. Chloe knew that Pepper would be no problem with her as Chloe kept her tack clean. The condition of the tack was so important in horse care.

Chloe's grandfather, Morgan, had always taught her to take pride in her care of horses. He told her many a time that the horse weighed over twelve hundred pounds. She needed to be sure to respect that and keep it in mind, but not to fear the horse.

She had been raised with horses since she was about two years old. She was taught to ride with some-one leading her around. Chloe did not ride with saddles when she was little, just bareback. Saddling up came when Chloe was old enough to handle both saddle and tack.

Leading Pepper out of the barn was easy, as Chloe knew she was anxious for a morning run, as well.

One gentle but firm nudge on Pepper's sides and off they went as fast as lightning. The cool breeze blew through Chloe's hair and Pepper's mane. This was the way to start a new day!

7. What happens when Chloe is finally ready to ride?

Ⓐ   She cannot go riding because Pepper is too excited to ride.
Ⓑ   She realizes that her mother is calling her home and puts up everything.
Ⓒ   She leads Pepper out of the stall, gives a nudge to the horse's sides, and takes off.
Ⓓ   None of the above

8. What could happen as a result of not pulling and tightening the girth?

Ⓐ   She could fall down setting the saddle and decide not to ride.
Ⓑ   Chloe could be seriously injured in a fall.
Ⓒ   She could ride anyway, because she is a pro at riding.
Ⓓ   None of the above

How to Design and Make Awesome Snowflakes

With the coming of winter, many people are lucky to see gorgeous snowflakes in the air. Some people do not have snow where they live. All of us can grace our window panes with paper snow flakes. We can decorate our windows and make other crafts with these easy to make snowflakes. You can occupy many hours in a day by cutting out dozens of paper snowflakes.

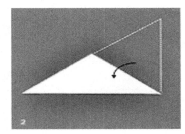

The following directions will help you make your awesome winter wonderland of snowflakes. First take a square piece of paper and fold it in half diagonally to make a triangle. Then fold it in half again to make the corners meet as shown in figure 2 below.

In figure 3, will notice that you will once again fold your triangle to make a smaller triangle. Be sure that the have your corners meeting and even.

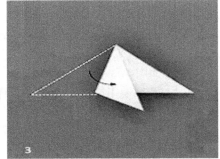

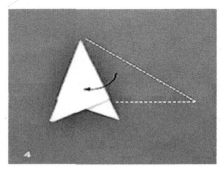

Now you fold it over again to make the shape shown in figure 4. Be careful as you might need to adjust these folds to get the sides to match up. Crease the paper after the folds are done just right.

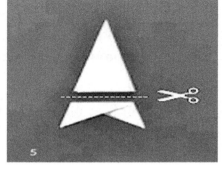

Cut straight across the bottom as shown in figure 5.

You are now ready to cut of various designs and shapes on your folded paper. Be careful not to cut straight across the entire fold.

Carefully unfold to see the awesome snowflake that you have designed and made. You can add color and, glitter. You can even make additional crafts out of multiple snowflakes. Enjoy your winter wonderland of snowflakes.

(Pictures taken from Martha Stewart online.)

9. The reason that you cut off the bottom of the folded triangles is_____

  Ⓐ   You have to make it littler.
  Ⓑ   You can make two out of it instead of one.
  Ⓒ   There is no reason to cut it off.
  Ⓓ   To be sure that your snowflake looks as much like a real snowflake as possible.

10. What is the most important part of making a paper snowflake?

  Ⓐ   Both answers C and D.
  Ⓑ   Getting the designs right when you cut them out.
  Ⓒ   Making sure that you do not cut all the way through after the final folding.
  Ⓓ   Making sure that you have corners meet every time you fold.

Chapter 2

Lesson 4: General Academic Vocabulary

Let us understand the concept with an example.

This standard asks you the reader to "Determine the meaning" of words or phrases in written text. If you don't know the meaning of a word or phrase, you have to either look it up in a dictionary or thesaurus (contains other words that mean the same thing) or enter it as a keyword in a search engine (ex. Google) or figure it out by using the meanings of the other words in the text. But sometimes a word or phrase can have different meanings, so you have to decide what the author of the text wanted the meaning to be.

Here are some examples of words and phrases with explanations of how to figure out their meanings by using the meanings of the other words in the text.

The words or phrases are underlined.

1. The author of the children's book used <u>personification</u> to allow the animals in the story to speak and play baseball. Explanation: You know that most animals cannot speak and none can play baseball, but humans can, so the author must be giving the animals human characteristics. When an author allows an animal or an object to do things it cannot ordinarily do, but that humans can do, the technique is called personification.

2. From my <u>point of view</u>, the school should allow students to bring their tablets and smartphones to school. On the other hand, the opinion of the school board is that this should not be allowed. Explanation: It should be clear to you, the reader, that the author is expressing his or her opinion or belief on the issue of bringing tablets and smartphones to school. Another word for expressing an opinion is expressing a point of view.

3. A group of students want the school to make the math courses more interesting, but without being <u>specific</u> about how these courses should be changed, it is unlikely the principal will change anything. Explanation: The key phrase is "how these courses should be changed." In order for the principal to take any action, he or she needs to understand why the students are making this request. They are not giving the principal any facts or details; they are not being definite. Another way of saying this is that they are not being specific.

4. The dress code in my school is <u>archaic</u>. I mean, what kid doesn't want to wear jeans some days of the week? And what girl wants to wear a dress to school every day? Someone should tell this principal to shape up and get with it. Explanation: It is obvious that the student thinks that the dress code is out of touch with reality, is old-fashioned. Old-fashioned is another word for archaic.

Name: _____   Date: _____

You can scan the QR code given below or use the url to access additional EdSearch resources including videos and mobile apps related to *General Academic Vocabulary.*

General Academic Vocabulary

URL	QR Code
http://www.lumoslearning.com/a/ri54	

1. What is a reference source?

Ⓐ Sets of information that an author can base an article or story from such as almanacs, newspapers, and interviews
Ⓑ The actual text that an author uses to write an article or story
Ⓒ A set of information that is only valid in its primary form
Ⓓ A set of information that is only valid in its secondary form

2. What does a 'prompt' mean with respect to "language?"

Ⓐ A prompt details what the passage is about.
Ⓑ A prompt is a basic idea of what to write about.
Ⓒ A prompt forms the middle part of an essay.
Ⓓ A prompt is the conclusion of the passage.

3. What is personification?

Ⓐ A figure of speech where human characteristics are given to an animal or object
Ⓑ A figure of speech where a word is used to describe a sound made by an object
Ⓒ A figure of speech where a word or phrase means something different from what it says
Ⓓ A figure of speech that draws a verbal picture by comparing two objects

4. What is point of view?

Ⓐ The basis for which a story is formed
Ⓑ The perspective from which the author tells the story
Ⓒ The perspective from which the reader tells the story
Ⓓ The sources where an author gains information to write a story

5. What is onomatopoeia?

Ⓐ A figure of speech where human characteristics are given to an animal or object
Ⓑ A figure of speech where a word is used to describe a sound made by an object
Ⓒ A figure of speech where a word or phrase means something different from what it says
Ⓓ A figure of speech that draws a verbal picture by comparing two objects

6. What is an idiom?

Ⓐ A figure of speech where human characteristics are given to an animal or object
Ⓑ A figure of speech where a word is used to describe a sound made by an object
Ⓒ A figure of speech where a word or phrase means something different from what it says
Ⓓ A figure of speech that draws a verbal picture by comparing two objects

Oranges have many medicinal values. Oranges are the fruit with the greatest concentration of vitamin C. The skin of the orange helps to keep the fruit inside from becoming damaged and to remain clean. The thick, oily, and bitter skin does not allow any insects to get into an orange. Many kinds of useful oils can be <u>extracted</u> from the thick skin. Oranges are healthy and delicious.

7. What is the meaning of the underlined word?

    Ⓐ put in
    Ⓑ concentrate
    Ⓒ taken out
    Ⓓ placed

Salmon

A fish that is a great favorite with people is salmon. It begins its life in a small pool up a river. Far from the sea, the fish lays its eggs in a pool in the river. When the baby fish are a few inches long, they begin to swim down the river. As they grow bigger, they make their way towards the sea.

They jump over rocks, often with their tails first. Suddenly, they find themselves in the sea. The fish live in the sea for three years. They swim far away from land. How do they find their way back? These fish have a wonderful sense of smell. They remember the scent of their journey easily, because the river flowed to the sea and carried them there. After three years, most salmon swim toward the pools.

As soon as they reach a pool, the females lay their eggs. They lay their eggs near the edge of the water and cover them with sand. Soon the eggs <u>hatch</u> and the pool is full of small fish, getting ready for the long journey out to the sea.

8. What is the meaning of the underlined word?

    Ⓐ devise
    Ⓑ produce
    Ⓒ shade
    Ⓓ emerge

We have been studying the <u>aftermath</u> of volcanos. Now I have to prepare an essay that includes this information.

9. What is the meaning of the underlined word?

    Ⓐ cause
    Ⓑ preparation
    Ⓒ consequences
    Ⓓ reason

The American colonists have to formulate a plan to declare independence from Great Britain. Although the reasons vary, at the core, they want independence because they believe Great Britain takes away the rights of the colonists. But, without any real <u>specificity</u> of those reasons, other countries will have a difficult time supporting this new nation, and they must accumulate support if they are going to be able to break away.

10. What is the meaning of the underlined word?

Ⓐ formulation
Ⓑ creation
Ⓒ definition
Ⓓ reason

Chapter 2

Lesson 5: Text Structure

Text structure refers to how the information within a written text is organized. The examples below include several different text structures.

Compare-Contrast Structure
This type of text examines the similarities and differences between two or more people, events, concepts, ideas, etc.

Example: Square dancing involves four couples lining up so each couple forms the side of a square, and everyone faces in toward the center of the square. A caller calls out the steps that the dancers follow. Country-western line dancing means each dancer gets into a straight line, all dancers in the line facing the same direction. The DJ calls out the name of the dance, and the dancers follow the steps that they have been taught for that dance in time to the music.

Cause-Effect Structure
This structure presents a relationship between the cause of an event, idea, or concept and the effects of carrying out that event, idea, or concept.

Example: Several days of heavy rain will probably cause some areas to be flooded.

Sequence Structure
This text structure gives readers a chronology of events or a list of steps in a procedure.

Example: How did I end up being the mayor of a large eastern city? I grew up in a small town in the mid-west. I went to college in the east as a political science major with a minor in project management. While there I met my future wife, who was from a large eastern city. We moved there and I worked my way up through the dominant political party.

Example: Recipe for making a cake. Step 1…, Step 2…, Step 3…

Problem-Solution Structure
This type of structure sets up a problem or problems, explains the solution, and then discusses the effects of the solution.

Example: Years ago, a serious disease called polio was prevalent in this country. Through research, a researcher discovered a cure for the disease. As a result, a vaccine was developed, and the disease was wiped out.

Descriptive Structure

This type of text structure features a detailed description of something to give the reader a mental picture.

Example: There is now a better phone available than the flip-phone. It is called a smartphone. It is a little larger than the flip-phone, about 3" wide and 6" long, because it features a larger screen that takes up most of the width. There is a border around the screen which comes in a choice of colors. There is an on/off button under the screen, and push buttons on the side to control volume, and ring or vibrate settings. There is no cover to open or close to use the phone. The screen is a touch screen with many icons that when touched, offer many different capabilities, from interacting with e-mails and text messages to selecting applications called apps.

Question-Answer Structure

This text structure starts by posing a question then goes on to answer that question.
Example: Here is what an online FAQ (frequently asked questions) structure looks like:

Q Is the green light glowing when you turn the unit on?
A If not, check to make sure the unit is plugged in. If so, plug it into a different electrical outlet.
If still not glowing, go to the next step.
Example: Questionnaire

Q1. Do you agree with the present immigration policy?
A1 _ Yes _ No _ Unsure

You can scan the QR code given below or use the url to access additional EdSearch resources including videos and mobile apps related to *Text Structure.*

Text Structure

URL	QR Code
http://www.lumoslearning.com/a/ri55	

1. What is a index?

Ⓐ It is a sequential arrangement of names, places, and topics along with the page numbers that they are discussed on.
Ⓑ It is a list that helps in finding things pertaining to the topic faster.
Ⓒ Both A and B
Ⓓ None of the above

2. What is a glossary?

Ⓐ A list of unusual words
Ⓑ A list explaining or defining the difficult words and expressions used in the text
Ⓒ A list of where a word can be found in the book
Ⓓ Both B and C

Salmon

A fish that is a great favorite with people is salmon. It begins its life in a small pool up a river. Far from the sea, the fish lays its eggs in a pool in the river. When the baby fish are a few inches long, they begin to swim down the river. As they grow bigger, they make their way towards the sea.

They jump over rocks, often with their tails first. Suddenly, they find themselves in the sea. The fish live in the sea for three years. They swim far away from land. How do they find their way back? These fish have a wonderful sense of smell. They remember the scent of their journey easily, because the river flowed to the sea and carried them there. After three years, most salmon swim toward the pools.

As soon as they reach a pool, the females lay their eggs. They lay their eggs near the edge of the water and cover them with sand. Soon the eggs hatch and the pool is full of small fish, getting ready for the long journey out to the sea.

3. What genre would the writing above be classified as?

Ⓐ A nonfiction passage
Ⓑ Informative writing
Ⓒ Realistic fiction
Ⓓ Both A and B

4. How is a Table of Contents helpful?

Ⓐ It organizes the text into manageable passages.
Ⓑ It lets the reader know where specific topics or chapters are and on what page number they begin.
Ⓒ It lists and defines some of the most difficult words in the text.
Ⓓ It is a list of unusual words.

5. Where is a Table of Contents located?

Ⓐ It is located at the beginning of the text.
Ⓑ It is located at the end of the text.
Ⓒ It is located in the middle of the text.
Ⓓ It is located at the beginning of each chapter of the text.

6. The heading of a letter usually includes which of the following?

Ⓐ An address and date
Ⓑ An introduction such as "Dear"
Ⓒ A conclusion and signature
Ⓓ None of the above

7. What is a comparison/contrast text structure?

Ⓐ It is writing that looks at how two or more pieces of information are similar or different.
Ⓑ It is writing that looks at how something occurs over a period of time.
Ⓒ It is writing that looks at why something happened and what else occurred as a result.
Ⓓ It is writing that looks at answers to different dilemmas.

8. What is a problem/solution text structure?

Ⓐ It is writing that looks at how two or more pieces of information are similar or different.
Ⓑ It is writing that looks at how something occurs over a period of time.
Ⓒ It is writing that looks at why something happened and what else occurred as a result
Ⓓ It is writing that looks at answers to different dilemmas.

I have been studying the water shortage crisis in several states. My report will include the facts I have found as well as various prevention techniques for future droughts.

9. What type of text structure would best address this information?

Ⓐ cause and effect
Ⓑ problem and solution
Ⓒ chronological order
Ⓓ compare and contrast

We have been studying the aftermath of volcanoes. Now I have to prepare an essay that includes this information.

10. What type of text structure would best address this information?

Ⓐ cause and effect
Ⓑ problem and solution
Ⓒ chronological order
Ⓓ compare and contrast

Chapter 2

Lesson 6: Point of View

Let us understand the concept with an example.

Media Rights: These are permissions given to media organizations, such as TV or radio networks, to film or record sporting or other events for broadcast to viewers or listeners.

In return for charging the media for these rights, the rights are only given to one or a few media outlets.

Sporting Associations and Media Rights

Ban the sale of media rights
by Vibhu Krishnaswamy

Sporting associations should be banned from selling media rights. A number of scams related to sporting associations such as FIFA, NFL and IOC have come to light in the recent past. Many sporting associations are acquiring huge sums of money by selling media rights and using some of the money for corrupt practices. I think this corrupt system needs to be changed so that the sole emphasis is on the games themselves instead of on money from media rights.

These are sporting associations, whose focus should be on running the sporting events efficiently and fairly instead of acquiring huge sums of money by selling media rights.

Nowadays, anyone can watch sporting events on their smartphones, television sets and computer. Broadcast companies should be able to record high quality live video at no charge and transmit it to their audiences, covering their costs and earning profits by charging their advertisers for ads.

By eliminating the charges for media rights, officials of the sponsoring associations are less likely to get involved in corrupt behavior. An opponent of this proposal might say that they need monetary resources to run their associations, but I say they can get funds through other channels, such as ad revenue and subscriber fees. They should be able to efficiently run sporting events with a fraction of the money instead of hundreds of millions of dollars.

Therefore, I believe that sports would be fun and fair if the financial incentive for corruption was removed. I would like to ban sporting associations from entering into large deals with broadcast companies.

Allow the sale of media rights
by George Smith

I am in favor of a sports association selling media rights to an event, providing they are obligated to spend some of that money on programs beneficial to the athletes and coaches who participate in the sport. Media rights provide a media outlet with a competitive advantage over other outlets without these rights to broadcast an event to their audience, an advantage appealing to advertisers who want to reach the largest audience possible. If media rights are free, hundreds of media outlets will broadcast the event, and the potential audience will be fragmented and smaller than if media rights were restricted to fewer outlets. Making a sporting event available to a widespread audience is considered good for the sport, but the broadcasters need to make a profit.

While the sports association will need to spend money to hire someone to manage media rights, the potential income will most likely exceed the salary and benefits expense, and will still leave other employees of the association free to focus on managing the sport itself. To meet their expenses, without revenue from selling media rights, a sports association would probably not earn enough from the admission charge for fans attending the event, and would have to make up the difference by charging members higher dues. Increasing their expenses is not a benefit for athletes and coaches.

As for corruption by some members of a sports association, the members should insist that management hire a competent accounting firm to perform periodic audits of the finances. Also, it would be beneficial for the athletes and coaches who are members of the association to pressure management to allocate a certain percentage of the fees received for media rights to programs that benefit them. Scholarships, training, travel expense and medical benefits are examples of such programs.

Your assignment: Review each point of view and document the similarities and differences.

This is what you might write.

Both positions recognize the benefits of allowing media coverage. But the "ban" group wants media rights granted free of charge, and assumes that the broadcasters can get the revenue they need by charging advertisers, and assumes the sports associations can also earn enough revenue from attendance fees at events to cover their expenses. Without revenue from media rights, the "allow" group does not think revenue from admission fees will be high enough to cover sports association expenses, including benefit programs for members, and the association will need to charge higher dues to members.

You can scan the QR code given below or use the url to access additional EdSearch resources including videos and mobile apps related to *Point of View*.

 **Point of View**

URL	QR Code
http://www.lumoslearning.com/a/ri56	

Mary sat in front of Peter in the classroom. She had two long blonde braids in the back of her hair. Peter reached out and tugged on her braids. Mary turned around and swatted Peter with her notebook.

1. Identify the point of view used in the paragraph above.

Ⓐ first person
Ⓑ second person
Ⓒ third person
Ⓓ none of the above

It was a cool, crisp morning. Lucy threw her backpack over her shoulders, jumped on her bicycle, and pedaled down Pine Street. Her tires made soft crunching noises as she drove through piles of brown, yellow, and orange leaves.

2. Identify the point of view used in the paragraph above.

Ⓐ first person
Ⓑ second person
Ⓒ third person
Ⓓ none of the above

Mrs. Davis lived in a great big apartment on the top floor of her building. As I walked into her spacious, clean apartment, I noticed fine, leather furniture and expensive works of art. Mrs. Davis sat up in her large, king-size bed wearing a beautiful, silk robe and smiled at me. She looked like she felt better than she had the last time I visited.

3. Identify the point of view used in the paragraph above.

Ⓐ first person
Ⓑ second person
Ⓒ third person
Ⓓ none of the above

At the bakery, Vince the baker was getting the muffins ready for baking. He mixed up flour, sugar, milk, and blueberries. He poured the mixture into a muffin pan and placed it into the oven. Then, he heard one of his employees call him from the front of the store. "A lady wants six blueberry muffins!" "Ok," Vince called back, "I'll have them ready in ten minutes!"

4. Identify the point of view of the paragraph above.

    Ⓐ first person
    Ⓑ second person
    Ⓒ third person
    Ⓓ none of the above

I took one look at the hideous creature and ran away as fast as I could. I had never been so scared in my whole life!

5. Identify the point of view in the sentences above.

    Ⓐ first person
    Ⓑ second person
    Ⓒ third person
    Ⓓ none of the above

Kara's mother wakes up at 5:30 A.M. every morning so that she'll have time to study for her college classes. This is the only time that she has to study before she has to go to work. She takes college classes two nights a week. Every weekend, she volunteers at the local homeless shelter. She has been helping out there for the past three years.

6. Identify the point of view in the paragraph above.

    Ⓐ first person
    Ⓑ second person
    Ⓒ third person
    Ⓓ none of the above

Victor took off his reading glasses and rubbed his eyes. He picked up his walking cane. Then he slowly used the cane to help himself up from the bench. Every day, it takes him a little bit longer to stand up. Every day, it becomes more difficult for him to walk.

7. Identify the point of view in the paragraph above.

    Ⓐ first person
    Ⓑ second person
    Ⓒ third person
    Ⓓ none of the above

Before each practice starts, make sure that everyone on your team is wearing the proper equipment. Be sure that everyone is wearing athletic shoes and a helmet. It's also important to remind your team-mates to remove any jewelry, because it could injure another player. You should also have a first-aid kit on hand.

8. Identify the point of view in the paragraph above.

   Ⓐ first person
   Ⓑ second person
   Ⓒ third person
   Ⓓ none of the above

Corky waddled toward the lake. When he reached the water, he flapped his wings, quacked, and jumped in.

9. Identify the point of view in the sentences above.

   Ⓐ first person
   Ⓑ second person
   Ⓒ third person
   Ⓓ none of the above

Once you have your computer desk assembled, the next thing to decide is where to put it. A desk-top computer requires electricity, so you will need to make sure you choose a spot where there's an electrical outlet available.

10. Identify the point of view in the paragraph above.

   Ⓐ first person
   Ⓑ second person
   Ⓒ third person
   Ⓓ none of the above

Chapter 2

Lesson 7: Locating Answers

Let us understand the concept with an example.

1. To find information about a famous person, such as a past President of the United States or an actor or an athlete:

- Enter his/her name into a web search engine to do a key word search
- Visit your local library and ask the research person where to look for information on this person. For example, the information could be in the biography or history sections. Also, the library may have a computer-search program for all of the information in the library, which can be searched by entering key words.
- Go to the website of a newspaper and use their search capabilities to locate information.
- Visit the person's web site if they have one. Request an interview, by phone or in person.
- Visit a local bookstore or online book publisher.

2. To find information about a health issue, a disease for example:

- Enter the name of the disease into a web search engine to do a key word search. The search results may list associations, publications and pharmaceutical companies that are involved with providing information and cures for the disease.
- Through the web search above or through another web search that included the words "association," locate an association that specializes in information about that disease.
- Interview a local doctor or other medical professional who specializes in that health issue.

3. To find information about a specific country:

- Look it up in an almanac (your library probably has one).
- Enter its name into a web search engine to do a key word search. The search might list books, promotional literature, facts, geography, history, points of interest
- Visit your local library and ask the research person where to look for information on this country.
- Visit a local bookstore or online book publisher.

Name: _____   Date: _____

You can scan the QR code given below or use the url to access additional EdSearch resources including videos and mobile apps related to *Locating Answers*.

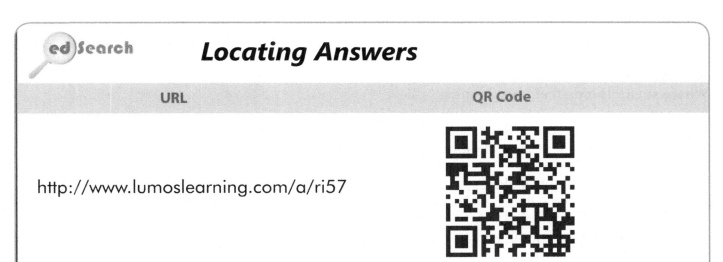

edSearch   **Locating Answers**

URL	QR Code
http://www.lumoslearning.com/a/ri57	

What is this life if, full of care,
We have no time to stand and stare?

No time to stand beneath the boughs
And stare as long as sheep or cows.

No time to see, when woods we pass,
Where squirrels hide their nuts in grass

No time to see, in broad daylight,
Streams full of stars, like skies at night.

No time to turn at Beauty's glance,
And watch her feet, how they can dance.

No time to wait till her mouth can
Enrich that smile her eyes began.

A poor life if, full of care,
We have no time to stand and stare.
- W. H. Davies

1. If you had to research the poet above, where would you look for information?

Ⓐ in the library
Ⓑ on the Internet
Ⓒ in a book about different poets
Ⓓ all of the above

I went for a run this morning. Although I usually run in the evening, I decided to go in the morning because of the weather. It has been so hot this summer, so hot in fact, that I cannot run in the evening. Therefore, until we have cooler weather, I will continue to enjoy a morning run.

2. Where might you find the passage above?

Ⓐ You might find it in a newspaper.
Ⓑ You might find it on the Internet.
Ⓒ You might find it in a journal or diary.
Ⓓ You might find it in a book report.

3. **If you wanted to write a report about a famous author, where would be the best place to look for information?**

   Ⓐ a biography or autobiography of the author
   Ⓑ the newspaper
   Ⓒ the Internet
   Ⓓ both A & C

4. **Where would you find the meaning of the word thespian?**

   Ⓐ in an encyclopedia
   Ⓑ in a dictionary
   Ⓒ in a journal
   Ⓓ in an almanac

5. **Where could you read the weather forecast for tomorrow?**

   Ⓐ dictionary
   Ⓑ almanac
   Ⓒ newspaper
   Ⓓ encyclopedia

6. **Where would you best look for a synonym for the word procrastinate?**

   Ⓐ thesaurus
   Ⓑ atlas
   Ⓒ almanac
   Ⓓ dictionary

7. **You want to find out the neighboring countries of France. What reference material should you use?**

   Ⓐ an almanac
   Ⓑ an atlas
   Ⓒ a newspaper
   Ⓓ a dictionary

8. **In a textbook, where would you look to locate the definition of a key word?**

   Ⓐ a glossary
   Ⓑ an index
   Ⓒ the table of contents
   Ⓓ copyright page

9. In a textbook, where would you look to locate the alphabetical list of important topics?

Ⓐ a glossary
Ⓑ an index
Ⓒ the table of contents
Ⓓ copyright page

10. In a textbook, where would you look to find out when the book was published?

Ⓐ a glossary
Ⓑ an index
Ⓒ the table of contents
Ⓓ copyright page

Chapter 2

Lesson 8: Using Evidence to Support Claims

Let us understand the concept with an example.

The Obesity Epidemic

In the United States population, 30% of adults and 17% of children are obese, according to the American Heart Association. And, by 2020, 83% of men and 72% of women are expected to be overweight or obese, according to research presented to the Heart Association's scientific meeting in 2011. More than one-third (36.5%) of U.S. adults have obesity, states the Centers for Disease Control and Prevention.

Being obese has negative health and health expense disadvantages. According to the Centers for Disease Control and Prevention:

Obesity-related conditions include heart disease, stroke, type 2 diabetes, high blood pressure, arthritis and certain types of cancer, some of the leading causes of preventable death.

The estimated annual medical cost of obesity in the U.S. was $147 billion in 2008 U.S. dollars; the medical costs for people who are obese were $1,429 higher than those of normal weight.

What is causing so many people to be obese? More sedentary lifestyles are one factor. Sitting and watching television, driving instead of walking, not exercising enough. Nutrition is another. So much of our food is processed, which means fat and sugar are added. Also, we frequently eat portions larger than our bodies need, and we often snack between meals.

What can people do about reducing their obesity?

Exercise: The Centers for Disease Control (CDC) recommends 2.5 hours of moderate aerobic exercise per week, along with 2 days of strength training. Americans are clearly not abiding by these minimum recommendations. But diet can have more effect on weight loss than exercise, although both are important solutions.

Nutrition: Controlling the intake of carbohydrates is one important action. Also, eating less processed food, less refined grains and bread and more vegetables are also important. You need to add lean protein to every meal and every snack, along with moderate amounts of healthy fats.

Your assignment: Write text that meets the requirements of the standard.

Here is what you might write.

The authors state their point of view that there is an obesity epidemic today among adults and children in America. They state evidence from the American Heart Association and the Centers for Disease Control and Prevention as proof. They also state that being obese has negative health and health expense disadvantages, and list diseases associated with obesity and the medical costs incurred by obese people.

The authors also speculate on the causes of the obesity epidemic, citing a more sedentary lifestyle, insufficient exercise and dietary factors. Lastly, the authors state what can be done to reduce obesity, citing suggestions for exercise and nutrition.

You can scan the QR code given below or use the url to access additional EdSearch resources including videos and mobile apps related to *Using Evidence to Support Claims.*

 *Using Evidence to Support Claims*

URL	QR Code
http://www.lumoslearning.com/a/ri57	

The Orange

Even though no one knows exactly where oranges come from, Southeast Asia is believed to be their first home. They are grown today in most of the warmer parts of the world. The ancient Greeks and Romans knew about oranges. It is possible that oranges were carried from India to Western Asia, and then to Europe.

The Spaniards took the sour oranges to the West Indies and from there to Florida, in America. Today, oranges are the most important fresh fruit in international trade. There are three different kinds of oranges: the sweet or common orange, the mandarin orange, and the sour or bitter orange.

One type of sweet orange is called the blood orange. It has a pulp with a deep red color. This type of orange is grown mostly in the Mediterranean region. Mandarin oranges are mainly found in Florida. Sour oranges are grown almost everywhere with Spain having the greatest number used for trade. These sour oranges are generally used to make marmalade.

However, they can be put to many other interesting uses, from making medicine to creating perfumes. Oranges have many medicinal values. Oranges are the fruit with the greatest concentration of vitamin C. The skin of the orange helps to keep the fruit inside from becoming damaged and to remain clean. The thick, oily, and bitter skin does not allow any insects to get into an orange. Many kinds of useful oils can be extracted from the thick skin. Oranges are healthy and delicious.

1. Which paragraph discusses the types of oranges?

Ⓐ paragraph one
Ⓑ paragraph two
Ⓒ paragraph three
Ⓓ paragraph four

2. Which paragraph discusses the health value of oranges?

Ⓐ paragraph one
Ⓑ paragraph two
Ⓒ paragraph three
Ⓓ paragraph four

Salmon

A fish that is a great favorite with people is salmon. It begins its life in a small pool up a river. Far from the sea, the fish lays its eggs in a pool in the river. When the baby fish are a few inches long, they begin to swim down the river. As they grow bigger, they make their way towards the sea.

They jump over rocks, often with their tails first. Suddenly, they find themselves in the sea. The fish live in the sea for three years. They swim far away from land. How do they find their way back? These fish have a wonderful sense of smell. They remember the scent of their journey easily, because the river flowed to the sea and carried them there. After three years, most salmon swim toward the pools.

As soon as they reach a pool, the females lay their eggs. They lay their eggs near the edge of the water and cover them with sand. Soon the eggs hatch and the pool is full of small fish, getting ready for the long journey out to the sea.

3. Which sentence in the first paragraph discusses where salmon begin their lives?

Ⓐ sentence one
Ⓑ sentence two
Ⓒ sentence three
Ⓓ sentence four

I went for a run this morning. Although I usually run in the evening, I decided to go in the morning because of the weather. It has been so hot this summer, so hot in fact, that I cannot run in the evening. Therefore, until we have cooler weather, I will continue to enjoy a morning run.

4. Which sentence indicates how long the author will continue to run in the morning time?

Ⓐ one
Ⓑ two
Ⓒ three
Ⓓ four

Sports can develop character. The players must abide by the rules of the game. Any departure from following these rules means foul play. Every foul stroke in a game involves a penalty. Therefore, players play a fair game. Fair play is a noble and moral quality.

Players become honest and punctual. The player develops the sportsman's spirit. Defeat does not dishearten a true sportsman. He does not feel over- excited if he wins a match. He learn to take both victory and defeat in stride. He never strikes an adversary.

5. Read the above paragraphs and identify the main idea.

Ⓐ Every foul stroke in a game involves a penalty.
Ⓑ Sports develop a player's character.
Ⓒ The players have to abide by the rules of the game.
Ⓓ Any departure from these rules means foul play.

My mother works extremely hard as a nurse. Each day she gives her all, and when she comes home she is dog tired. I like to help her take a load off, so I try and make dinner for her. I also clean the house and mow the yard outside. Today was even more difficult though. It rained like cats and dogs all afternoon, so I couldn't take care of the yard. Then, when I came inside to clean, I realized the kitchen sink was clogged and the washing machine seemed broken. I couldn't catch a break! By the time Mom came home, I had given up, called a plumber, and ordered a pizza. It's a good thing my mom always taught me that where there is a will, there is a way!

6. Which sentence explains why today was difficult?

Ⓐ two
Ⓑ four
Ⓒ six
Ⓓ eight

7. Which sentence explains what happened when the author tried to clean?

Ⓐ one
Ⓑ three
Ⓒ five
Ⓓ seven

8. Which detail explains why the mother is so tired?

Ⓐ She works hard as a nurse.
Ⓑ She has to clean the house.
Ⓒ She has to do the laundry.
Ⓓ She has to mow the lawn.

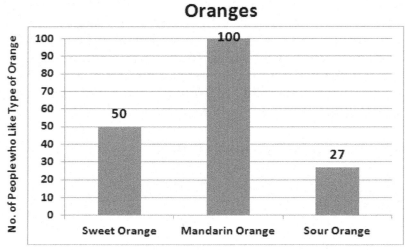

Oranges

9. According the graph, which type of orange is the most popular?

Ⓐ Sweet Orange
Ⓑ Mandarin Orange
Ⓒ Sour Orange

10. Evidence to support details can be found _____.

Ⓐ in the text and title only
Ⓑ in the text only
Ⓒ in the text, illustrations, graphs, and headings
Ⓓ in the conclusion

Chapter 2

Lesson 9: Integrating Information

Let us understand the concept with an example.

Text #1: Search and Rescue Mission: Lost in the Woods

One day, 10 year old Tessa invited her friend Carol to come to her house to spend the afternoon together. Because it was a nice warm day and Tessa had recently moved here, they decided to take a walk and explore the woods near her house. They told Tessa's mother that they were going for a short walk in the woods. They followed a trail into the woods, and as they walked, they came across several intersecting trails and just picked any trail and continued on. They just kept walking and talking. Finally, deep in the woods, they came upon a little pond, so they scrambled down an embankment to reach it and sat there in a clearing talking for a long time, basking in the warm sunshine. After a while they became sleepy and took a nap. They did not realize that several hours had passed.

Meanwhile, Tessa's mother went out to run errands, and when she returned several hours later, she noticed the girls were not there. It was early evening and the sun was low in the sky. She walked a short distance into the woods and called for the girls but there were no answers. She decided to call 911 just to be safe.

Within a short time, several police officers and other volunteers arrived and fanned out into the woods looking for the girls. They did not find them; no one responded to their calls. Fortunately, a police officer brought a search-and-rescue dog. He asked Tessa's mom to get a few of her clothes so the dog could sniff them to recognize Tessa's scent.

The dog's handler asked the searchers which trails they had taken, and identified one trail they had missed. He took the dog down that trail, and it kept sniffing for Tessa's scent. All at once the dog veered off the trail and headed down an embankment toward a pond. In a clearing by the pond they found the two girls fast asleep. The handler woke the girl's up; they were startled to see a police officer and the search dog, and felt badly when the handler explained how worried Tessa's mother had been about them and had called the police and had involved an entire group of people trying to find them. When he returned with the girls, everyone was relieved and they rewarded the dog with some great treats.

Text #2: SAR (search and rescue) Dogs

SAR (search and rescue) dogs are specially trained dogs with a keen sense of smell that are trained to sniff a missing person's clothing and then use their familiarity with that scent to search for the person who is missing. They have handlers who get a piece of clothing and hold it near the dog's nose so the dog can recognize the missing person's scent, then accompany the dog as they search for a missing or trapped person. They can often locate a person that rescuers have not been able to find, especially a person who is unconscious and can't respond to calls from rescuers.

These dogs have been used find victims in the rubble from earthquakes or people trapped in their homes after devastating hurricanes, floods tornadoes or other natural disasters.

Your assignment: As stated in the standard, your assignment is to integrate (join together; unify; make one text from several texts) the key points from these two texts into one text.

This is what you might write.

SAR (search and rescue) dogs are specially trained dogs with a keen senses of smell that are trained to sniff a person's clothing and then recognize that scent when searching for the actual person who is missing. They have handlers who get a piece of the missing person's clothing and then hold it near the dog's nose so the dog can recognize the missing person's scent, then accompany the dog as it searches for the missing or trapped person.

Here is a true story of how an SAR dog was used to find two girls lost in the woods.

Two ten year old girls went for a walk in a woods they had never been in before. They were so busy walking and talking that they did not keep track of which trails they followed. Even if they had tried, they probably would not have been able to find their way back home. Publisher's Note: the previous sentence was not in either text, but it could have been added by you as an example of an inference (a conclusion from a set of facts) that you could have realized from the statement "...as they walked, they came across several intersecting trails and just picked any trail and continued on."

Far into the woods they reached a clearing by a pond and while sitting there basking in the sun they fell asleep. One of their parents became concerned after several hours when they did not return, and called the police. All of the searchers were unsuccessful in finding them except for an SAR dog who was brought to the scene, given an article of one girl's clothing to sniff to get her scent, and then managed to lead its handler to the clearing where the girls were sleeping. A happy ending and another successful find by an SAR dog.

Name: _____   Date: _____

You can scan the QR code given below or use the url to access additional EdSearch resources including videos and mobile apps related to *Integrating Information*.

 **Integrating Information**

URL	QR Code
http://www.lumoslearning.com/a/ri59	

1. In which situation would you possibly need to read multiple texts?

Ⓐ to locate an answer to a question
Ⓑ to write or speak about a topic knowledgeably
Ⓒ to fully understand a historical or scientific concept
Ⓓ all of the above

2. If you are studying World War II, you might _____.

Ⓐ read a chapter from your social studies textbook about World War II
Ⓑ look at a book of photographs from the war
Ⓒ read a magazine article written by someone who fought in the war
Ⓓ all of the above

3. If you wanted to start a recycling club at your school, where could you learn more information?

Ⓐ Go to the library and read books about recycling.
Ⓑ Search the Internet to find web sites about recycling.
Ⓒ Both A and B
Ⓓ None of the above

4. In which of the following texts would an author most likely use a "subjective" point of view?

Ⓐ a chapter in a history textbook
Ⓑ a letter which was written by a soldier to his father found in the war
Ⓒ a memoir written years after the war by a woman whose son died in the war
Ⓓ both b and c

5. In which of the following texts would an author most likely use an "objective" point of view?

Ⓐ a newspaper article about how the American Red Cross helps during natural disaster
Ⓑ a book of photographs of natural disasters
Ⓒ Both A and B
Ⓓ None of the above

Suppose your parents asked you to attend your little sister's softball game.

6. Choose the sentence below that is written in a subjective point of view.

Ⓐ The final score was 12 to 11.
Ⓑ The game was really boring.
Ⓒ My sister's team won the game.
Ⓓ None of the above

Lost in the Woods

One day, a little girl named Tessa asked her mom if she could invite her friend Katelyn over for a sleepover. Her mom agreed. When Katelyn arrived at Tessa's house the next afternoon, the girls decided to go exploring in the woods close to Tessa's house. When the girls did not come back inside the house after a while, Tessa's mom decided to go looking for them. She walked to the edge of the woods and called out to them, but she heard no reply. After looking for them for about an hour, she decided to call 911.

Within hours, nearly 100 police officers and volunteers were searching for them in the woods. One of the officers brought Nickel, a search-and-rescue dog. Tessa's mom let the dog sniff one of Tessa's shirts so the dog could track the girl's scent. Nickel and her handler set off to look for the girls.

As they were walking down a trail, Nickel suddenly veered off the trail and headed downhill. Nickel led the volunteers down an embankment, and under a tree they found the two girls scared, but un-hurt. In less than an hour, Tessa and Katelyn were back with their relieved families. The girls were thankful Nickel had found them. Nickel went home to wait for his next mission.

SAR Dogs

Search-and-rescue (SAR) dogs are special dogs with an acute sense of smell that are called in when a person is lost or trapped. SAR dogs search in remote areas and in places struck by natural disasters such as earthquakes, tornadoes, and hurricanes. SAR dogs are very effective and can often locate people when many volunteers can't.

Dogs make great searchers because of their powerful sense of smell. SAR dogs are trained to use their incredible sense of smell to search for people.

In 2010, SAR dogs from the United States found people trapped in the rubble after a devastating earthquake in Haiti. In 2012, SAR dogs helped locate people who were trapped in their homes after Hurricane Sandy hit the East Coast. These are only a few instances of when SAR dogs have helped people.

7. What is the purpose of the second passage "SAR Dogs?"

Ⓐ To teach readers about earthquakes
Ⓑ To provide readers with information about search-and-rescue dogs
Ⓒ To give examples of types of search-and-rescue dogs
Ⓓ To tell a story about a rescue effort

8. In "Lost in the Woods," what is the girls' attitude toward SAR dogs?

Ⓐ They are scared of them.
Ⓑ They are angry at them.
Ⓒ They are thankful for them.
Ⓓ They make them sad.

9. How does information from "SAR Dogs" add to your understanding of the story "Lost in the Woods?"

Ⓐ It explains that the dogs' sense of smell helps them find people.
Ⓑ It helps the reader to understand the setting of the story.
Ⓒ It allows helps the reader to get to know the characters better.
Ⓓ It informs helps the reader about natural disasters of the past.

10. From which type of point of view is SAR Dogs told?

Ⓐ first person
Ⓑ objective
Ⓒ subjective
Ⓓ none of the above

End of Reading: Informational Text

Answer Key and Detailed Explanations

Chapter 2: Reading: Informational Text

Lesson 1: Inferences and Conclusions

Question No.	Answer	Detailed Explanations
1	A	The following clues in the passage hint that it is fall: "cool, crisp morning," and "piles of brown, yellow, and orange leaves." In the fall, mornings are typically cool. Also, leaves change from green to brown, and yellow and orange during the fall.
2	C	Lucy is likely going to school. Clues from the passage are "morning" and "threw her backpack over her shoulder." Students go to school during the morning and they also take a backpack. Choice A is incorrect, because students would be going home during the afternoon, not in the morning. Choices B and C are incorrect, because Lucy probably wouldn't take her backpack to visit friends or to the supermarket.
3	A	In this passage, the writer implies that Mrs. Davis is a wealthy woman. The following pieces of evidence are clues that she is wealthy: "great big apartment on the top floor," "fine, leather furniture," "expensive works of art," and "silk robe."
4	A	Dr. Thomas is visiting Mrs. Davis, because she had been sick. The following clues from the passage help readers make this inference: Mrs. Davis was in bed. Dr. Thomas commented that she seems to be feeling better, which implies that she had been sick.
5	B	Jan must have been scared of the creature. Choice A is incorrect, because the sentence said the creature was "hideous," not cute. Choice C is incorrect, because running away is not a reaction Jan would have if she actually felt sorry for the creature. Choice B "She thinks the creature is scary" is the best answer, because of the fact that the creature is "hideous" and Jan's reaction was to run away.
6	B	Choice B is correct. Choice A is incorrect, because the paragraph does not mention a husband. Choice C is incorrect, because the paragraph does not imply that Kara's mother is tired. Choice B is correct, because there is evidence in the paragraph that Kara's mother is hard-working such as the fact that she wakes up early to study, works at a job during the day, takes college classes at night, and volunteers on the weekends.

Question No.	Answer	Detailed Explanations
7	C	Victor is probably an old man, because he wears reading glasses, uses a cane to walk, and has trouble standing up and walking. Choice B is incorrect, because the paragraph does not state or imply that Victor is happy or unhappy. Choice D is incorrect, because the paragraph says that Victor has a difficult time standing and walking, meaning that he is not in good health.
8	D	Choice D, all of the above, is the correct choice. All of the choices are supported by evidence from the paragraph.
9	B	If Corky has wings, waddles, quacks, and likes water, he must be a duck. This is a logical conclusion about Corky.
10	D	Readers do all of these behaviors when they read, helping them to make inferences or draw conclusions. This is called "reading between the lines."

Lesson 2: Main Idea and Supporting Details

Question No.	Answer	Detailed Explanations
1	A	In the first paragraph, the author provides specific details of how the orange has been dispersed all over the world and as one of the most important internationally traded products, it now grows in the warmer parts of the world. We don't have evidence about how the ancient Romans and Greeks knew about oranges. There is also no information to support how oranges were traded.
2	D	According to the second sentence of the first paragraph, oranges are grown in most of the warmer parts of the world.
3	A	In the third and fourth sentences of the second paragraph, there are details about who grows sour oranges and where they are grown. It's essential to go back and find the evidence to support your answer choice.
4	C	The fact that when someone touches an orange, they are not touching the fleshy part until the skin is peeled, and the orange's thick, oily, bitter skin protects it from insects, makes the orange a clean fruit, according to the passage.
5	D	According to the first sentence of the second paragraph, the passage is about the types of oranges and their usefulness and where they are grown.
6	D	The sentence "As they grow bigger, they make their way towards the sea, "and" They jump over the rocks, often with their tails first," is evidence that the salmon jump backwards over the rocks. If they didn't jump backwards, they would jump with their head first.
7	B	Sentence eight in the passage tells that live in the sea, for three years. Look for the evidence to support your choice in the passage, right down to the paragraph or sentence
8	B	According to the passage, a tasty, healthy kind of honey is made from the orange flowers. While this might be considered an opinion statement, it is the one that is used in the passage. However, there is no mention of other opinions stating whether the honey is bad or unhealthy.
9	A	According to the passage, sports help individuals mentally, physically, and emotionally. There is no evidence in the passage to support that sports are not useful, that they do not require special skills, or that they require players to develop their bodies instead of their minds.
10	D	The main idea of the passage is that sports develop strong character in players. The rest of the sentences are detail sentences, which include players abiding by the rules, playing fair, and being honest and punctual or on time.

Lesson 3: Text Relationships

Question No.	Answer	Detailed Explanations
1	D	In the story, Joshua asks his mother where his fishing stuff is at. Answer A is not found in the story. Answer B states that she tells him where she hid it. She does not tell him the exact location of it in his room. Answer C is not found either. Answer D gives the best information.
2	B	Joshua's mother got advice from his grandmother on how to correct Joshua's bad habit of not doing chores. B is the correct answer.
3	C	Daniel stopped surfing after he was hurt while surfing. The passage is entirely about surfing, so Answers A, B, D would not apply.
4	B	The reason Daniel tried again was because his father encouraged him without making him feel badly. Answer B is correct.
5	C	The traveler grabbed his shoes and ran off, because he had overheard Sam's wife say that Sam would cut off the traveler's ears and feed them to the son. Choice A is incorrect, because the passage never gave the traveler's opinion about Sam's wife. Choice B is incorrect, because the traveler did not do anything to anger Sam. Choice D is incorrect. It is true that there were no chickens left to eat, but that is not the reason the traveler ran away. He did not know that weren't any chickens left.
6	D	Since Sam's wife had a habit of eating as she cooked, she ate all of the chickens that she had prepared. Therefore, there were no curried chickens left to eat. Choices A and B are incorrect, there was only one traveler or guest mentioned in the story. Choice C is incorrect. Sam's wife's appearance was not mentioned in the passage.
7	C	Answer C tells what Chloe does when she is finally ready to ride. The other answers are not stated, implied, or found as evidence in the story.
8	B	As noted in the passage, a person could get hurt if the girth is not put on and fastened correctly. Answer B is correct.
9	D	Only answer D is supported in the text because it indicates how to make a snowflake.
10	A	As noted in the text and shown by the diagrams, both cutting the designs without cutting through the folds, and making certain that the corner meet are important steps. Therefore, A is the best answer.

Lesson 4: General Academic Vocabulary

Question No.	Answer	Detailed Explanations
1	A	A reference source is a set of information that an author can base an article or story. Almanacs, newspapers, and interviews are references to sources. One usually cannot check references out from the library. However, many of the same resources are accessible online. References contain different kinds of information. The reference source is not the information but it is the location of the information that is gathered to write a report.
2	B	With respect to language, the "prompt" is generally given in the form of a question. There may be many ways to answer the question. However, its purpose is not to tell you exactly what a paper is about, but to give you a basic idea of what to write about. If the "prompt' is for an essay, the essay will still have the three basic parts, which are the introduction, body, and conclusion.
3	A	Personification is a figure of speech that is used when human qualities are given to a non-human thing. The non-human thing cannot literally do what the human can do, but it is colorful and has interesting language that makes the writing more engaging to read. It adds variety to the writing. To help you remember the definition of personification, look at the first part of the word that you see at the beginning of it. It is person, this should remind a reader that the figure of speech uses actions, thoughts, and feelings of a human being to bring a non-human object to life.
4	B	After an author finds the basis for the story, he/she decides on a point of view to tell the story to the readers. The story can be told in the first, second, or third person.
5	B	Onomatopoeia is the use of words to imitate sounds. Choice A is a personification which is the figure of speech that gives human characteristics to non-human objects. Choice C is an idiom, a figure of speech that is not meant to be literal because it means something different from what is stated. Choice D is a metaphor.
6	C	An idiom is a figure of speech where a literal meaning should not be taken, because the phrase means something different than what it says. A personification is the figure of speech that gives human characteristics to non-human objects. Words that imitate sounds are a type of figurative language called onomatopoeia.

Question No.	Answer	Detailed Explanations
7	C	The word extracted means to take out. The phrase "extracted from this thick skin" shows that something is being removed from the skin.
8	D	The reader can use the context clues around the word "hatch". The meaning of the word "hatch" in this context refers to fish breaking out of the eggs and filling the pool.
9	C	The reader can look at the parts of the word aftermath, "after" is a clue that it's referring to what happened after the volcanos (erupted). So, the best answer is consequences. You can test the word when you substitute consequences for the word aftermath, and the meaning of the sentence is similar. The words aftermath and consequences both mean that something is a result of something else that happens. The word cause can be used in the sentence and the sentence still sounds the same, the words cause and aftermath are not the same.
10	C	When substituting words, they must be the same part of speech. The word "specificity" is a noun, as are all words that end with "ity." So, from the choices, the word "definition" makes the most sense and can replace the word "specificity". One has a specificity of reasons or a definition of reasons. The meaning of the sentence is the same.

Lesson 5: Text Structure

Question No.	Answer	Detailed Explanations
1	C	The index of a text, usually found at the back of a book, is a sequential listing of topics with page numbers. Rather than reading the entire book, sometimes a student only need to gather information about a specific topic, so the index will help a student to locate specified information quickly.
2	B	The glossary is a specialized dictionary inside of a particular text that explains difficult words. It is very helpful because it is quick and provides the definition as it relates to the text. A dictionary may have more meanings, and it may be difficult to select the definition that applies to the usage of the word that is encountered. This could cause one to misinterpret the content if wrong meaning of a word or phrase is chosen.
3	D	Since the passage has factual information, it is considered to be a work of nonfiction. It provides information. Realistic fiction is a story that requires the use of characters and has a plot that is actually false but is based on real people, events, and places.
4	B	A table of contents will help the reader to see what chapters are in the book with the corresponding page number. If the reader is looking for specific information quickly, it is helpful. A glossary, located in the back of the book, will help define selected words found in the book. Headings are used to organize the text into more manageable passages.
5	A	A table of contents with each chapter in a book is located at the beginning of the text. The index and glossary are often found at the back of the text.
6	A	According to the parts of a letter, the heading includes the address and date. Dear is used as the salutation or greeting. The signature is used as the closing of the letter.
7	A	The compare and contrast text structure looks at how two or more things are alike and also different. The word similar can be used in place of like, and the word unlike or dissimilar can be used in place of different.
8	D	A problem/solution text structure is a writing that presents solutions to different dilemmas.

Question No.	Answer	Detailed Explanations
9	B	The problem and solution text structure should be used because the report will provide factual information about the problem of the water shortage crisis or drought and the prevention techniques that can solve this problem for the future.
10	A	When writing a report about the aftermath of volcanoes, using the cause and effect text structure will explain the causes of volcanoes, and then the aftermath or the result of the volcanoes. Because the volcanoes (erupted), damaged homes and lost lives were the aftermath or the result of what happened.

Lesson 6: Point of View

Question No.	Answer	Detailed Explanations
1	C	This paragraph was written in the 3rd person point of view, because the author was not in the story. It was told from an observer's point of view. We know this, because the characters (Mary and Peter) are named. If it was told from the 1st person point of view, the pronoun I would be used. If it was told in the 2nd person point of view, it would use the pronoun "you."
2	C	This paragraph was written in the 3rd person point of view, because the author was not in the story. It was told from an observer's point of view. We know this, because the character (Lucy) is named. If it was told in the 1st person point of view, the pronoun I would be used. If it was told in the 2nd person point of view, it would use the pronoun "you."
3	A	This passage was written in the 1st person point of view. The author is one of the characters in the story. The author is the person visiting Mrs. Davis. We know this, because the pronouns "I" and "me" are used.
4	C	The paragraph was written in the 3rd person point of view, because the author was not in the story. It was told from an observer's point of view. We know this, because the character (Vince) is named. If it was told in the 1st person point of view, the pronoun I would be used. If it was told in the 2nd person point of view, it would use the pronoun "you." When Vince called back to the employee stating that he would have the muffins ready in ten minutes, he used the pronoun "I," but it was used in dialogue. The author was reporting what he said. So this does not mean it was in the 1st person point of view.
5	A	These sentences are written in the 1st person point of view. The author was the person in the story running away from the hideous creature. When the author used pronouns such as "I" or "me," one can tell that it is from the 1st person point of view.
6	C	The paragraph was written in the 3rd person point of view, because the author was not in the story. It was told from an observer's point of view. We know this, because the character (Kara's mother) is named. If it was told in the 1st person point of view, the pronoun I would be used. If it was told in the 2nd person point of view, it would use the pronoun "you."

Question No.	Answer	Detailed Explanations
7	C	The paragraph was written in the 3rd person point of view, because the author was not in the story. It was told from an observer's point of view. We know this, because the character (Victor) is named. If it was told in a 1st person point of view, the pronoun I would be used. If it was told in the 2nd person point of view, it would use the pronoun "you."
8	B	This paragraph was written in the 2nd person point of view. The 2nd person point of view means that the author is talking to the reader. A clue is the use of the pronoun "you." The 2nd person point of view is often used in instructional manuals and how-to articles.
9	C	The paragraph was written in the 3rd person point of view, because the author was not in the story. It was told from an observer's point of view. We know this, because the character (Corky) is named. If it was told in 1st person point of view, the pronoun I would be used. If it was told in the 2nd person point of view, it would use the pronoun "you."
10	B	This paragraph was written in the 2nd person point of view. The 2nd person point of view means that the author is talking to the reader. A clue is the use of the pronoun "you." The 2nd person point of view is often used in instructional manuals and how-to articles.

Lesson 7: Locating Answers

Question No.	Answer	Detailed Explanations
1	D	Information about W. H. Davies, the author of the poem, can be found in the library, on the Internet, or in a book about different poets. All of the resources have a variety of information that can provide information about the poet.
2	C	Information from the passage may be found in a personal journal or diary, because it includes information that is relevant to the author, which may be considered in some cases opinions, rather than facts. Factual information is generally found in newspaper articles, unless it's an editorial, and also on the Internet or in a book report.
3	D	Factual information about a specific author may be found in an autobiography, a biography, or on the Internet. The newspaper is usually ideal for searching for current events.
4	B	The dictionary primarily contains word meanings. To locate the meaning of thespian, you would use a dictionary.
5	C	The newspaper contains current events. If you are looking for the weather forecast for tomorrow or even for a one week period, the newspaper will have a meteorologist or weather reporter's predictions.
6	A	While you could use the dictionary to find a synonym for procrastinate, the easiest way to get several words that have the same meanings is to use a thesaurus. A thesaurus provides synonyms and antonyms of words.
7	B	An atlas is a group of maps, so if you wanted to locate neighboring countries of France, you would use an atlas. Neighboring means that the countries share a border.
8	A	A glossary is a textbook specific dictionary that has some of the words or phrases that might be difficult to understand, like the definition of a key word.
9	B	The back of a book often has on index, which is an alphabetical listing of important topics covered in the book with page numbers. The glossary, a text-based dictionary, is located in the back. The table of contents and the copyright page are located in the front of the book.
10	D	If you are looking for when (and where) a book was published, you can locate that information on the copyright page found in the front of the book.

Lesson 8: Using Evidence to Support Claims

Question No.	Answer	Detailed Explanations
1	B	Paragraph two, which begins with "there are three different kinds of oranges..." tells what the paragraph is about. Types and kinds mean essentially the same thing. There isn't a paragraph four, so that could not possibly be the correct answer. Make sure that you examine each answer choice for the evidence. If the evidence is not there, then eliminate the answer choice.
2	C	The first sentence of the third paragraph states that oranges have many medicinal values. Since this refers to caring for one's health, then this paragraph discusses the health benefits of oranges.
3	B	Choice B is correct. The second sentence in the paragraph explains where salmon begin their lives. It directly states that salmon begin their lives in a pool up a river. This type of question, which points to the paragraph, requires the reader to look for evidence to support the question or claim. It is one of the easiest types of questions.
4	D	The author states in the last sentence that until there is cooler weather, he will continue to run in the morning. If you look at sentences one, two, and three, you will not find evidence to support this.
5	B	The first sentence, the topic sentence or main idea, discusses the details about how sports develop character.
6	C	In the paragraph, following the sentence that said the day was difficult, is the sentence that tells why the day was difficult. The day was difficult, because it rained like cats and dogs.
7	D	Sentence seven tells what happened when the author tried to clean--the kitchen sink was clogged and the washing machine seemed broken.
8	A	The first sentence states that the mother worked very hard as a nurse. Since she worked so hard, this would explain why she is so tired.
9	B	According to the graph, the color of the highest bar in the middle represents mandarin oranges.
10	C	Evidence for supporting details found in the text, includes charts, illustrations, graphs, and headings.

Lesson 9: Integrating Information

Question No.	Answer	Detailed Explanations
1	D	As a reader or a writer, you will often need to use more than one text or source at a time. It is important to be able to make comparisons and connections between these sources.
2	D	Sometimes there is a need to read different texts about a subject. This adds to knowledge about the subject. When several different pieces of information about the same subject and are combined connections are made, it can broaden one's understanding about the topic.
3	C	When you read about a subject using multiple sources, you will be able to write or speak about the subject more knowledgeably. You may also need to research using multiple sources to answer a question or solve a problem such as figuring out how to start a recycling club.
4	D	Choices B and C are both examples of an author writing in a subjective point of view. When an author uses a subjective point of view, it means that the author offers his or her own feelings, emotions, or opinions about a subject. A subjective point of view is usually used when an author is directly involved in the events of the text.
5	C	Choices A and B are both examples of texts that an author would most likely write in an objective point of view. Choice B is written from a subjective point of view, in that it was "boring" in the authors opinion.
6	B	Nonfiction texts are usually written in an objective point of view. A text written in an objective point of view is about an event, subject, person, or concept. It does not include the author's opinions, just facts.
7	B	The purpose of "SAR Dogs" is to provide readers with information about search-and-rescue dogs. Choice A is incorrect, because it does not teach readers anything about earthquakes. Choice C is incorrect, because examples of types of SAR dogs are not included in this passage. Choice D is incorrect, because it is not a story.
8	C	The first sentence in the last paragraph of "Lost in the Woods" reads that the girls are thankful for SAR dogs. There isn't any evidence in the passage to support Choices A, B, or D.

Question No.	Answer	Detailed Explanations
9	A	"SAR Dogs" tells readers how dogs' sense of smell helps them to find people. In the story "Lost in the Woods," two girls were lost and the dogs found them. After reading "SAR Dogs," readers can figure out how the dog was able to locate the two lost girls (with its sense of smell).
10	B	"SAR Dogs" is told from an objective point of view. Information about the topic was presented without including any of the author's opinions or emotions about the subject.

Chapter 3 - Language

The objective of the Language standards is to ensure that the student is able to accurately use grade appropriate general academic and domain specific words and phrases related to Grade 5.

To support each student to master the necessary skills, we encourage the student to go through the resources available online on EdSearch to gain an in-depth understanding of these concepts. EdSearch page for each lesson can be accessed with the help of the url or the QR code provided.

Chapter 3

Lesson 1: Prepositional Phrases

You can scan the QR code given below or use the url to access additional EdSearch resources including videos and mobile apps related to *Prepositional Phrases*.

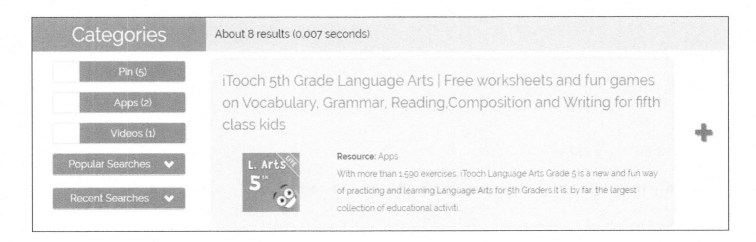

Categories | About 8 results (0.007 seconds)

Pin (5)
Apps (2)
Videos (1)
Popular Searches ⌄
Recent Searches ⌄

iTooch 5th Grade Language Arts | Free worksheets and fun games on Vocabulary, Grammar, Reading,Composition and Writing for fifth class kids

L. Arts 5th

Resource: Apps
With more than 1,590 exercises, iTooch Language Arts Grade 5 is a new and fun way of practicing and learning Language Arts for 5th Graders.It is, by far, the largest collection of educational activiti...

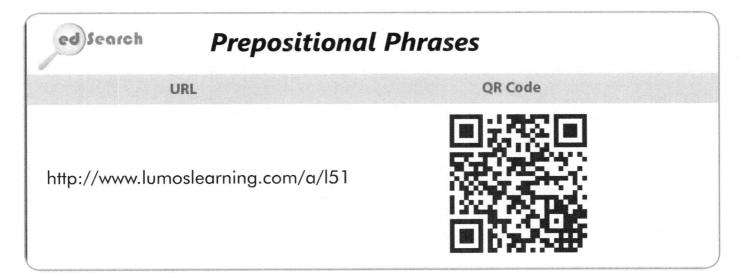

ed)Search **Prepositional Phrases**

URL	QR Code
http://www.lumoslearning.com/a/l51	

1. Prepositions are _____.

Ⓐ words that introduce or connect
Ⓑ words that confuse
Ⓒ words that show action
Ⓓ words that end a sentence

We met at the loud concert.

2. Identify the preposition in the above sentence.

Ⓐ we
Ⓑ met
Ⓒ at
Ⓓ concert

We met at the loud concert.

3. Identify the object of the preposition in the above sentence.

Ⓐ we
Ⓑ met
Ⓒ at
Ⓓ concert

4. The object of a preposition is _____.

Ⓐ the actual preposition
Ⓑ the noun or pronoun that follows the preposition
Ⓒ a word that identifies
Ⓓ a word that shows direction

5. A prepositional phrase always _____.

Ⓐ begins with a preposition
Ⓑ ends with a preposition
Ⓒ has a preposition in the middle
Ⓓ none of the above

My mother plants orange trees in the backyard that give us wonderful fruit.

6. Identify the preposition in the above sentence.

- (A) plants
- (B) in
- (C) backyard
- (D) wonderful

My mother plants orange trees in the backyard that give us wonderful fruit.

7. Identify the object of the preposition in the above sentence.

- (A) plants
- (B) in
- (C) backyard
- (D) wonderful

Grandpa drives a yellow school bus each morning to the school.

8. Identify the preposition in the above sentence.

- (A) drives
- (B) bus
- (C) to
- (D) school

Grandpa drives a yellow school bus each morning to the school.

9. Identify the prepositional phrase in the above sentence.

- (A) drives a
- (B) yellow school bus
- (C) to the school
- (D) to school

The pen is behind the chair.

10. Identify the preposition in the above sentence.

- (A) pen
- (B) behind
- (C) chair
- (D) is

Chapter 3

Lesson 2: Verbs

You can scan the QR code given below or use the url to access additional EdSearch resources including videos and mobile apps related to *Verbs*.

ed)Search   ***Verbs***

URL	QR Code
http://www.lumoslearning.com/a/l51	

Mrs. Smith <u>teach</u> us math this year.

1. What is the correct way to write the underlined verb?

Ⓐ teaches
Ⓑ taught
Ⓒ teaching
Ⓓ teached

2. In which sentence is the verb *have* used correctly?

Ⓐ Emily have a wonderful dinner last night.
Ⓑ I have lemon cake for dessert tomorrow.
Ⓒ She have chocolate chip cookies today.
Ⓓ I have brownies for a snack.

My uncle <u>have</u> the greatest music collection, and I cannot wait to borrow some of his songs!

3. What is the correct way to write the underlined verb?

Ⓐ had
Ⓑ has
Ⓒ have
Ⓓ having

4. In which sentence is the verb *sing* used correctly?

Ⓐ Jose wants to sing at the end of the year talent show.
Ⓑ Bill sing every Friday night.
Ⓒ Last week, Jimmy sing at Sue's party.
Ⓓ My favorite part of the night was sing with everyone on the hayride.

5. In which sentence is the verb *climbing* used correctly?

Ⓐ I _____ the mountain last year.
Ⓑ My mother and I _____ three flights of stairs.
Ⓒ Maggie went rock _____ at the gym yesterday.
Ⓓ Yesterday, my sister said I could _____ to the top of the highest hill.

Gerry and I <u>be</u> going fishing tomorrow to catch dinner for our family.

6. What is the correct way to write the underlined verb?

- Ⓐ been
- Ⓑ are
- Ⓒ am
- Ⓓ is

Last year, I <u>dance</u> a solo at my end of the year recital.

7. What is the correct way to write the underlined verb?

- Ⓐ dancing
- Ⓑ dances
- Ⓒ dance
- Ⓓ danced

8. In which sentence is the verb *make* used correctly?

- Ⓐ I make cupcakes right now.
- Ⓑ I usually make dinner for my family.
- Ⓒ My mother make homemade ice cream tonight.
- Ⓓ Billy make dinner for his family tonight.

A weary traveler <u>visit</u> my farm yesterday.

9. What is the correct way to write the underlined verb?

- Ⓐ visiting
- Ⓑ visited
- Ⓒ visits
- Ⓓ visit

The two brothers <u>fight</u> yesterday, but today they both apologized.

10. What is the correct way to write the underlined verb in the sentence?

- Ⓐ fighting
- Ⓑ fights
- Ⓒ fought
- Ⓓ fighted

Chapter 3

Lesson 3: Subject-Verb Agreement

You can scan the QR code given below or use the url to access additional EdSearch resources including videos and mobile apps related to *Subject-Verb Agreement.*

 **Subject-Verb Agreement**

URL	QR Code
http://www.lumoslearning.com/a/l51	

The video game my sister ____ _____ broke, and it is all her fault.

1. Select the correct form of the verb to complete the above sentence.

Ⓐ are playing
Ⓑ were playing
Ⓒ was playing
Ⓓ will play

_____ are the reason we are late today.

2. Select the correct subject to complete the above sentence.

Ⓐ She
Ⓑ They
Ⓒ He
Ⓓ Her

Her father is cooking breakfast before school tomorrow morning. The menu will include eggs, bacon, and biscuits. My sister and _____ cannot wait to wake up and eat!

3. Select the correct subject to complete the above sentence.

Ⓐ I
Ⓑ we
Ⓒ me
Ⓓ None of the above

He _____ the chickens out of the yard and ran off with them!

4. Select the correct verb to complete the above sentence.

Ⓐ snatch
Ⓑ snatched
Ⓒ snatching
Ⓓ snatcher

5. The traveler, who had gone to wash his hands, _____.

Ⓐ returned
Ⓑ has returns
Ⓒ returning
Ⓓ return

The skateboarding show really _____ soon.

6. Identify the correct verb phrase from the above sentence.

Ⓐ be starting
Ⓑ started
Ⓒ should be starting
Ⓓ start

_____ performed beautifully yesterday, and I'm sure they will again today.

7. Select the correct subject to complete the above sentence.

Ⓐ Them choir
Ⓑ They choir
Ⓒ The choir
Ⓓ There choir

My mother and I were racing against each other in the video game, and she kept winning. Now, _____ and my brother are going to compete!

8. Select the correct subject to complete the above sentence.

Ⓐ I
Ⓑ she
Ⓒ her
Ⓓ None of the above

One type of sweet orange _____ the blood orange.

9. Select the correct verb to complete the above sentence.

Ⓐ called
Ⓑ call
Ⓒ is called
Ⓓ is call

She danced so beautifully. She dances so beautifully.

10. Which two verb tenses, in the given order, are used in the above sentences?

Ⓐ present, past
Ⓑ past, present
Ⓒ present, future
Ⓓ future, perfect

Chapter 3

Lesson 4: Adjectives and Adverbs

You can scan the QR code given below or use the url to access additional EdSearch resources including videos and mobile apps related to *Adjectives and Adverbs.*

 **Search**   **Adjectives and adverbs**

URL	QR Code
http://www.lumoslearning.com/a/l51	

1. These words are used to modify and describe nouns and pronouns.

Ⓐ Adjectives
Ⓑ Adverbs
Ⓒ Nouns
Ⓓ Verbs

2. These words are used to modify or describe verbs or adverbs.

Ⓐ Adjectives
Ⓑ Adverbs
Ⓒ Nouns
Ⓓ Verbs

She teaches her class <u>patiently</u>.

3. What part of speech is the underlined word in the above sentence?

Ⓐ Noun
Ⓑ Verb
Ⓒ Adjective
Ⓓ Adverb

She is a <u>patient</u> teacher.

4. What part of speech is the underlined word in the sentence above?

Ⓐ Noun
Ⓑ Verb
Ⓒ Adjective
Ⓓ Adverb

This <u>exciting</u> movie is wonderful. The plot is quite <u>suspenseful</u>. Several parts are also very <u>funny</u>, and the <u>humor</u> adds much to the movie.

5. Which underlined word is NOT an adjective?

Ⓐ exciting
Ⓑ suspenseful
Ⓒ several
Ⓓ humor

My cousin used to be one of the _____ basketball players in the world. Now, there are only two players that are _____ than him.

6. Select the answer that has the correct adjectives in the correct order to complete the sentence.

Ⓐ taller, tallest
Ⓑ tallest, taller
Ⓒ most tall, more tall
Ⓓ tallest, more tall

My brother is a good driver. He drives very <u>well</u>.

7. What part of speech is the underlined word in the sentence?

Ⓐ adjective
Ⓑ noun
Ⓒ adverb
Ⓓ verb

Orange trees produce <u>wonderful</u> fruit and flowers all year long.

8. What is the underlined word in the sentence?

Ⓐ adjective
Ⓑ noun
Ⓒ adverb
Ⓓ verb

She makes the most _____ chocolate chip cookies. They are so good that the most _____ bakery in the nation wants her recipe.

9. Select the answer that has the correct adjectives in the correct order to complete the sentence.

Ⓐ delicious, famous
Ⓑ famous, delicious
Ⓒ deliciouser, famouser
Ⓓ delicious, all famous

This is the <u>craziest</u> movie I have seen in a long time. So far it has had the <u>ugliest</u> monsters, the <u>scariest</u> vampires, and the <u>strangest</u> <u>werewolves</u>.

10. Which underlined word is NOT an adjective?

Ⓐ craziest
Ⓑ ugliest
Ⓒ scariest
Ⓓ werewolves

Chapter 3

Lesson 5: Correlative Conjunctions

You can scan the QR code given below or use the url to access additional EdSearch resources including videos and mobile apps related to *Correlative Conjunctions.*

Correlative Conjunctions

URL	QR Code
http://www.lumoslearning.com/a/l51	

Danielle wants _____ pizza _____ pasta for lunch, because she doesn't like Italian food.

1. Which set of conjunctions correctly completes the sentence?

- Ⓐ either, or
- Ⓑ neither, and
- Ⓒ neither, nor
- Ⓓ either, and

I can't decide _____ I should take Spanish class next year _____ German class.

2. Which set of conjunctions correctly completes the sentence?

- Ⓐ either, or
- Ⓑ whether, or
- Ⓒ neither, nor
- Ⓓ whether, nor

_____ my mom _____ my dad can take me to the library.

3. Which set of conjunctions correctly completes the sentence?

- Ⓐ Whether, or
- Ⓑ Neither, nor
- Ⓒ Either, nor
- Ⓓ Whether, nor

_____ you give back my sweater you borrowed last week, _____ I won't loan you my new dress.

4. Which set of conjunctions correctly completes the sentence?

- Ⓐ Either, or
- Ⓑ Neither, nor
- Ⓒ Whether, or
- Ⓓ Either, nor

_____ we go to the mountains for vacation _____ to the beach, I'll be happy.

5. Which set of conjunctions correctly completes the sentence?

Ⓐ Either, nor
Ⓑ Either, or
Ⓒ Neither, nor
Ⓓ Whether, or

_____ we can go for a walk in the park tomorrow afternoon, _____ we can go watch a ballgame instead.

6. Which set of conjunctions correctly completes the sentence?

Ⓐ Either, or
Ⓑ Either, nor
Ⓒ Neither, nor
Ⓓ Whether, or

I'm sorry, but I have _____ the money _____ the time to shop for new clothes right now.

7. Which set of conjunctions correctly completes the sentence?

Ⓐ either, or
Ⓑ either, whether
Ⓒ neither, nor
Ⓓ whether, or

I can't decide _____ to join the marching band next year _____ try out for the football team.

8. Which set of conjunctions correctly completes the sentence?

Ⓐ whether, nor
Ⓑ neither, or
Ⓒ neither, nor
Ⓓ whether, or

_____ Donna _____ Natalie won the art contest, even though they are both very talented.

9. Which set of conjunctions correctly completes the sentence?

Ⓐ Either, or
Ⓑ Neither, or
Ⓒ Neither, nor
Ⓓ Whether, or

10. Which of the following are pairs of correlative conjunctions?

Ⓐ either, or
Ⓑ neither, nor
Ⓒ whether, or
Ⓓ all of the above

Chapter 3

Lesson 6: Capitalization

You can scan the QR code given below or use the url to access additional EdSearch resources including videos and mobile apps related to *Capitalization*.

)Search

Capitalization

URL	QR Code
http://www.lumoslearning.com/a/l52	

1. Which sentence is written correctly?

Ⓐ My Cat, Katie, is black and white.
Ⓑ My cat, Katie, is black and white.
Ⓒ my Cat, Katie, is black and white.
Ⓓ My cat, katie, is black and white.

2. Select the sentence that uses capital letters correctly.

Ⓐ Nana has two Dogs, named Hank and Sugar, who love the Back Porch.
Ⓑ Nana has two Dogs, named Hank and Sugar, who love the back porch.
Ⓒ Nana has two dogs, named Hank and Sugar, who love the back porch.
Ⓓ nana has two dogs, named Hank and Sugar, who love the back porch.

3. Select the sentence that uses capital letters correctly.

Ⓐ "You just missed the bus!" Marrah's mother yelled. "Why can't you ever be on time?"
Ⓑ "You just missed the bus!" Marrah's Mother yelled. "Why can't you ever be on time?"
Ⓒ "you just missed the bus!" Marrah's mother yelled. "why can't you ever be on time?"
Ⓓ "You just missed the bus!" marrah's Mother yelled. "Why can't you ever be on time?"

4. Select the sentence that uses capital letters correctly.

Ⓐ With her eyes closed, she imagined her Mother helping her get dressed and ready for tonight.
Ⓑ With Her eyes closed, she imagined her Mother helping Her get dressed and ready for tonight.
Ⓒ With her eyes closed, she imagined her mother helping her get dressed and ready for tonight.
Ⓓ with her eyes closed, she imagined her mother helping her get dressed and ready for tonight.

5. Select the sentence that uses capital letters correctly.

Ⓐ A Person good at sports is usually given preference over others for admission to colleges.
Ⓑ A person good at sports is usually given preference over others for admission to Colleges.
Ⓒ a person good at sports is usually given preference over others for admission to colleges.
Ⓓ A person good at sports is usually given preference over others for admission to colleges.

6. Which of the following words or terms are capitalized correctly?

Ⓐ I, You, Texas, Katie
Ⓑ I, you, Texas, Katie
Ⓒ I, You, Texas, katie
Ⓓ I, You, texas, Katie

7. Which of the following words or terms are capitalized correctly?

Ⓐ Winter, Thanksgiving, Bobby, Cat
Ⓑ Winter, Thanksgiving, bobby, cat
Ⓒ winter, Thanksgiving, Bobby, cat
Ⓓ Winter, Thanksgiving, Bobby, cat

8. Select the sentence that uses capital letters correctly.

Ⓐ Sam's Wife could not resist food.
Ⓑ sam's wife could not resist food.
Ⓒ Sam's wife could not resist food.
Ⓓ sam's Wife could not resist food.

9. Select the sentence that uses capital letters correctly.

Ⓐ My mother works Extremely hard as a nurse.
Ⓑ My Mother works extremely hard as a Nurse.
Ⓒ My mother works extremely hard as a nurse.
Ⓓ My Mother works extremely hard as a nurse.

10. Select the sentence that uses capital letters correctly.

Ⓐ The President lives in the White House which is located in Washington, D.C.
Ⓑ The president lives in the White House which is located in Washington, D.C.
Ⓒ The President lives in the White House which is located in Washington, d.c.
Ⓓ The President lives in the white house which is located in Washington, D.C.

Chapter 3

Lesson 7: Punctuation

You can scan the QR code given below or use the url to access additional EdSearch resources including videos and mobile apps related to *Punctuation*.

 Search   ***Punctuation***

URL	QR Code
http://www.lumoslearning.com/a/l52	

1. Which sentence is written correctly?

Ⓐ Will your mom take us to school, or do we have to take the bus!
Ⓑ Will your Mom, take us to school, or do we have to take the bus.
Ⓒ Will your Mom, take us to school, or do we have to take the bus?
Ⓓ Will your Mom take us to school, or do we have to take the bus.

2. Which sentence has the correct punctuation?

Ⓐ After I scraped the gum off my shoes I went into the house!
Ⓑ After I scraped the gum off my shoes, I went into the house.
Ⓒ After I scraped the gum off my shoes I went into the house?
Ⓓ After, I scraped the gum off my shoes I went into the house.

3. Which sentence has the correct punctuation?

Ⓐ I have already seen the movie you want to see.
Ⓑ I have already seen, the movie you want to see!
Ⓒ I have already seen, the movie you want, to see.
Ⓓ I have, already seen the movie you want to see.

4. Which sentence has the correct punctuation?

Ⓐ My sister, who will be fifteen soon is learning to drive
Ⓑ My sister who will be fifteen soon is learning to drive.
Ⓒ My sister, who will be fifteen soon, is learning to drive.
Ⓓ My sister who will be fifteen, soon, is learning to drive!

5. Which sentence has the correct punctuation?

Ⓐ The boss entered the room and the workers became silent.
Ⓑ The boss, entered the room, and the workers became silent?
Ⓒ The boss entered the room, and the workers, became silent.
Ⓓ The boss entered the room, and the workers became silent.

6. Which sentence has the correct punctuation?

Ⓐ Please don't sing, until I have the webcam ready.
Ⓑ Please don't sing until I have the webcam ready.
Ⓒ Please, don't sing, until I have the webcam ready!
Ⓓ Please, don't sing until I have the webcam ready?

7. Which sentence has the correct punctuation?

Ⓐ Although the moon was out, the sky was dark.
Ⓑ Although, the moon was out the sky was dark
Ⓒ Although, the moon was out the sky was dark.
Ⓓ Although, the moon was out, the sky was dark.

8. Which sentence has the correct punctuation?

Ⓐ The armadillo which is the state animal, is native to Texas.
Ⓑ The armadillo, which is the state animal is native to Texas.
Ⓒ The armadillo which is the state animal is native to Texas.
Ⓓ The armadillo, which is the state animal, is native to Texas.

9. Which sentence has the correct punctuation?

Ⓐ I took my backpack with me as I was headed to school.
Ⓑ I took my backpack with me, as I was headed to school.
Ⓒ I took my backpack with me as I was headed, to school.
Ⓓ I took, my backpack with me, as I was headed to school.

10. Which sentence has the correct punctuation?

Ⓐ Whole milk has more vitamins but skim milk has less fat.
Ⓑ Whole milk, has more vitamins, but skim milk, has less fat.
Ⓒ Whole milk has more vitamins, but skim milk has less fat.
Ⓓ Whole milk, has more vitamins but skim milk has less fat.

Chapter 3

Lesson 8: Commas in Introductory Phrases

You can scan the QR code given below or use the url to access additional EdSearch resources including videos and mobile apps related to *Commas in Introductory Phrases.*

 **Search**

Commas in Introductory Phrases

URL	QR Code
http://www.lumoslearning.com/a/l52	

An introductory phrase comes at the _____ of a sentence.

1. Which word correctly completes the sentence above?

Ⓐ beginning
Ⓑ middle
Ⓒ end
Ⓓ none of the above

2. Which sentence uses a comma in the correct place?

Ⓐ After, the class returned from the playground they took a math test.
Ⓑ After the class, returned from the playground they took a math test.
Ⓒ After the class returned, from the playground they took a math test.
Ⓓ After the class returned from the playground, they took a math test.

3. Which sentence uses a comma in the correct place?

Ⓐ If you, always eat breakfast you will be more successful in school.
Ⓑ If you always eat breakfast, you will be more successful in school.
Ⓒ If you always eat breakfast you will be more successful, in school.
Ⓓ If, you always eat breakfast you will be more successful in school.

4. Which sentence uses a comma in the correct place?

Ⓐ Until, the whole class gets quiet we will not start watching the video.
Ⓑ Until the whole class, gets quiet we will not start watching the video.
Ⓒ Until the whole class gets quiet, we will not start watching the video.
Ⓓ Until the whole class gets quiet we will not start, watching the video.

5. Which sentence uses a comma in the correct place?

Ⓐ By the way you left your book on the table, in the library.
Ⓑ By the way you left your book, on the table in the library.
Ⓒ By the way you, left your book on the table in the library.
Ⓓ By the way, you left your book on the table in the library.

6. Which sentence uses a comma in the correct place?

Ⓐ Every Christmas, my family travels to Vermont to visit my grandmother.
Ⓑ Every Christmas my family, travels to Vermont to visit my grandmother.
Ⓒ Every Christmas my family travels, to Vermont to visit my grandmother.
Ⓓ Every Christmas my family travels to Vermont, to visit my grandmother.

7. Which sentence uses a comma in the correct place?

Ⓐ After, we all were seated the speaker began his presentation.
Ⓑ After we all were seated, the speaker began his presentation.
Ⓒ After we all were seated the speaker began, his presentation.
Ⓓ After we all, were seated the speaker began his presentation.

8. Which sentence uses a comma in the correct place?

Ⓐ At, the next meeting new officers will be elected.
Ⓑ At the next meeting new officers, will be elected.
Ⓒ At the next, meeting new officers will be elected.
Ⓓ At the next meeting, new officers will be elected.

9. Which sentence uses a comma in the correct place?

Ⓐ Last, Saturday Fred attended a play at the Berlin Theater.
Ⓑ Last Saturday Fred attended a play, at the Berlin Theater.
Ⓒ Last Saturday, Fred attended a play at the Berlin Theater.
Ⓓ Last Saturday Fred attended a play at the Berlin, Theater.

10. Which sentence uses a comma in the correct place?

Ⓐ By tomorrow, morning the train will have reached Atlantic City.
Ⓑ By tomorrow morning the train will have reached, Atlantic City.
Ⓒ By tomorrow morning the train, will have reached Atlantic City.
Ⓓ By tomorrow morning, the train will have reached Atlantic City.

Chapter 3

Lesson 9: Using Commas

You can scan the QR code given below or use the url to access additional EdSearch resources including videos and mobile apps related to *Using Commas*.

 Search

Using Commas

URL	QR Code
http://www.lumoslearning.com/a/l52	

1. Which sentence uses a comma in the correct place?

Ⓐ Sammy, may I go with you to the mall?
Ⓑ Sammy may I go, with you to the mall?
Ⓒ Sammy may I go with you, to the mall?
Ⓓ Sammy may I, go with you to the mall?

2. Which sentence uses commas correctly?

Ⓐ If I could play the guitar, like you Wally I would join a band.
Ⓑ If I could play the guitar like you, Wally I would join a band.
Ⓒ If I could play the guitar like you, Wally, I would join a band.
Ⓓ If I could play the guitar like you Wally, I would join a band.

3. Which sentence uses a comma in the correct place?

Ⓐ Yes, I would like to go to the theme park.
Ⓑ Yes I would like to go, to the theme park.
Ⓒ Yes I would, like to go to the theme park.
Ⓓ Yes I would like to go to the theme, park.

4. Which sentence uses a comma in the correct place?

Ⓐ No I can't, babysit your little sister after school today.
Ⓑ No I can't babysit, your little sister after school today.
Ⓒ No I can't babysit your little sister, after school today.
Ⓓ No, I can't babysit your little sister after school today.

5. Which sentence uses a comma in the correct place?

Ⓐ The movie, starts at 7 o'clock right?
Ⓑ The movie starts at, 7 o'clock, right?
Ⓒ The movie starts at 7 o'clock, right?
Ⓓ The movie starts at 7, o'clock right?

6. Which sentence uses a comma in the correct place?

Ⓐ Kathy, will you drive me to the golf course?
Ⓑ Kathy will you drive, me to the golf course?
Ⓒ Kathy will you drive me, to the golf course?
Ⓓ Kathy will you drive me to the golf, course?

7. Which sentence uses a comma in the correct place?

Ⓐ I promise, to be home before 9:30 Mom.
Ⓑ I promise to be home, before 9:30 Mom.
Ⓒ I promise to be home before 9:30, Mom.
Ⓓ I promise to be home before, 9:30, Mom.

8. Which sentence uses a comma in the correct place?

Ⓐ This is the funniest, book don't you think?
Ⓑ This is the funniest book, don't you think?
Ⓒ This is the funniest book don't you, think?
Ⓓ This is, the funniest book don't you think?

9. Which sentence uses a comma in the correct place?

Ⓐ Yes, I can help you edit your English essay.
Ⓑ Yes I can help you, edit your English essay.
Ⓒ Yes I can help, you edit your English essay.
Ⓓ Yes I can help you edit your English, essay.

10. Which sentence uses a comma in the correct place?

Ⓐ Beau can I come over, and play video games with you?
Ⓑ Beau, can I come over and play video games with you?
Ⓒ Beau, can I come over, and play video games with you?
Ⓓ Beau can I come over and play video games, with you?

Chapter 3

Lesson 10: Writing Titles

You can scan the QR code given below or use the url to access additional EdSearch resources including videos and mobile apps related to *Writing Titles.*

Writing Titles

URL	QR Code
http://www.lumoslearning.com/a/l52	

My favorite Shel Silverstein poem is _____.

1. Select a choice to complete the sentence above that displays the title correctly.

Ⓐ *Hector the Collector*
Ⓑ "Hector the Collector"
Ⓒ Hector the Collector
Ⓓ None of the above

Richard just wrote a new short story called _____.

2. Select a choice to complete the sentence above that displays the title correctly.

Ⓐ *My Time in China*
Ⓑ "My Time in China"
Ⓒ My Time in China
Ⓓ None of the above

My cousin's favorite song is _____.

3. Select a choice to complete the sentence above that displays the title correctly.

Ⓐ *Don't Rain on My Parade*
Ⓑ "Don't Rain on My Parade"
Ⓒ Don't Rain on My Parade
Ⓓ None of the above

Last week, my parents saw the movie _____.

4. Select a choice to complete the sentence above that displays the title correctly.

Ⓐ *Superman*
Ⓑ "Superman"
Ⓒ Superman
Ⓓ Both A and C

Most newsstands sell issues of _____.

5. Select a choice to complete the sentence above that displays the title correctly.

Ⓐ *The New York Times*
Ⓑ "The New York Times"
Ⓒ The New York Times
Ⓓ Both A and C

_____ is one of the longest novels ever written.

6. Select a choice to complete the sentence above that displays the title correctly.

Ⓐ *War and Peace*
Ⓑ "War and Peace"
Ⓒ <u>War and Peace</u>
Ⓓ Both A and C

Has your little brother watched the movie _____?

7. Select a choice to complete the sentence above that displays the title correctly.

Ⓐ *Bambi*
Ⓑ "Bambi"
Ⓒ <u>Bambi</u>
Ⓓ Both A and C

My science teacher read us an article called _____ yesterday.

8. Select a choice to complete the sentence above that displays the title correctly.

Ⓐ *Exploring Neutrons*
Ⓑ "Exploring Neutrons"
Ⓒ <u>Exploring Neutrons</u>
Ⓓ None of the above

I will use some of my birthday money to buy a subscription to _____.

9. Select a choice to complete the sentence above that displays the title correctly.

Ⓐ *Sports Illustrated for Kids*
Ⓑ "Sports Illustrated for Kids"
Ⓒ <u>Sports Illustrated for Kids</u>
Ⓓ Both A and C

Martha's sister starts dancing whenever she hears the song _____.

10. Select a choice to complete the sentence above that displays the title correctly.

Ⓐ *I Love Rock and Roll*
Ⓑ "I Love Rock and Roll"
Ⓒ <u>I Love Rock and Roll</u>
Ⓓ Both A and C

Chapter 3

Lesson 11: Spelling

You can scan the QR code given below or use the url to access additional EdSearch resources including videos and mobile apps related to *Spelling*.

   **Spelling**

URL	QR Code
http://www.lumoslearning.com/a/l52	

The birthday party was wonderful! Everyone had so much fun playing and swimming. The birthday presents were great, but my favorite part was the cake. It was incredble!

1. Which word is spelled incorrectly?

Ⓐ wonderful
Ⓑ swimming
Ⓒ favorite
Ⓓ incredble

I went for a run this morning. Although I usualy run in the evening, I decided to go in the morning because of the weather.

2. Which word is spelled incorrectly?

Ⓐ morning
Ⓑ usualy
Ⓒ decided
Ⓓ weather

Sports devlop our character. The players have to abide by the rules of the game. Any departure from these rules means foul play.

3. Which word is spelled incorrectly?

Ⓐ devlop
Ⓑ abide
Ⓒ rules
Ⓓ departure

A weary traveler stopped at Sam's house and asked him for shelter for the night. Sam was a friendly soul. He not only agreed to let the traveler stay for the night, he decided to treat his guest to some curried chiken.

4. Which word is spelled incorrectly?

Ⓐ weary
Ⓑ friendly
Ⓒ traveler
Ⓓ chiken

So as she cooked the meat, she smelled the rich steam and could not help tasteing a piece. It was tender and delicious, and she decided to have another piece.

5. Which word is spelled incorrectly?

Ⓐ smelled
Ⓑ tasteing
Ⓒ tender
Ⓓ delicious

Frantic now, Marrah lifted her sheets to look under them before droping to her knees in front of her bed. She pushed mounds of clothes out of the way as she continued to search for her backpack.

6. Which word is spelled incorrectly?

Ⓐ frantic
Ⓑ droping
Ⓒ mounds
Ⓓ continued

Katie stood before the crowd blushing and ringing her hands. She looked out and saw the room full of faces.

7. Which word is spelled incorrectly?

Ⓐ blushing
Ⓑ ringing
Ⓒ looked
Ⓓ saw

They all had wonderful things to say about her song and how proud they were because she kept going even when it seemed like she might give up. She shruged her shoulders and shared a smile with her mother. "I just did my best," she answered.

8. Which word is spelled incorrectly?

Ⓐ wonderful
Ⓑ because
Ⓒ shruged
Ⓓ shoulders

Once there was a severe drout. There was little water in Tony's well, and he didn't know what would happen to the fruit trees in his garden.

9. Which of the word is spelled incorrectly?

Ⓐ drout
Ⓑ little
Ⓒ happen
Ⓓ garden

Then, when I came inside to clean, I realized the kitchen sink was clogged, and the washing machine seamed broken.

10. Which underlined word is spelled incorrectly?

Ⓐ inside
Ⓑ realized
Ⓒ clogged
Ⓓ seamed

Chapter 3

Lesson 12: Sentence Structure

You can scan the QR code given below or use the url to access additional EdSearch resources including videos and mobile apps related to *Sentence Structure*.

 **Search**

Sentence Structure

URL	QR Code
http://www.lumoslearning.com/a/l53	

A group of words that expresses a complete thought with a subject and a verb is _____.

1. Select the phrase that best completes the sentence.

- Ⓐ a clause
- Ⓑ an independent clause
- Ⓒ a dependent clause
- Ⓓ a coordinating conjunction

A group of words that does not express a complete thought, but has a subject and a verb is called _____.

2. Select the phrase that best completes the sentence.

- Ⓐ a complete sentence
- Ⓑ an independent clause
- Ⓒ a dependent clause
- Ⓓ a coordinating conjunction

When Juan studied for his quiz at the library.

3. The sentence is an example of _____.

- Ⓐ a complete sentence
- Ⓑ an independent clause
- Ⓒ a dependent clause
- Ⓓ a coordinating conjunction

Miguel loves cars, but he can never find the time to work on one.

4. This is an example of _____.

- Ⓐ a simple sentence
- Ⓑ a compound sentence
- Ⓒ a complex sentence
- Ⓓ an incomplete sentence

Please help your father wash the car.

5. This is an example of _____.

- Ⓐ a simple sentence
- Ⓑ a compound sentence
- Ⓒ a complex sentence
- Ⓓ an incomplete sentence

My father warned us about the dangers of forest fires before he took us camping.

6. This is an example of _____.

- Ⓐ a simple sentence
- Ⓑ a compound sentence
- Ⓒ a complex sentence
- Ⓓ an incomplete sentence

My puppy always chews my slippers.

7. This is an example of _____.

- Ⓐ a simple sentence
- Ⓑ a compound sentence
- Ⓒ a complex sentence
- Ⓓ an incomplete sentence

The sleepy cat is.

8. This is an example of _____.

- Ⓐ a simple sentence
- Ⓑ a compound sentence
- Ⓒ a complex sentence
- Ⓓ an incomplete sentence

Would you like a cookie, or would you rather have a piece of cake?

9. This is an example of _____.

- Ⓐ a simple sentence
- Ⓑ a compound sentence
- Ⓒ a complex sentence
- Ⓓ an incomplete sentence

Although Jason takes drum lessons, he also plays the tuba in the band.

10. This is an example of _____.

- Ⓐ a simple sentence
- Ⓑ a compound sentence
- Ⓒ a complex sentence
- Ⓓ an incomplete sentence

Chapter 3

Lesson 13: Varieties of English

You can scan the QR code given below or use the url to access additional EdSearch resources including videos and mobile apps related to *Varieties of English*.

Varieties of English

URL	QR Code
http://www.lumoslearning.com/a/l53	

Francine: Well aren't you as refreshing as a cold glass of lemonade on a hot summer day! I'm delighted to meet you! My name is Francine.

Adam: It is a pleasure to make your acquaintance. I am Adam.

1. Based on the dialogue above, which word best describes Francine?

  Ⓐ arrogant
  Ⓑ friendly
  Ⓒ serious
  Ⓓ bored

2. Based on the dialogue above, which word best describes Adam?

  Ⓐ casual
  Ⓑ rude
  Ⓒ proper
  Ⓓ silly

3. Based on the dialogue above, where do you think Francine might be from?

  Ⓐ Europe
  Ⓑ Alaska
  Ⓒ the South
  Ⓓ Canada

4. Which sentence indicates use of dialect?

  Ⓐ Would you like for me to help you paint the fence?
  Ⓑ Abe thought about it, but he changed his mind.
  Ⓒ I reckon I don't have time.
  Ⓓ That's ok with me.

"I appreciate you taking time out of your busy day to meet with me."

5. What type of character would use this style of English?

  Ⓐ a student speaking with a college professor
  Ⓑ two teenage boys watching a basketball game
  Ⓒ a patient talking to his doctor
  Ⓓ a woman talking to her best friend

"Yo, I'm psyched that we could do this today!"

6. What type of character would use this style of English?

Ⓐ a student speaking with a college professor
Ⓑ two teenage boys watching a basketball game
Ⓒ a patient talking to his doctor
Ⓓ a woman talking to her best friend

_____ is always spelled correctly, and _____ is spelled the way the character speaks the words.

7. Choose the pair of words that correctly completes the sentence above.

Ⓐ Standard English, dialect
Ⓑ Dialect, standard English
Ⓒ British English, expressions
Ⓓ None of the above

8. Dialect conveys a character's _____, and standard English does not.

Ⓐ accent
Ⓑ locality
Ⓒ physical appearance
Ⓓ Both A and B

Choose the style of speech that would be the most appropriate for the situation below.

9. A student speaking to a school librarian

Ⓐ "Do you have a book about insects?"
Ⓑ "Give me a book about insects."
Ⓒ "Would you please tell me if you have a book about insects?"
Ⓓ "I want a book about insects."

Chapter 3

Lesson 14: Context Clues

You can scan the QR code given below or use the url to access additional EdSearch resources including videos and mobile apps related to *Context Clues*.

 Search

Context Clues

URL	QR Code
http://www.lumoslearning.com/a/l54	

The snake <u>slithered</u> across the back porch when my mother chased it with a broom.

1. Select the best definition for the underlined word based on the context clues.

Ⓐ stopped
Ⓑ moved
Ⓒ slept
Ⓓ ate

Our dog <u>gnawed</u> through the rope, allowing him to get loose and leave the backyard.

2. Select the best definition for the underlined word based on the context clues.

Ⓐ stopped
Ⓑ moved
Ⓒ slept
Ⓓ chewed

Jan took one look at the <u>hideous</u> creature and ran away in disgust.

3. Select the best definition of the underlined word based on the context clues.

Ⓐ very ugly and frightful
Ⓑ beautiful but frightful
Ⓒ very happy and excited
Ⓓ very scared and alone

Emily's mother <u>sternly</u> told her to finish practicing the piano, because she had taken long enough.

4. Select the best definition for the underlined word based on the context clues.

Ⓐ happily
Ⓑ beautifully
Ⓒ sadly
Ⓓ strictly

Her mother called again, and she could hear the <u>impatience</u> in her voice downstairs.

5. Select the best definition for the underlined word based on the context clues.

   Ⓐ patience
   Ⓑ annoyance
   Ⓒ endurance
   Ⓓ persistence

He <u>snatched</u> the chickens out of the yard and ran off with them!

6. Select the best definition for the underlined word based on the context clues.

   Ⓐ stole
   Ⓑ gave
   Ⓒ smelled
   Ⓓ glowed

Ellen peered between the red curtains and realized she was truly nervous. She couldn't believe this many people were here to see her. She was a <u>novice!</u> Most new performers never had this large of a crowd.

7. Select the best definition of the underlined word based on the context clues.

   Ⓐ average
   Ⓑ experienced
   Ⓒ beginner
   Ⓓ regular

Words that provide the definition of an unknown word explicitly stated in the text are considered _____.

8. Select the phrase that best completes the above sentence.

   Ⓐ inferential context clues
   Ⓑ unusual context clues
   Ⓒ written context clues
   Ⓓ direct context clues

Keely was bored. She spent each day counting buttons, and she did not believe that there could be a more <u>monotonous</u> task. But even though it was repetitive and boring, she knew it was important.

9. Select the best definition of the underlined word based on the context clues.

Ⓐ dull
Ⓑ exciting
Ⓒ advantageous
Ⓓ varied

My father told me it would not be <u>prudent</u> to eat too much candy at one time. Now that I am sick to my stomach, I wish I had listened to him.

10. Select the best definition of the underlined word based on the context clues.

Ⓐ unwise
Ⓑ unexpected
Ⓒ expected
Ⓓ wise

Chapter 3

Lesson 15: Roots and Affixes

You can scan the QR code given below or use the url to access additional EdSearch resources including videos and mobile apps related to *Roots and Affixes.*

 **Roots and Affixes**

URL	QR Code
http://www.lumoslearning.com/a/l54	

1. Which of the following is a true statement?

Ⓐ A suffix or ending is an affix, which is placed at the end of a word.
Ⓑ A prefix or beginning is an affix, which is placed at the beginning of a word.
Ⓒ A suffix is attached at the beginning of a word.
Ⓓ Both A and B

2. What is the prefix in the word unhappy?

Ⓐ unh
Ⓑ u
Ⓒ un
Ⓓ None of these

3. What prefix changes the word cycle to mean "a moving device with two wheels?"

Ⓐ tri
Ⓑ dual
Ⓒ bi
Ⓓ quad

4. Which of the following words does not contain a suffix?

Ⓐ lemonade
Ⓑ resident
Ⓒ dormitory
Ⓓ liquidate

5. What is the prefix of the word retroactive?

Ⓐ retro
Ⓑ ret
Ⓒ re
Ⓓ tive

6. What is the suffix of the word strengthen?

Ⓐ then
Ⓑ stre
Ⓒ en
Ⓓ st

7. Which suffix would be the correct addition to the word music?

Ⓐ tian
Ⓑ sion
Ⓒ ian
Ⓓ tion

8. Which suffix would be the correct addition to the word friend?

Ⓐ er
Ⓑ y
Ⓒ ly
Ⓓ est

9. Identify the root word in the longer word unsuitable.

Ⓐ unsuit
Ⓑ suitable
Ⓒ suit
Ⓓ table

10. Identify the root word in the longer word uncomfortable.

Ⓐ uncomfort
Ⓑ comfort
Ⓒ table
Ⓓ comfortable

Chapter 3

Lesson 16: Reference Sources

You can scan the QR code given below or use the url to access additional EdSearch resources including videos and mobile apps related to *Reference Sources.*

 **Reference Sources**

URL	QR Code
http://www.lumoslearning.com/a/l54	

1. If you want to know how to say a word, look at the _____.

Ⓐ guide work
Ⓑ part of speech
Ⓒ pronunciation
Ⓓ definition

Zadey is reading a mystery book.

2. Where would be the best place for her to look up the meaning of a word she doesn't know?

Ⓐ another mystery book
Ⓑ the book's glossary
Ⓒ a thesaurus
Ⓓ a dictionary

marine

Synonyms: sea, saltwater, maritime, oceanic

3. In which source would you find this entry?

Ⓐ a glossary
Ⓑ a book about seas
Ⓒ a dictionary
Ⓓ a thesaurus

tissue: a group of plant or animal cells that are similar in form and function

4. In which resource would you find this entry for the word "tissue?"

Ⓐ a magazine
Ⓑ a dictionary
Ⓒ a thesaurus
Ⓓ a glossary

abacus (n) Pronunciation: AB uh kuhss History: 14th century
an instrument made from beads and wires that is used to perform arithmetic

5. What resource is this reference from?

Ⓐ a dictionary
Ⓑ a glossary
Ⓒ a thesaurus
Ⓓ a math textbook

kindle: to start (a fire) burning

6. In what source would you find this text?

Ⓐ a pamphlet about camping
Ⓑ a thesaurus
Ⓒ a glossary
Ⓓ a dictionary

7. _____ is a book that contains facts and figures about all kinds of topics.

Ⓐ An almanac
Ⓑ An atlas
Ⓒ An autobiography
Ⓓ A brochure

8. _____ is a book of maps.

Ⓐ An almanac
Ⓑ An atlas
Ⓒ A dictionary
Ⓓ An encyclopedia

9. You can use a dictionary to learn _____.

Ⓐ correct spellings
Ⓑ definitions
Ⓒ parts of speech
Ⓓ all of the above

10. _____ is a type of reference source that gives lists of synonyms and antonyms.

   Ⓐ An almanac
   Ⓑ An atlas
   Ⓒ An encyclopedia
   Ⓓ A thesaurus

Chapter 3

Lesson 17: Interpreting Figurative Language

You can scan the QR code given below or use the url to access additional EdSearch resources including videos and mobile apps related to *Interpreting Figurative Language*.

 **Interpreting Figurative Language**

URL	QR Code
http://www.lumoslearning.com/a/l55	

1. What is the meaning of the simile below?

The boys ran off like rockets shooting up to the stars.

- Ⓐ The boys ran toward the stars.
- Ⓑ The boys ran away quickly.
- Ⓒ The boys were shooting guns.
- Ⓓ The boys drove rockets.

2. What is the meaning of the metaphor below?

Dad's business is a well-oiled machine.

- Ⓐ Dad's business runs smoothly.
- Ⓑ Dad's business uses a lot of machines.
- Ⓒ Dad's business sells oil.
- Ⓓ Dad's business is putting oil on machines.

3. What is the meaning of the simile below?

My best friend and I are like two peas in a pod.

- Ⓐ The two friends like to eat peas.
- Ⓑ The two friends are very similar.
- Ⓒ The two friends are like vegetables.
- Ⓓ The two friends live in a pod.

4. What is the meaning of the simile below?

Without my glasses, I'm as blind as a bat.

- Ⓐ The person lives in a cave.
- Ⓑ The person is black like a bat.
- Ⓒ The person is blind.
- Ⓓ The person can't see very well without his or her eyeglasses.

5. What is the meaning of the simile below?

My teacher was as mad as an old wet hen when three kids didn't do their homework.

- Ⓐ The teacher lived on a farm.
- Ⓑ The teacher was crazy.
- Ⓒ The teacher was very angry.
- Ⓓ The teacher didn't assign any homework.

6. What is the meaning of the metaphor below?

Nick is a pig when he eats.

- Ⓐ Nick eats on the ground.
- Ⓑ Nick eats a lot, and he is messy.
- Ⓒ Nick is very fat.
- Ⓓ Nick makes pig-like sounds when he eats.

7. What is the meaning of the metaphor below?

My room is a disaster after my little cousins come over and play.

- Ⓐ An earthquake hit my room.
- Ⓑ My room is very messy.
- Ⓒ My cousins were involved in a disaster.
- Ⓓ My room is full of cousins.

8. What is the meaning of the simile below?

I felt like a fish out of water in the foreign city.

- Ⓐ I'm a good swimmer.
- Ⓑ I'm very wet.
- Ⓒ I can speak a foreign language.
- Ⓓ I feel like I don't belong.

9. What is the meaning of the simile below?

The little girl was as good as gold at the church service.

- Ⓐ She was golden colored.
- Ⓑ She wore lots of jewelry.
- Ⓒ She behaved very well.
- Ⓓ She wore a gold dress.

10. What is the meaning of the metaphor below?

My husband is the apple of my eye.

- Ⓐ My husband is one of my favorite people.
- Ⓑ My husband looks like a fruit.
- Ⓒ My husband has nice eyes.
- Ⓓ My husband brings me apples.

Chapter 3

Lesson 18: Idioms, Adages, and Proverbs

You can scan the QR code given below or use the url to access additional EdSearch resources including videos and mobile apps related to *Idioms, Adages, and Proverbs.*

 **Search**

Idioms, Adages, and Proverbs

URL	QR Code
http://www.lumoslearning.com/a/l55	

1. What is a phrase which contains advice or a generally accepted truth called?

Ⓐ adage
Ⓑ idiom
Ⓒ proverb
Ⓓ simile

Do not put all your eggs in one basket.

2. Which sentence is an example of the above proverb?

Ⓐ Do not put all your golf balls in one game.
Ⓑ Do not keep all your information a secret.
Ⓒ Do not store all your data on just one computer.
Ⓓ Do not eat all your breakfast at dinner.

If anything can go wrong, it will.

3. This famous saying is an example of _____.

Ⓐ an idiom
Ⓑ an adage
Ⓒ a proverb
Ⓓ an alliteration

She is really rubbing me the wrong way.

4. The above sentence is an example of _____.

Ⓐ an idiom
Ⓑ a proverb
Ⓒ an adage
Ⓓ a simile

Mrs. Smith's class is going bananas!

5. The above sentence is an example of _____.

Ⓐ an idiom
Ⓑ an adage
Ⓒ a proverb
Ⓓ a simile

A friend in need is a friend indeed.

6. The above sentence is an example of _____.

Ⓐ an idiom
Ⓑ an adage
Ⓒ a proverb
Ⓓ a simile

Actions speak louder than words.

7. What does this adage mean?

Ⓐ Actions make a lot of noise compared to words.
Ⓑ It is better to do and show rather than simply talk without doing anything.
Ⓒ What you actually *do* is more important than what you *say* you will do.
Ⓓ Both B and C

Remember, don't let the cat out of the bag and tell dad about the surprise party for his birthday.

8. The idiom, don't let the cat out of the bag means _____.

Ⓐ keep it a secret
Ⓑ tell everyone
Ⓒ keep the cat in the bag safely
Ⓓ none of the above

9. Which of the proverbs given in the choices below means the same as the sentence below?

When a bad thing happens, there is always a positive aspect to it.

Ⓐ Every dog has its day.
Ⓑ Every cloud has a silver lining.
Ⓒ A bird in hand is worth two in the bush.
Ⓓ Patience pays.

10. Which of the proverbs given in the choices below means the same as the following sentence?

You should be happy with what you have, even if it is less than what you want.

Ⓐ Where there is a will, there is a way.
Ⓑ Cut your coat according to the cloth.
Ⓒ Half a loaf is better than no bread.
Ⓓ None of the above

Chapter 3

Lesson 19: Synonyms and Antonyms

You can scan the QR code given below or use the url to access additional EdSearch resources including videos and mobile apps related to *Synonyms and Antonyms*.

Synonyms and Antonyms

URL	QR Code
http://www.lumoslearning.com/a/l55	

The murmur of the stoves,
The chuckles of the water pipes

1. Choose the set of antonyms of the word murmur.

Ⓐ roar, growl, loud
Ⓑ silent, quiet, still
Ⓒ silent, roar, quiet
Ⓓ silent, loud, rumble

2. What are synonyms?

Ⓐ Words that have similar meanings
Ⓑ Words that have different meanings
Ⓒ Words that have the same meanings and are spelled the same
Ⓓ None of the above

3. What are antonyms?

Ⓐ Words that have the same meanings
Ⓑ Words that have different meanings
Ⓒ Both A and B
Ⓓ Words that have opposite meanings

4. Choose the set of words that are antonyms of one another.

Ⓐ return, march
Ⓑ alive, dead
Ⓒ opened, broke
Ⓓ collect, take

Once there was a severe drought; there was little water in Tony's well, and he didn't know what would happen to the fruit trees in his garden. Just then, he noticed three men looking intently at his house. He was certain that the three were planning to rob his house.

5. What is a synonym for the word rob as it is used in the above paragraph?

Ⓐ cheat
Ⓑ thieves
Ⓒ steal
Ⓓ borrow

6. What is a synonym for the word intently as it is used in the paragraph?

Ⓐ lightly
Ⓑ watchfully
Ⓒ attentively
Ⓓ both B and C

7. Which words below are both antonyms for the word fragile in the below paragraph?

The king ordered his servants to collect all the pieces of glass and melt them down and make them into a globe with all the countries of the world upon it, to remind himself and others, that the earth is as fragile as that glass cupboard.

Ⓐ breakable, delicate
Ⓑ beautiful, strong
Ⓒ sturdy, unbreakable
Ⓓ delicate, unbreakable

8. Read the following sentence and identify the words that are synonyms.

After guests ate dinner, they devoured the dessert with delight.

Ⓐ devoured, delight
Ⓑ ate, devoured
Ⓒ dessert, delight
Ⓓ dinner, dessert

9. Read the following sentence and identify the words that are antonyms.

The stars appear tiny from earth, but they are actually huge objects in the universe.

Ⓐ tiny, huge
Ⓑ stars, earth
Ⓒ appear, actually
Ⓓ earth, universe

10. Read the following sentence and identify the words that are synonyms.

My math teacher and my gym instructor are good tennis players.

Ⓐ teacher, player
Ⓑ instructor, player
Ⓒ gym, tennis
Ⓓ teacher, instructor

Chapter 3

Lesson 20: Vocabulary

You can scan the QR code given below or use the url to access additional EdSearch resources including videos and mobile apps related to *Vocabulary*.

Vocabulary

URL	QR Code
http://www.lumoslearning.com/a/l56	

1. Choose the definition of the underlined word in the sentence below.

It is difficult to find a movie store that sells video tapes, because video tapes are nearly <u>obsolete</u>.

- Ⓐ very loud and disturbing
- Ⓑ simple to operate
- Ⓒ no longer produced or used
- Ⓓ a traditional story

2. Choose the definition of the underlined word in the sentence below.

If you will <u>provide</u> me with your phone number, I will call you when your order is ready to be picked up.

- Ⓐ make available for use
- Ⓑ leave one's job and stop working
- Ⓒ hold onto
- Ⓓ keep secret and confidential

3. Choose the definition of the underlined word in the sentence below.

It is a wise idea to <u>retain</u> a copy of your receipt when making a purchase in case you need to return it.

- Ⓐ make available for use
- Ⓑ hold onto or keep
- Ⓒ throw away or dispose of
- Ⓓ make a photocopy

4. Choose the definition of the underlined word in the sentence below.

My uncle plans to <u>retire</u> from the steel factory when he turns sixty-five years old in October.

- Ⓐ hide or conceal
- Ⓑ work additional hours
- Ⓒ clean up an area
- Ⓓ leave one's job and stop working

5. Choose the definition of the underlined word in the sentence below.

My favorite Greek <u>myth</u> is the story about Pandora's Box.

- Ⓐ a box to keep special belongings
- Ⓑ a family heirloom
- Ⓒ a traditional story
- Ⓓ a writing assignment

6. Choose the word that correctly completes the sentence below.

The people of the village were tired of being treated badly, so they made the decision to _____ the king.

- Ⓐ budge
- Ⓑ convert
- Ⓒ revert
- Ⓓ overthrow

7. Choose the word that correctly completes the sentence below.

She pushed as hard as she could, but the heavy bookshelf would not _____.

- Ⓐ budge
- Ⓑ convert
- Ⓒ revert
- Ⓓ overthrow

8. Choose the word that correctly completes the sentence below.

I need to know where to go to _____ my American dollars to Mexican pesos.

- Ⓐ budge
- Ⓑ convert
- Ⓒ revert
- Ⓓ overthrow

9. Choose the word that correctly completes the sentence below.

When a child no longer has parents, the court will appoint a _____.

- Ⓐ babysitter
- Ⓑ guardian
- Ⓒ monitor
- Ⓓ bookkeeper

10. Choose the word that correctly completes the sentence below.

It is difficult to see on a foggy morning, because it is _____.

- Ⓐ beautiful
- Ⓑ hazy
- Ⓒ rainy
- Ⓓ sunny

End of Language

Answer Key and
Detailed Explanations

Chapter 3: Language

Lesson 1: Prepositional Phrases

Question No.	Answer	Detailed Explanations
1	A	Prepositions are words that introduce and connect. A prepositional phrase begins with a preposition and ends with a noun or pronoun. Verbs show action. Punctuation marks are used to end a sentence.
2	C	The preposition "at" introduces the prepositional phrase "at the loud concert." We is a pronoun, met is a verb, and concert is a noun.
3	D	Concert, which is a noun, is the object of the preposition at. The object of a preposition is the first noun that follows the preposition.
4	B	The object of a preposition is the noun or pronoun that follows the preposition. Generally, any word/words that are between the preposition and object of the preposition are adjectives.
5	A	A prepositional phrase begins with a preposition and always ends with a noun or pronoun.
6	B	The word "in" is the preposition that begins the prepositional phrase, in the backyard. Plants and backyard are nouns. Wonderful is an adjective.
7	C	In the prepositional phrase, in the backyard, backyard is the object of the preposition in.
8	C	The word "to" is the preposition. Drives is an action verb. Bus is a noun. School is a noun.
9	C	The prepositional phrase is "to the school."
10	B	The word "behind" is the preposition.

Lesson 2: Verbs

Question No.	Answer	Detailed Explanations
1	A	The singular subject Mrs. Smith takes the singular present tense verb teaches. This year indicates present tense. Taught is past tense. Teached is an incorrect form. Using teaching in the position of the sentence would require a singular present tense helping verb such as "is."
2	D	Choice A requires the past tense "had." Choice B requires the helping verb "will" along with "have" to agree with the future tense. Choice C requires the third person present tense "has."
3	B	The subject, my uncle, of the first independent clause requires the use of the third person singular verb (has). Had is past tense. Having is the progressive or continuous tense and requires a helping verb.
4	A	Joe wants to sing at the end of the year talent show. Choice B requires sings, present tense (3rd person singular - Bill). Choice C requires the past tense, sang. Last week is a clue to the past tense. Choice D, with the helping verb "was," requires singing.
5	C	Maggie went rock climbing at the gym yesterday. Choices A and B require the past tense (climbed), and Choice D requires climb.
6	B	Gerry and I are going fishing tomorrow to catch dinner for our family. Remember that the word "be" is not used alone as a verb. "Be" may be used as a helping verb with a main verb or a form of "be" such as is, am, are, was, and were.
7	D	Last year (indicates past), I danced a solo at my end of the year recital.
8	B	I usually make dinner for my family. Choice A requires the helping verb "am" making. Choice C requires the helping verb "is"or "was", making. Choice D requires the past tense, made.
9	B	The word "yesterday" is a clue that it's past tense. The verb visit(ed) is past tense also.
10	C	The word "yesterday" indicates that the action took place in the past. The past tense of fight is fought. Fought is an irregular verb because it doesn't follow the usual rule of adding "ed" to the end of the verb to form the past tense.

Lesson 3: Subject-Verb Agreement

Question No.	Answer	Detailed Explanations
1	C	The phrase "was playing" is in a singular present tense form. The word were (plural-past) are (plural), and will (future) are incorrect in number and tense. Remember that the number of the subject (whether it is singular or plural) determines the verb because a singular subject must have a singular verb and a plural subject must have a plural verb.
2	B	The verb "are" is plural and requires a plural subject. She and he are all singular subjects and would not agree with a plural verb.
3	A	When referring to yourself and another subject as the subjects of a sentence, you should mention yourself last, so the answer should be my sister and "I". "I" is a subject pronoun. If you read the sentence without the other subject, you would read the sentence with "I". You never begin a sentence with the pronoun "me (an object pronoun), so you should use "I".
4	B	The verb tense has to agree with the subject, the verb "snatched" is correct. There is a compound verb in this sentence. The other verb, "ran," is in past tense, so both verbs must be in past tense. Adding "ed" to the end of the present tense "snatch" makes it past tense. Snatcher is not a verb. The "er" makes it a noun.
5	A	Traveler is the singular subject and requires a singular verb. Returned (past tense) agrees with the subject. If you read each of the choices in the sentence, the others do not fit because they do not agree in tense or number.
6	C	The adverb "soon" is a future time, so the verb has to be in the future tense. The phrase should be starting (soon) is correct. Choice B is past tense, and choices A and D are the wrong tense.
7	C	It's important not to begin a sentence with an object pronoun (them). If you read the sentence beginning with "them," it doesn't sound right. They choir and there choir are incorrect, because they should function as a possessive pronoun. The spelling is incorrect. The choir is in the correct form.
8	B	A compound subject that uses a noun and a pronoun, must be a subject pronoun in order to agree with the other pronoun. She is a subject pronoun. Without "I" in the subject, she would still be correct.
9	C	If you try to read the sentence with called, call, and is call, they do not read correctly. The verb forms are not correct and do not agree with the subject and tense of the sentence.
10	B	Danced is past tense, and dances is present tense. A helping verb is required for the future and perfect tenses.

Lesson 4: Adjectives and Adverbs

Question No.	Answer	Detailed Explanations
1	A	Adjectives modify nouns and pronouns. Nouns name persons, places, things, and ideas. Adverbs tell when, where, how, and to what extent. Verbs may be an action or linking and tell what the subject is or does.
2	B	Adverbs are used to modify or describe verbs or even other adverbs. Verbs may be an action or describe the state of being. Adjectives modify nouns. Nouns names persons, places, things, or ideas.
3	D	Patiently is an adverb that modifies the verb teaches and tells how she teaches the class.
4	C	Patient as it's used in the sentence is an adjective that describes the teacher. It tells what kind of teacher she is. Teacher is a noun.
5	D	Humor is a noun. Remember that words that follow "the" (which is an article and adjective), should be a noun, except for any adjectives that may precede the noun. Choices A, B, and C are adjectives.
6	B	Choice B, tallest and taller, is correct. Tallest is the superlative form of an adjective that is comparing more than two things, whereas the adjective taller, the comparative form, is used to compare only two things.
7	C	The word well in the sentence is an adverb describing how he drives. As you might note, good is an adjective and is used to describe nouns. However, well as an adverb can describe how something is done or one's state of health.
8	A	The adjective wonderful is used to describe fruit and flowers. It tells "what kind" of fruit and flowers.
9	A	The most delicious chocolate chip cookies, and the most famous bakery are the correct answers. Because delicious and famous are two syllable words, you should not add er or est to either of them.
10	D	Werewolves is correctly identified as a noun. Each of the other underlined words, which all end in -est, are adjectives that modify or describe nouns.

Lesson 5: Correlative Conjunctions

Question No.	Answer	Detailed Explanations
1	C	Danielle wants neither pizza nor pasta for lunch, because she doesn't like Italian food. Pizza and pasta are both types of Italian food, so since Danielle doesn't like Italian food, she doesn't want it. That makes Choice A incorrect. Choices B and D don't make sense.
2	B	I can't decide whether I should take Spanish class next year or German class. If you're deciding between two options, use the correlating conjunction pair "whether" and "or."
3	B	Neither my mom nor my dad can take me to the library. When you are saying that two options are negative, use the correlative conjunctions "neither" and "nor."
4	A	Either you give back my sweater you borrowed last week, or I won't loan you my new dress. When you have two options, use the correlative conjunctions "either" and "or."
5	D	Whether we go to the mountains for vacation or to the beach, I'll be happy. Use the correlative conjunction "whether" in place of the word "if," and use the correlative conjunction "or" when you are expressing two different options.
6	A	When you're giving someone two options, use the correlative conjunctions "either" and "or." Answer D is incorrect, because using "whether" and "or" would form an incomplete or fragmented sentence.
7	C	I'm sorry, but I have neither the money nor the time to shop for new clothes right now. When you are expressing that two options are both negative, use the correlative conjunctions "neither" and "nor."
8	D	I can't decide whether to join the marching band next year or try out for the football team. When you are expressing two actions to participate in, use the correlative conjunctions "whether" and "or."
9	C	Neither Donna nor Natalie won the art contest, even though they are both very talented. When you are expressing that two options are both negative, use the correlative conjunctions "neither" and "nor."
10	D	All of the choices are pairs of correlative conjunctions. Correlative conjunctions are pairs of conjunctions that work together. A writer must use the context of a sentence to choose the appropriate pair of correlative conjunctions to use.

Lesson 6: Capitalization

Question No.	Answer	Detailed Explanations
1	B	My cat Katie is black and white. Remember that the first word of a sentence must be capitalized. Cat should not be capitalized because it is a common noun; however, Katie is the name of the cat so it needs to be capitalized. You do not capitalize the verb is, adjectives black, white, or the conjunction and.
2	C	Nana has two dogs, named Hank and Sugar, who love the back porch. Nana should be capitalized because it's the first word of a sentence and it's a proper noun. Hank and Sugar are the names of dogs, so they should be capitalized. However, back porch and dogs should not be capitalized because they are common nouns.
3	A	"You just missed the bus!" Marrah's mother yelled. "Why can't you ever be on time?" In this sentence, the first word of each of the two sentences should be capitalized (You and Why). Marrah should be capitalized because it is a proper noun and names a specific person. However, mother, a common noun, should not be capitalized.
4	C	The first word should be capitalized. Mother should not be capitalized unless you can substitute a name for mother. For example, without the possessive pronoun "her" in front of mother, you could put her mother's name or any name to test whether you should capitalize mother.
5	D	The only word that should be capitalized is the first word of the sentence. People and college do not need to be capitalized because they are not specific names.
6	B	I is always capitalized unless it is used to spell a word that is not the first word of a sentence. Texas is the name of a state, and Katie is the name of a girl. However, you is a pronoun and should not be capitalized unless it is used as the first word of a sentence.
7	C	Winter, unless it's the first word of a sentence, should not be capitalized because it is not a specific name. Seasons are not capitalized. Thanksgiving, like all holidays, should be capitalized. Bobby is the name of a person, so it should be capitalized. However, cat is a common noun and isn't the specific name of a cat, so it should not be capitalized. Also, winter is capitalized if use as a proper noun.
8	C	"Sam's" should be capitalized because it is the name of a person, and it is the first word of the sentence. However, wife should not be capitalized because it is a common noun.

Question No.	Answer	Detailed Explanations
9	C	My, the first word of the sentence, should be capitalized. Mother should not be capitalized because you cannot substitute "mother" with a name. Extremely is an adverb and doesn't need to be capitalized. Nurse is a common noun and not a specific name, so it shouldn't be capitalized.
10	B	The president does not come before a name. Therefore, it doesn't need to be capitalized. White House is also the specific name of a place (the official residence of the President of the United States of America), so it should be capitalized. The name of the city, Washington, should be capitalized as well as D.C., which is the abbreviation for the District of Columbia (which is not a state), but a federal district.

Lesson 7: Punctuation

Question No.	Answer	Detailed Explanations
1	A	"Will your mom take us to school, or do we have to take the bus?" You must capitalize the first word of the sentence. However, you do not capitalize mom in this sentence. You should capitalize mom if it's the first word of the sentence or if you just use the word mom without a pronoun.
2	B	The first word of the sentence should be capitalized. It is a statement so it needs a period at the end. Since "After I scraped the gum off my shoes" begins the sentence, it requires a comma to separate it from the independent clause that follows. It is a subordinate or dependent clause which cannot stand alone. However, if the same phrase were put at the end of the sentence like this, "I went into the house after I scraped the gum off my shoes," then, it doesn't need a comma.
3	A	The first word is capitalized. There are no proper nouns, and the sentence should end with a period because it's a statement. The other choices have the incorrect use of a comma.
4	C	The reason that a comma is needed behind sister and fifteen is because "who will be fifteen soon" is an appositive phrase that explains who sister is. Since it is not essential or necessary, you need the commas. The sentence would be just fine without the appositive phrase.
5	D	The comma and the conjunction "and" are used to separate the two sentences. Without the conjunction, the sentence would be a run-on.
6	B	This is a complex sentence because it has an independent clause (which can stand alone as a sentence) and a dependent clause, until I have the webcam ready, (which cannot stand alone as a sentence.)
7	A	The comma separates the dependent clause (on the left), from the independent clause (on the right). This is called a complex sentence. Therefore, it needs a comma to separate the clauses.
8	D	This is a simple sentence. The commas separate an adjective clause, which is not essential or necessary, but gives an additional description of the armadillo. The first letter should be capitalized and the proper noun Texas.

Question No.	Answer	Detailed Explanations
9	B	Choice B is correct. I took my backpack with me, for I was headed to school. The comma is separating a participle (prepositional phrase) that is functioning as an adverb to tell where I took my backpack.
10	C	The comma and conjunction (but) separate the two independent clauses of this compound sentence. Remember that independent clauses have a subject and verb and are able to stand alone.

Lesson 8: Commas in Introductory Phrases

Question No.	Answer	Detailed Explanations
1	A	An introductory phrase comes at the beginning of a sentence. It is not the main part of a sentence, but it often gives important information about the sentence. Use a comma to separate the introductory phrase from the rest of the sentence.
2	D	"After the class returned from the playground" is an introductory phrase. Use a comma to separate the introductory phrase from the rest of the sentence.
3	B	"If you always eat breakfast" is an introductory phrase. Use a comma to separate the introductory phrase from the rest of the sentence.
4	C	"Until the whole class gets quiet" is an introductory phrase. Use a comma to separate the introductory phrase from the rest of the sentence.
5	D	"By the way" is an introductory phrase. You should use a comma to separate the introductory phrase from the rest of the sentence.
6	A	"Every Christmas" is an introductory phrase. YUse a comma to separate the introductory phrase from the rest of the sentence.
7	B	"After we all were seated" is an introductory phrase. Use a comma to separate the introductory phrase from the rest of the sentence.
8	D	"At the next meeting" is an introductory phrase. Use a comma to separate the introductory phrase from the rest of the sentence.
9	C	"Last Saturday" is an introductory phrase. Use a comma to separate the introductory phrase from the rest of the sentence.
10	D	"By tomorrow morning" is an introductory phrase. Use a comma to separate the introductory phrase from the rest of the sentence.

Lesson 9: Using Commas

Question No.	Answer	Detailed Explanations
1	A	Sammy, may I go with you to the mall? Use a comma to set off a person's name when you are speaking directly to that person.
2	C	If I could play the guitar like you, Wally, I would join a band. Use a comma to set off a person's name when you are speaking directly to that person.
3	A	Yes, I would like to go to the theme park. Use a comma to set off "yes" and "no" from the rest of the sentence.
4	D	No, I can't babysit your little sister after school today. Use a comma to set off "yes" and "no" from the rest of the sentence.
5	C	The movie starts at 7 o'clock, right? Use a comma to set off a tag question (right?) from the rest of the sentence.
6	A	Kathy, will you drive me to the golf course? Use a comma to set off a direct address (a person's name such as Kathy) from the rest of the sentence.
7	C	I promise to be home before 9:30, Mom. Use a comma to set off a direct address (a person's name such as Mom) from the rest of the sentence.
8	B	This is the funniest book, don't you think? Use a comma to set off a tag question (don't you think?) from the rest of the sentence.
9	A	Yes, I can help you edit your English essay. Use a comma to set off "yes" and "no" from the rest of the sentence.
10	B	Beau, can I come over and play video games with you? Use a comma to set off a direct address (a person's name such as Beau) from the rest of the sentence.

Lesson 10: Writing Titles

Question No.	Answer	Detailed Explanations
1	B	Choice B is the correct answer. You should use quotation marks to emphasize titles of poems, short stories, songs, and other short written works.
2	B	Choice B is correct. You should use quotation marks to emphasize titles of poems, short stories, songs, and other short written works.
3	B	Choice B is correct. You should use quotation marks to emphasize titles of poems, short stories, songs, and other short written works.
4	D	Choice D is correct. You can use underlining (Choice C) or italics (Choice A) to indicate titles of plays, books, newspapers, magazines, movies, and other complete works. Typically, these titles are underlined when they are handwritten and in italics when they are typed.
5	D	Choice D is correct. You can use underlining (Choice C) or italics (Choice A) to highlight titles of plays, books, newspapers, magazines, movies, and other complete works.
6	D	Choice D is correct. You can use underlining (Choice C) or italics (Choice A) to indicate titles of plays, books, newspapers, magazines, movies, and other complete works.
7	D	Choice D is correct. You can use underlining (Choice C) or italics (Choice A) to emphasize titles of plays, books, newspapers, magazines, movies, and other complete works.
8	B	Choice B is the correct answer. You should use quotation marks to indicate titles of poems, short stories, songs, and other short written works.
9	D	Choice D is correct. You can use underlining (Choice C) or italics (Choice A) to emphasize titles of plays, books, newspapers, magazines, movies, and other complete works.
10	B	Choice B is the correct answer. You should use quotation marks to highlight titles of poems, short stories, songs, and other short written works.

Lesson 11: Spelling

Question No.	Answer	Detailed Explanations
1	D	The correct spelling is incredible. The prefix is in-, the root word is cred, and the suffix is -ible. There are many words that end with this suffix.
2	B	The correct spelling should be usually. Be aware of the word weather because it is often confused with whether.
3	A	The correct spelling should be develop. It has three syllables.
4	D	The correct spelling is chicken. Remember this rule: there is always an a, e, i, o, u before ck.
5	B	The correct spelling is tasting. The rule for adding -ing to the base word taste, which ends with an e, is to drop the e and add -ing.
6	B	The correct spelling is dropping. The general rule for adding -ing to the end of a word that ends with a consonant "p", preceded by a vowel "o", is to double the final consonant before adding -ing.
7	B	The correct spelling is wringing. If you read the context, the word that is required is a twisting and squeezing of the hands. You ring a bell, but you wring out your clothes if they are wet.
8	C	The correct spelling is shrugged. If a word that ends with a consonant is preceded by a vowel, you have to double the consonant when you add -ed to the end. Shrugged is the past tense.
9	A	The correct spelling is drought. There are many words that can be spelled in the -ought family, such as bought and thought.
10	D	The correct spelling for the past tense of the linking verb seem is seemed.

Lesson 12: Sentence Structure

Question No.	Answer	Detailed Explanations
1	C	Choice C is correct. An independent clause is a group of words that has a subject and a verb, expresses a complete thought, and can stand alone. A dependent clause has a subject and a verb, but it does not express a complete thought and cannot stand alone. It must be attached to an independent clause. We call this a complex sentence when you have an independent and a dependent clause joined together. A coordinating conjunction is just one of the parts of speech that is used to join words, phrases, or sentences.
2	C	A group of words that has a subject and a verb, does not express a complete thought, and cannot stand alone is called a dependent clause. Remember that an independent clause doesn't need a dependent clause, but a dependent clause needs an independent clause. It's just like an independent person who can take care of himself or herself, but a dependent person requires the aid and support of someone else who should be and is most likely independent.
3	C	"When Juan studied for his quiz at the library" is not a complete sentence or an independent clause. Although it has a subject (Juan) and a verb (studied), it does not express a complete thought and cannot stand on its own. The subordinating conjunction "when" makes the sentence dependent. Without the first word, "when", the group of words would be an independent clause. Remember that subordinating conjunctions turn independent clauses into dependent clauses.
4	B	Miguel loves cars, but he can never find the time to work on one. This is an example of a compound sentence that is joined together by the comma and a coordinating conjunction. Both sentences have a subject and a verb (Miguel loves... and he can (never) find). Both sentences can stand alone, because they express a complete thought. You could make this a complex sentence by adding a subordinating conjunction to the beginning of the sentence which would turn the independent clause into a dependent clause (Although Miguel loves cars). Although Miguel loves cars, he can never find the time to work on one. This is a complex sentence, because it is composed of a dependent clause and an independent clause.

Question No.	Answer	Detailed Explanations
5	A	"Please help your father wash the car" is an imperative (command or request) sentence. Its subject is understood "you." The verb of the sentence is help. The sentence expresses a complete thought and can stand alone. Using the word "please" makes the sentence more polite, rather than direct, in tone.
6	C	This is an example of a complex sentence. "My father warned us about the dangers of forest fires" has a subject and a verb and is an independent clause. It can stand alone, because it has a subject and a verb and expresses a complete thought. However, "before he took us camping" has a subject and a verb, but it does not express a complete thought and cannot stand alone. Remember that a complex sentence has an independent and a dependent clause.
7	A	"My puppy always chews my slippers" is an example of a simple sentence that has a subject and a verb and expresses a complete thought.
8	D	The sleepy cat is. This is an incomplete sentence, because it does not express a complete thought even though it has a subject and a verb. The linking verb "is" should link the subject (cat) to something. To make the sentence complete, add an adjective like irritable after the verb "is" or a noun like Persian. The sleepy cat is irritable. The sleepy cat is Persian.
9	B	This is an example of a compound sentence with two independent clauses that are joined together by a comma and the conjunction "or."
10	C	"Although Jason takes drum lessons (dependent clause), he also plays the tuba in the band (independent clause)" is an example of a complex sentence. Remember that both clauses of this complex sentence have a subject and a verb. However, only the independent clause expresses a complete thought and can stand alone without the dependent clause. The dependent clause requires the independent clause.

Lesson 13: Varieties of English

Question No.	Answer	Detailed Explanations
1	B	Choice A is incorrect, because Francine wouldn't bother to introduce herself to a stranger if she was arrogant. Choice C is incorrect, because Francine shows that she's not serious by comparing Adam to a cold glass of lemonade. Choice D is incorrect, because Francine seems excited which is the opposite of bored.
2	C	Adam can be described as proper due to the way he formally introduces himself to Francine. Choices A and D are incorrect, because casual and silly are nearly opposites of proper. Choice B is incorrect, because William would have ignored Francine if she was rude.
3	C	Francine is likely from the southern part of the United States. Because she compared meeting Adam to a cold glass of water on a hot summer day, it seems she is from the South. Southern people often use expressions such as this one and are known for their friendliness.
4	C	"I reckon" means "I think." This is an example of a dialect and it is often used in the southern region of the United States.
5	A	The sentence is respectful and formal. Also "your busy day" is another clue that a student could be talking to a college professor. Choices B and D are incorrect, because these are informal settings. Choice C is incorrect, because an appointment would be required to speak to a doctor. People use different styles of English for particular purposes and in different social settings. Different situations require different styles.
6	B	This is likely a statement said by a teenage boy to another teenage boy while watching a basketball game. "Yo" and "psyched" are informal terms used by young people in casual settings.
7	A	Standard English is always spelled correctly, and a dialect is spelled the way the character speaks the words. Unique spellings are a way to identify dialect in text.
8	D	A dialect conveys a character's accent and locality (where they are from), and standard English does not. Dialect and accent are synonyms. You can often tell a character's locality from his or her dialect or accent.
9	C	If a student is speaking to a librarian, a very respectful and mannerly style of speech is used as in Choice C. Choices B and D are rude and inappropriate for a student speaking to an adult who works at a school. Choice A is incorrect, because it lacks manners which should be used when speaking to an adult who works at a school.

Lesson 14: Context Clues

Question No.	Answer	Detailed Explanations
1	B	A clue to this meaning is that my mother chased it with a broom.
2	D	If you insert the word chewed in place of gnawed, the meaning is still workable.
3	A	Jan ran away in disgust. The fact that she ran indicates that she was frightened of what she saw, so it must have been ugly. It's not typical to run away from something that is beautiful.
4	D	The clue in the sentence is that sternly tells how mother spoke to Emily. Since she said that she had practiced long enough, it indicates that mother strictly meant what she said.
5	B	The clue in the sentence is that her mother called her again. Her mother is waiting downstairs for her to come down, and she seems to be taking longer than her mother expected since she called her a second time.
6	A	The clue in the sentence is that he took the chicken out of the yard and ran. The chicken was not given to him, which is why he ran. Taking without permission and running off is considered stealing.
7	C	The clues in the sentence which reflect that she was a beginner are that she was peering and nervous, couldn't believe people were there to see her, and surprised that so many people came to see a new performer.
8	D	Direct context clues explicitly define a word in a sentence. There are no unusual clues, and it's not necessary to infer or read between the lines. The meaning is directly stated.
9	A	According to the context clues in the sentence, counting buttons all day was the monotonous task. The use of the word "but" in the last sentence indicates an exception. The work was repetitive, boring, and, at the same time, important.
10	D	According to the clues in the sentence the father said that eating too much candy was not prudent. In the second sentence, the clues that the child's stomach hurt and that the child wished he/she had listened and not eaten too much candy, also suggests the meaning of wise.

Lesson 15: Roots and Affixes

Question No.	Answer	Detailed Explanations
1	D	Suffixes are added to the end of a word, such as the word quickly. The suffix is -ly. A prefix is added to the beginning of a word, such as restate. Re- is a prefix. An affix means that something can be attached to a word and it changes the meaning.
2	C	The word unhappy has a prefix of un, which means "not." Unhappy literally means not happy. So, if you are unhappy about something, it means you are the opposite of happy (sad).
3	C	The prefix bi-, added to cycle forms the word bicycle, meaning two wheels. The prefix tri, means three, and quad means four. The word dual means having two like parts or a double.
4	B	The word resident, does not have a suffix. However, lemon - ade, dormit- ory, and liquid - ate, each have a suffix at the end.
5	A	The prefix retro- , is attached to the beginning of the word retroactive, meaning actively going back in time.
6	C	The suffix -en, is attached to the end of the word strength to form strengthen. The suffix -en makes strengthen mean to make stronger.
7	C	The suffix -ian is added to the end of the word music to create the word musician, meaning one who plays an instrument.
8	C	The suffix -ly is the correct suffix to add to the word friendly which means in a manner or way of acting like a friend.
9	C	The word suit, is the root word in the word unsuitable, which has a prefix (un) and a suffix (able).
10	B	The word comfort, is the root word in the word uncomfortable. Uncomfortable has a prefix and a suffix. The word means not able to be comfortable.

Lesson 16: Reference Sources

Question No.	Answer	Detailed Explanations
1	C	When you look up a word in a dictionary, you will see its pronunciation. That means that you will get a phonetic spelling of the word so that you will know how to say it.
2	D	A dictionary provides meanings of unknown words. Choice A is incorrect, because another mystery book would not provide a definition. Choice B is incorrect, because mystery books do not usually contain glossaries. Choice C is incorrect, because a thesaurus provides a list of synonyms.
3	D	A thesaurus is a reference book that synonyms. Use a thesaurus to find different, interesting words when you are writing.
4	D	Glossaries give word meanings. A thesaurus provides a list of synonyms. A dictionary provides a lot of information (pronunciation, part of speech, definition), while a magazine doesn't typically offer any definitions.
5	A	A dictionary provides a word's part of speech, its pronunciation, its history, and its definition. A thesaurus, glossary, and a math textbook would not contain all of that information.
6	C	Glossaries give the meaning of a word. A thesaurus provides a list of synonyms. A dictionary offers many components of information (part of speech, pronunciation, definitions). A pamphlet would not likely offer any definitions at all.
7	A	An almanac is a book that contains facts and figures about all kinds of topics. It is published every year, so the information is current and up-to-date. Much of the information in an almanac is in list form.
8	B	An atlas is a book of maps. An almanac is a book that contains facts and figures. A dictionary contains definitions. An encyclopedia contains specific information about particular topics.
9	D	All of the following information can be found in a dictionary: correct spellings, definitions, parts of speech (verb, noun, adjective, etc.), and also word origins.
10	D	A thesaurus is a type of reference source that gives lists of words with similar meanings (synonyms) as well as opposite meanings (antonyms).

Lesson 17: Interpreting Figurative Language

Question No.	Answer	Detailed Explanations
1	B	The boys ran off like rockets shooting up to the stars means that the boys ran away quickly. Rockets shooting up to the stars would have to be extremely fast. The boys running away were extremely fast. A simile compares two unlike objects using like or as.
2	A	Dad's business runs like a well-oiled machine means that the business is run or managed very smoothly. That means everyone knows what they're supposed to do, and there are rarely any difficulties. A metaphor is a direct comparison of two unlike objects.
3	B	My best friend and I are like two peas in a pod means that the two friends are very similar. They might look alike, act alike, and like similar things. This is a simile, because it compares two unlike things using like or as.
4	D	Without my glasses, I'm as blind as a bat means that the person can't see very well without eyeglasses. Bats live in the dark, and without glasses the person can't see very well, it's like they're in the dark.
5	C	The teacher was very angry, because three of the kids didn't do their homework. A hen gets mad when it gets wet. A teacher gets mad when kids don't do their homework. This is a simile, because it compares two unlike objects using like or as.
6	B	Nick is a pig when he eats means that Nick eats a lot and is messy when he eats. Pigs eat a lot, and they are messy because they're animals. When Nick eats, he probably gets food on his face and on the table. This is a metaphor, because it is a direct comparison of two unlike objects.
7	B	My room is a disaster means that it is very messy. The cousins probably helped scatter toys and other belongings all around the room. The literal meaning of disaster is a natural tragedy such as an earthquake or tornado. An actual storm did not occur in the room – only a mess.
8	D	I felt like a fish out of water means that I felt out of place and I didn't belong. Someone who goes somewhere and feels like an outsider could be compared to a "fish out of water." This is a simile because two unlike things are being compared using like or as.

Question No.	Answer	Detailed Explanations
9	C	"As good as gold" means behaved very well. Gold is a very good metal, because it very valuable. A little girl acting "good as gold" means she behaved very well. A church service is a place where children have to be quiet. A simile compares two unlike objects using like or as.
10	A	My husband is the apple of my eye means that he is one my favorite people. Apples are fruits that represent love in Greek Mythology. A metaphor is a direct comparison of two unlike objects.

Lesson 18: Idioms, Adages, and Proverbs

Question No.	Answer	Detailed Explanations
1	C	A proverb is a phrase which contains advice or a generally accepted truth. An example of a proverb is "look before you leap."
2	C	Do not put all your eggs in one basket" has a similar meaning to "do not store all of your data on one computer." It means that you shouldn't keep important data in one place, because something destructive might happen where it's stored.
3	B	Alliteration is the repetition of a particular sound in a series of words like tongue twisters. A proverb and an adage can be confused, but proverbs tend to give advice or wisdom, whereas an adage is a short memorable phrase that is passed around and becomes accepted as a truth.
4	A	It is not a literal interpretation, so the meaning has to be inferred. This idiom means that someone is getting on your nerves or they say or do something that one considers unkind.
5	A	The phrase "going bananas" generally means that there is a lot of excitement, chaos, or silliness.
6	B	A friend in need is a friend indeed has come to mean that if you help someone who is in need, they may be considered your friend or become your friend. They may be able to return a favor one day.
7	D	Choice D is correct because Both B and C explain the idiom, "Action speaks louder than words." It is better to do and show than talk about doing, just as what you do is more important than what you say. In other words, seeing is believing.
8	A	Keep it a secret, is what the idiom "don't let the cat out of the bag," means. It is not a literal meaning to keep a real cat in a bag.
9	B	Choice B, 'every cloud has a silver lining,' means the same as when bad things happen, there is always a positive aspect to it. Choice A means that if you do mean things, one day you may have mean things done to you. Some people call this Karma. 'A bird in the hand is worth two in the bush' is an adage that means be thankful for what you actually have, whether it's a job or a house, instead of hoping for more that is harder to get. Having and hoping to have are not the same thing. 'Patience pays' means that as hard as it is to wait, if you do, you will benefit or win in the end.

Question No.	Answer	Detailed Explanations
10	C	"A half a loaf of bread is better than no bread is similar in meaning to "You should be happy with what you have, even if it's less than what you want." "Where there is a will, there is a way" means that if you have enough determination, you can do anything. "Cut your coat according to the cloth" means that you should only buy what you can afford, or do what you are capable of doing.

Lesson 19: Synonyms and Antonyms

Question No.	Answer	Detailed Explanations
1	A	Antonyms are words that are opposite in meaning. Roar, growl, and loud are similar in meaning, but opposite to the meaning of the word murmur, which means a very low sound that's barely audible.
2	A	Synonyms are words that have similar meanings.
3	D	Antonyms are words that have opposite meanings. A way to remember the difference between antonym and synonym is to recall the letter "a" (antonym) and link it with the word against (opposite), and recall the letter "s" (synonym) and link it with the word same or similar.
4	B	Since antonyms are opposite in meaning. The words "alive" and "dead" are opposite in meaning. Choice D contains synonyms. Choice A and Choice B are neither antonyms nor synonyms.
5	C	The word cheat is not a synonym even though stealing could be considered a way of cheating someone. Remember that if you have two words that have some similarity in meaning, you should choose the best answer. Also, practice the words in the sentence to see if they read with the same meaning as the underlined word. Thieves rob or steal. If someone borrows something, it is assumed that they will return what they borrowed.
6	D	The word watchfully and attentively are both similar to the word intently. All three of these words are adverbs that describe the manner in which something is being viewed.
7	C	Fragile means breakable or delicate. Something that is sturdy is the opposite of fragile.
8	B	Both of these words are verbs in the past tense. However, they differ by degree because to devour something means to eat in a manner of being very hungry. Delight is an adjective that describes being very happy or pleased. Dinner is a noun that generally describes the last meal of the day that is often eaten in the evenings after lunch. Dessert is a noun and describes a type of food that is generally sweet and may be fruit, pie, cake, ice cream, etc.
9	A	Tiny and huge, are antonyms because they are opposite in meaning. The stars and the planet earth are each part of the universe. Appear is a word that means to come into view, while the word actually is an adverb that adds emphasis. The earth is a part of the Universe.
10	D	The word teacher and instructor, are synonyms because they both describe someone who provides information and assists others in learning. A gym is a place to exercise and play sports. A player is someone who plays games, such as tennis, which is a sports game.

Lesson 20: Vocabulary

Question No.	Answer	Detailed Explanations
1	C	The word obsolete means no longer produced or used. Video tapes are nearly obsolete, because movies are more commonly sold in DVD format now.
2	A	The word provide means to make available for use. When you provide someone your phone number, it means you are giving it to them so that they can use it to call you.
3	B	Retain means to hold onto or keep. One may retain a receipt which means to keep it in case the item needs to be returned something in the future.
4	D	The word retire means to leave one's job and stop working. People in the United States normally retire at the age of sixty-five when they are able to receive social security payments.
5	C	A myth is a traditional story usually about gods and goddesses of ancient Greece. Pandora's Box is a popular Greek myth.
6	D	The people of the village were tired of being treated badly, so they decided to overthrow the king. Overthrow means to remove from leadership.
7	A	She pushed as hard as she could, but the heavy bookshelf would not budge. Budge means move. Since the bookshelf was heavy, the girl couldn't move it.
8	B	I need to know where to go to convert my American dollars to Mexican pesos. Convert means to change. In the sentence, a person wants to change American dollars to Mexican pesos.
9	B	When a child no longer has parents, the court will appoint a guardian. A guardian is the person legally in charge of a child under the age of 18.
10	B	It is difficult to see on a foggy morning, because it is hazy. Hazy means that the air is thick, and one can't see very far ahead.

SBAC FAQ

What will SBAC English Language Assessments Look Like?

In many ways, the SBAC assessments will be unlike anything many students have ever seen. The tests will be conducted online, requiring students complete tasks to assess a deeper understanding of the CCSS. The students will be assessed once 75% of the year has been completed in two different assessments - a Computer Adaptive Testing (CAT) and a Performance Task (PT).

The time for each ELA portion is described below:

Estimated Time on Task in Minutes		
Grade	CAT	PT
3	90	120
4	90	120
5	90	120
6	90	120
7	90	120
8	90	120

Bacause the assessment is online, the test will consist of a combination of new types of questions:

1. Drag and Drop
2. Drop Down
3. Essay Response
4. Extended Constructed Response
5. Hot Text Select and Drag
6. Hot Text Selective Highlight
7. Matching Table In-line
8. Matching Table Single Reponse
9. Multiple Choice – Single Correct Response, radial buttons
10. Multiple Choice – Multiple Response, checkboxes
11. Numeric Response
12. Short Text
13. Table Fill-in

What is this SBAC Test Practice Book?

Inside this book, you will find practice sections aligned to each CCSS. Students will have the ability to review questions on each standard, one section at a time, in the order presented, or they can choose to study the sections where they need the most practice.

In addition to the practice sections, you will have access to two full-length CAT and PT practice tests online. Completing these tests will help students master the different areas that are included in newly aligned SBAC tests and practice test taking skills. The results will help the students and educators get insights into students' strengths and weaknesses in specific content areas. These insights could be used to help students strengthen their skills in difficult topics and to improve speed and accuracy while taking the test.

Because the SBAC assessment includes newly created, technology-enhanced questions, it is necessary for students to be able to regularly practice these questions. The Lumos online StepUp program includes thirteen technology enhanced questions that mimic the types students will see during the assessments. These include:

Why Practice with Repeated Reading Passages?

Throughout the Lumos Learning Common Core Practice workbooks, students and educators will notice many passages repeat. This is done intentionally. The goal of these workbooks is to help students practice skills necessary to be successful in class and on standardized tests. One of the most critical components to that success is the ability to read and comprehend passages. To that end, reading fluency must be strengthened. According to Hasbrouck and Tindal (2006), "Helping our students become fluent readers is absolutely critical for proficient and motivated reading" (p. 642). And, Nichols et al. indicate, (2009), "fluency is a gateway to comprehension that enables students to move from being word decoders to passage comprehenders" (p. 11).

Lumos Learning recognizes there is no one-size-fits-all approach to build fluency in readers; however, the repeated reading of passages, where students read the same passages at least two or more times, is one of the most widely recognized strategies to improve fluency (Nichols et al., 2009). Repeated reading allows students the opportunity to read passages with familiar words several times until the passage becomes familiar and they no longer have to decode word by word. As students reread, the decoding barrier falls away allowing for an increase in reading comprehension.

The goal of the Lumos Learning workbooks is to increase student achievement and preparation for any standardized test. Using some passages multiple times in a book offers struggling readers an opportunity to do just that.

References
Hasbrouck, J., and Tindal, G. (2006). Oral reading fluency norms: A valuable assessment tool for reading teachers. Reading Teacher, 59(7), 636644. doi:10.1598/RT.59.7.3.
Nichols, W., Rupley, W., and Rasinski, T. (2009). Fluency in learning to read for meaning: going beyond repeated readings. Literacy Research & Instruction, 48(1). doi:10.1080/19388070802161906.

What if I buy more than one Lumos Study Program?

Step 1

Visit the URL and login to your account.
http://www.lumoslearning.com

Step 2

Click on 'My tedBooks' under the "Account" tab.
Place the Book Access Code and submit.

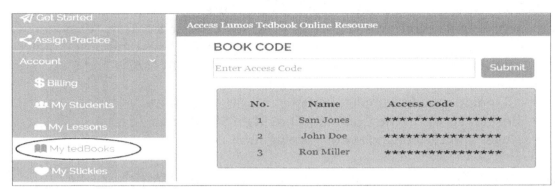

Step 3

To add the new book for a registered student, choose the
○ Existing Student button and select the student and submit.

Assign To ⓘ

- ● Existing Student
- ○ Add New student
- ○ Sam Jones
- ○ John Doe
- ○ Ron Miller

Submit

To add the new book for a new student, choose the ○ Add New student
button and complete the student registration.

Assign To ⓘ

○ Existing Student   ● Add New student

Register Your TedBook

Student Name:*   Enter First Name   Enter Last Name

Student Login*

Password*

Submit

Lumos StepUp® Mobile App
FAQ For Students

What is the Lumos StepUp® App?

It is a FREE application you can download onto your Android Smartphones, tablets, iPhones, and iPads.

What are the Benefits of the StepUp® App?

This mobile application gives convenient access to Practice Tests, Common Core State Standards, Online Workbooks, and learning resources through your Smartphone and tablet computers.

- Eleven Technology enhanced question types in both MATH and ELA
- Sample questions for Arithmetic drills
- Standard specific sample questions
- Instant access to the Common Core State Standards
- Jokes and cartoons to make learning fun!

Do I Need the StepUp® App to Access Online Workbooks?

No, you can access Lumos StepUp® Online Workbooks through a personal computer. The StepUp® app simply enhances your learning experience and allows you to conveniently access StepUp® Online Workbooks and additional resources through your smart phone or tablet.

How can I Download the App?

Visit **lumoslearning.com/a/stepup-app** using your Smartphone or tablet and follow the instructions to download the app.

**QR Code
for Smartphone
Or Tablet Users**

Lumos StepUp® Mobile App FAQ For Parents and Teachers

What is the Lumos StepUp® App?

It is a free app that teachers can use to easily access real-time student activity information as well as assign learning resources to students. Parents can also use it to easily access school-related information such as homework assigned by teachers and PTA meetings. It can be downloaded onto smart phones and tablets from popular App Stores.

What are the Benefits of the Lumos StepUp® App?

It provides convenient access to

- Standards aligned learning resources for your students
- An easy to use Dashboard
- Student progress reports
- Active and inactive students in your classroom
- Professional development information
- Educational Blogs

How can I Download the App?

Visit **lumoslearning.com/a/stepup-app** using your Smartphone or tablet and follow the instructions to download the app.

QR Code
for Smartphone
Or Tablet Users

Progress Chart

Standard	Lesson	Page No.	Practice		Mastered	Re-practice /Reteach
CCSS			Date	Score		
RL.5.1	Supporting Statements	7				
RL.5.1	Drawing Inferences	17				
RL.5.2	Theme	27				
RL.5.2	Characters	37				
RL.5.2	Summarizing Texts	46				
RL.5.3	Events	55				
RL.5.3	Setting	64				
RL.5.4	Figurative Language	74				
RL.5.5	Structures of Text	79				
RL.5.6	Styles of Narration	86				
RL.5.7	Visual Elements	91				
RL.5.9	Compare and Contrast	96				
RI.5.1	Inferences and Conclusions	126				
RI.5.2	Main Idea and Supporting Details	133				
RI.5.3	Text Relationships	140				
RI.5.4	General Academic Vocabulary	149				
RI.5.5	Text Structure	154				
RI.5.6	Point of View	158				
RI.5.7	Locating Answers	164				
RI.5.8	Using Evidence to Support Claims	169				
RI.5.9	Integrating Information	175				

Standard	Lesson	Page No.	Practice		Mastered	Re-practice /Reteach
CCSS			Date	Score		
L.5.1.A	Prepositional Phrases	197				
L.5.1.B	Verbs	200				
L.5.1.C	Subject verb Agreement	203				
L.5.1.D	Adjectives and Adverbs	206				
L.5.1.E	Correlative Conjunctions	210				
L.5.2.A	Capitalization	214				
L.5.2.A	Punctuation	217				
L.5.2.B	Commas in Introductory Phrases	220				
L.5.2.C	Using commas	223				
L.5.2.D	Writing titles	226				
L.5.2.E	Spelling	229				
L.5.3.A	Sentence Structure	233				
L.5.3.B	Verities in English	236				
L.5.4.A	Context clues	239				
L.5.4.B	Roots & Affixes	243				
L.5.4.C	Reference sources	246				
L.5.5.A	Interpreting Figurative Language	250				
L.5.5.B	Idioms, Adages & Proverbs	253				
L.5.5.C	Synonyms and Antonyms	256				
L.5.6	Vocabulary	259				

Grade **5**

★ **Lumos Learning**
Developed By Expert Teachers

SBAC Practice
Math
Test Prep

(((tedBook)))

Smarter Balanced Study Guide

ONLINE

2 Performance Tasks (PT)

2 Computer Adaptive Tests (CAT)

30+ SKILLS

www.LumosLearning.com

Available

• At Leading book stores

• Online www.LumosLearning.com